ABOUT THE AUTHOR

Dr. Hossamaldin Alzawawi, a seasoned clinical pathologist, passionately explores the intersection of medicine, philosophy, physics, and cognitive neuroscience. His journey through medical expertise and philosophical inquiry has ignited a fascination with the enigmas of consciousness and intelligence.

Believing in the power of interdisciplinary knowledge, Dr. Alzawawi aims to bridge ancient wisdom and modern science. He envisions applying these insights to illuminate human cognition and enhance human experience.

Join Dr. Alzawawi on this intellectual odyssey and discover the hidden architect within you.

I0530140

BOOKS BY AUTHOR

Arcanum of Awareness Series

1. Book 1: The Spark of Creativity

2. Book 2: The Evolution of Thought

3. Book 3: The Labyrinth of Cognitexis

4. Book 4: The Supremacy of Selective Awareness

5. Book 5: Architects of a Future Dawn

Other Book by Author

- The Thermodynamic Universe and Beyond: How Nature's Laws Reveal the Secrets of Time, Biology, Information, and Quantum Reality

BOOK 5

ARCHITECTS OF A FUTURE DAWN

PILLARS OF TOMORROW'S CIVILIZATION

ARCANUM OF AWARENESS SERIES

Library of Congress Control Number: 2024919198

ISBN (PB):	**978-1-964328-10-2**
ISBN (E):	**978-1-964328-11-9**

Dedication

To my treasured mother, loving wife, and dear brother and sisters. To the future generations who will carry the torch of wisdom and hope, guiding their way through the darkness. To all the souls I have met along my journey and those I have yet to encounter, each one an essential part of this story.

To everyone who works tirelessly for a brighter future, this Arcanum of Awareness series serves as a tribute to our shared aspirations and hard work.

May this book and the entire Arcanum of Awareness series shine as a light, fostering awareness and fueling the desire for a better world.

ACKNOWLEDGMENTS

This work is a tribute to the great thinkers whose contributions have paved the way for me. **Professor Roger Penrose's Shadows of the Mind** has been a guiding light, encouraging me to explore the consciousness conundrum further. I am immensely grateful to **Napoleon Hill,** whose influential book **How to Own Your Mind** was a map through the maze of mental ownership. Their priceless insights have deepened my comprehension and inspired me to write this book. I hope you will discover, within these pages, the same glimmer of insights that have led me through the enchanting terrain of the mind.

Although I have a strong command of English as a second language, I have sought assistance refining my writing to make it more engaging and accessible. For that reason, I am compelled to offer my editorial board my most profound gratitude; their unwavering encouragement was crucial to the success of our project. **My Dear Wife, Basma,** I am writing to tell you how much you mean to me. I greatly appreciate your thoughtful analysis of my intricate concepts and theories; it helped me distill them into a more understandable story. You helped me tremendously develop narratives out of scientific principles by suggesting various forms my ideas may take and suggesting appropriate language. I am grateful for your contributions and the positive impact you have had on this project. Although my effort was focused on the ideas, descriptions, core concepts, and logical deduction and reasoning that made the skeleton of this work, the flourishment was to be carried out with the support from the AI, where various enrichment, examples, and illustrations were generated through passionate discussion. Also, the addition of diverse tones related to each book was not accessible without the support of AI. My work's varied topics and tones owe much to **Google AI,** our joint efforts, and the hours we devoted to working together. Your feedback substantially improved my writing process, producing more lyrical and narratively compelling works. **Microsoft AI,** thank you for all the hard work we put together. You played an essential and much-appreciated role in guiding us through various ideas and keeping the process moving smoothly. ChatGPT was the instrumental revisor and editor of this final book of the series. **ChatGPT,** I wanted to celebrate the time we worked together on this final book to enrich and enhance the contents and add valuable insight and suggestions to raise this book to the next level of enlightenment.

"Arcanum of Awareness" is a series that memorializes the great experiences and locations I've traveled. My deepest appreciation goes to **Queen's University Belfast's MBC and the McClay Libraries.** There was peace in these hallowed places of learning, perfect for serious study and deep thought. Libraries were more than simply locations where one could learn; they were also sanctuaries for new ideas and a love of learning. Being by my wife's side as she completed her degree at Queen's University Belfast has brought an incalculable amount of happiness to our trip. Knowledge, shared experiences, and personal progress were abundant during that time. What I learned and my experiences throughout this time will always be with me.

My sincere regards, Hossamaldin Alzawawi, M.D.

ARCHITECTS OF A NEW DAWN

THE PILLARS OF TOMORROW'S CIVILIZATION

The future whispers to us through the winds of change, beckoning us to build the pillars of a new civilization, one where harmony and progress resonate in the symphony of human eternal journey.

"Your cure is within you, and you do not perceive it; your ailment is from you, and you do not feel it... Do you claim that you are a small entity while the greater world is contained within you? And you are the clear book, in which the hidden is revealed by its letters."

— Ali ibn Abi Talib

"Look back along the endless corridors of time, and you will see that four things have built civilization: the spirit of religion, the spirit of creative art, the spirit of research, and the spirit of business enterprise."

— Neil Carothers

CONTENTS

A CALL TO ARCHITECTS THE DAWN

᠍᠍᠍᠍᠍᠍ 6᠍᠍᠍ 6᠍᠍᠍ 6᠍᠍᠍

Fearless wanderer! Having navigated the trials of the earlier books, you stand not merely as a sovereign of your fate but with an exhilarating awareness – you possess the capacity to shape the contours of a nascent era. The murmurs of what is yet to come, once mere shadows, now reverberate with clarity deep within your being. This transcends the mere act of carving out one's own journey; it embodies the essence of establishing the groundwork for the civilizations that will emerge, illuminated by the promise of a more hopeful future.

Well done! Through the mastery of the principles revealed to you, you have forged the foundation of your odyssey – a mind tempered by discipline. This powerful instrument surpasses the intricacies of the now, granting you the agency to deliberately shape what is yet to come.

Book Five transcends the ordinary; it serves as a time capsule intricately designed to bridge the vast expanse from the past to the future. It conveys an essential message for our current reality: a forward-thinking outline for the attributes that will shape the flourishing societies of the future. In this moment, we shall embark on a path of introspection, advocating for a shift leading us toward a more profound understanding of our collective existence.

Envision a grand structure, a symbol of human endeavor, yet one that demands robust foundations to uphold its grandeur. The foundational elements – governance, social structures, and the intricacies of individual consciousness – are what will support a robust, enlightened, and progressive future. This chapter, Genesis of Tomorrow: A Manifesto for a New Era, stands as a visionary compass, illuminating the essential principles that will shape our future.

This resonant summons confronts antiquated beliefs, championing a future where collaboration and unity transcend the divisive paradigms of "us vs. them." Envision it as a declaration for a transformative age, a shared enlightenment to the vast possibilities that await us, should we endeavor to create a genuinely civilized society. In this exploration, we will unravel the misunderstandings that cloud the notion of a "socialized" civilization, illuminating a future where advancement is not hindered but invigorated by a collective ethos of cooperation. This segment transforms into a Vision for an Ideal Future: The Foundations of Advancement.

As we embark on the exploration of a future civilization, let us contemplate the attributes that shape a robust, enlightened, and progressive nation's governance structure. This section acts as an in-depth exploration, contemplating the qualities that contribute to a nation's strength, fairness, and genuine civilization. In this exploration, we will delve into the governance frameworks while also contemplating the foundational principles that sustain them.

The future we imagine is not a realm that shuns transformation; rather, it is a landscape that welcomes it with open arms. We shall delve into the significance of nurturing a society in which transformation is not merely tolerated but embraced, intricately interlaced into the essence of its being. In this chapter, we shall delve into the essence of these pillars while simultaneously unraveling the misconceptions that loom over their very foundations, threatening to undermine their significance.

Embrace your curiosity, for it serves as the catalyst that ignites the flames of innovation. Allow valor to illuminate your path, for it is courage that serves as the guiding compass through the vast, uncharted realms of a future yet to unfold. Open the depths of your understanding and ready yourself to respond to the summons – the summons to shape the new beginning.

Here lies an invitation for you to become one with the visionaries of the new beginning. Are you prepared to heed the summons?

SECTION 1

FROM ASHES TO ASCENDANCY: CRAFTING A RESILIENT AND VISIONARY FUTURE

The world lay in silence, a silence not of peace but of aftermath—the echo of a storm that had unraveled everything humanity once held sacred. Cities were reduced to skeletal remains, forests replaced by ashen fields, and skies painted in hues of despair. Yet, amidst this devastation, the faint spark of life endured. Within the brokenness was still the hum of potential, a whisper of a future waiting to be reborn. This is not the end but the prologue of a story yet unwritten.

In this void of certainty, humanity stands at a precipice. The path forward is not paved; it is obscured by shadows of doubt and labyrinths of challenge. But within each of us lies the architect—a force capable of turning ruins into foundations, ashes into legacies. This chapter is not merely a reflection on survival; it is a manifesto for resilience, a blueprint for crafting a visionary future from the fragments of the past. It is a call to rise—not as victims of circumstance but as the phoenix reborn.

I. The Phoenix Rises: Rebuilding from the Ashes

Imagine a world ravaged by the storms of undisciplined thought. A civilization fractured by short-sightedness, consumed by the allure of immediate gratification. Perhaps it succumbed to the pitfalls of unchecked ambition or the poisonous whispers of societal discord. History is littered with such cautionary tales. Yet, within the embers of this metaphorical collapse lies the potential for a new dawn.

Here, the disciplined mind stands as the architect of a new future. It is not a singular, monolithic force but rather a tapestry woven from diverse threads – the ingenuity of the scientist, the foresight of the visionary leader, and the unwavering determination of the survivor. They are the architects of a new dawn, individuals who have honed their minds into instruments of progress and resilience.

Imagine a band of survivors emerging from the ruins, their minds not clouded by despair but ignited by a flicker of hope. They possess the blueprints of the past, not just in the form of technology or forgotten knowledge, but in the very essence of disciplined thought. They understand sustainability principles, the importance of long-term planning, and the immense power of collaboration, which unites them in their shared vision for a better future.

This new civilization wouldn't be built overnight. It would require a constant ascent fueled by the unwavering resolve of a disciplined mind. Each step, from establishing sustainable resource management to fostering social cohesion, would be a testament to the power of focused thought and action. This ascent wouldn't be without challenges. The whispers of old habits and the allure of instant gratification may still linger. But the architects of this new dawn would be prepared, armed with the knowledge that true progress comes from a disciplined and strategic approach to every facet of life – social, economic, and governmental.

This is not just a metaphorical journey; it is a call to action! Just as the survivors in our narrative unearthed the blueprints from the ruins, you, too, can excavate the power of the disciplined mind within yourself. By harnessing the lessons gleaned from the 'Arcanum of Awareness,' you can become the architect of your own personal and societal ascent, laying the foundation for a future brimming with resilience and vision.

Historical Context and Lessons

History offers powerful lessons about humanity's capacity to rise from the depths of devastation. Consider post-World War II Europe, a continent in ruins yet reborn through the Marshall Plan. This initiative fostered economic recovery, rebuilt infrastructure, and, most importantly, solidified international cooperation. Similarly, the Renaissance blossomed in the wake of the Black Plague, driven by adaptability and a renewed thirst for knowledge. These stories reveal that unity, strategic foresight, and collective effort are the keystones of recovery.

Every rebirth carries a psychological edge—the resilience to see opportunity where others perceive despair. It is not merely infrastructure that must be rebuilt but the human spirit itself, capable of rising to unprecedented heights when guided by shared purpose and unwavering will.

Technology and Future-Centric Vision

As we peer into the future, technology emerges as both the chisel and the canvas of our rebuilding efforts. Artificial intelligence, renewable energy, and biotechnology hold the promise of reshaping the world's foundations. Imagine cities powered entirely by solar grids, sustainable urban ecosystems integrating AI to optimize resources, or biotechnology healing both humanity and the environment. However, these tools come with risks. Without equitable access and ethical oversight, technology could widen societal rifts rather than bridge them.

The architect of tomorrow must wield these tools judiciously, ensuring innovation uplifts rather than isolates. They must weave a vision where humanity's progress harmonizes with its ethical and philosophical foundations, a future not dictated by machines but enhanced by their presence.

Individual Responsibility and Collective Action

Rebirth is neither a solitary act nor a collective accident. The phoenix's fire burns within each individual and spreads through collective action. Visionary thinkers like Viktor Frankl emphasized the power of personal discipline, and in these embers lies the core of rebuilding. Yet, it is the interplay between individual effort and societal collaboration that creates lasting legacies.

Imagine a mosaic of actions—from the lone artist whose resilience inspires a community to the international coalitions tackling global challenges. Each act, no matter how small, contributes to a greater whole. It is within this synergy that societies rediscover their purpose and forge a shared path forward.

Ecological and Environmental Rebuilding

Nature, too, must be an integral player in our resurrection. Ecological harmony is not an optional endeavor but a foundational necessity. Reforestation, biodiversity preservation, and sustainable urban planning serve as antidotes to humanity's destructive tendencies. The Great Green Wall initiative, combatting desertification in Africa, exemplifies ecological rebuilding's dual power: restoring ecosystems and uplifting communities.

The phoenix rises not just from human effort but from the soil, water, and air. Progress must intertwine with nature's rhythms, creating a symphony of coexistence rather than a cacophony of exploitation.

Examples of Visionary Leadership

Visionary leaders illuminate the path through darkness, shaping the rebirth of societies with courage and determination. Franklin D. Roosevelt's New Deal during the Great Depression redefined the government's role in economic and social welfare, showcasing the transformative power of bold leadership. On a different scale, Malala Yousafzai's advocacy for education exemplifies the ripple effect of individual resilience, proving that one voice can ignite global change.

Leadership, whether at the community or global level, inspires action and anchors the collective will need to rebuild.

Global Unity and Shared Challenges

Our world's interconnectedness amplifies both risks and opportunities. Challenges like climate change, pandemics, and resource scarcity transcend borders, necessitating global cooperation. The Paris Agreement and global vaccination initiatives underscore humanity's capacity to unite against shared threats. Yet, more must be done to cultivate trust, prioritize shared goals, and dissolve divisions.

The phoenix's flames must not remain isolated embers but a collective blaze that lights the way for all.

Emotional and Cultural Resilience

In the shadows of despair, culture and art provide light. Music, storytelling, and rituals serve as emotional scaffolding, fostering hope and shared identity. After the devastation of World War II, Beethoven's 9th Symphony became a symbol of unity, echoing across divided Germany. Cultural resilience ensures that societies do not merely survive but thrive, rooted in shared histories and aspirations.

Practical Frameworks for Progress

Reconstruction requires structure. Assessing damage, setting clear goals, pooling resources, and monitoring progress are essential steps. Public-private partnerships, grassroots movements, and inclusive policy-making ensure that rebuilding reflects diverse voices and priorities. Imagine urban regeneration projects that balance technological advancement with cultural preservation, creating spaces that honor the past while embracing the future.

The Role of Education

At the heart of resilience lies education. Transformative systems that prioritize critical thinking, sustainability, and adaptability equip future generations to confront uncertainty with confidence. Blending STEM with the arts fosters well-rounded innovators prepared to tackle multi-faceted challenges.

Conclusion

From the ashes of collapse rises a civilization redefined. The phoenix's rebirth is a metaphor for humanity's boundless potential—a future where unity, innovation, and resilience craft a world of unparalleled peace and prosperity. Let us act with the courage of visionaries, the wisdom of philosophers, and the resolve of survivors, forging a legacy that outshines the flames of adversity. Together, we ascend.

II. The Pillars of Progress: Building a Sustainable Future

The Pillars of Progress: Building a Sustainable Future

Envision a civilization emerging from the ashes of the past, not simply echoing history but crafting a bright tomorrow filled with possibility. This new dawn shall rise not upon the fragile foundations of fleeting desires but upon the solid ground of enduring advancement. The creators of this society would not succumb to the temptations of short-term rewards but would instead be steered by the tenets of enduring prosperity.

Here, the power of the disciplined mind manifests in the form of scientific advancement. The echoes of past mistakes still resonate as a constant reminder of the need for responsible innovation. Renewable energy sources, harnessed by the ingenuity of scientists, would become the lifeblood of their society. Technologies wouldn't be developed in isolation; their impact on the environment would be carefully considered, ensuring progress wouldn't come at the cost of ecological devastation. Artificial intelligence, a double-edged sword from the past, would be wielded with caution, its potential for good harnessed while its destructive tendencies are kept in check.

Historical Context: Lessons from Resilient Civilizations

History teaches that sustainable progress arises not from transient success but from deeply rooted foresight. Reflect upon the rise of civilizations such as Ancient Mesopotamia, where early innovations in agriculture, irrigation, and social organization laid the foundation for prosperity. Contrast this with the lessons of overreach, as seen in the fall of Easter Island's society, where unchecked consumption of natural resources led to collapse. These tales remind us that enduring progress demands a balance between ambition and restraint.

Innovation: The Lifeblood of a Resilient Society

A sustainable future is built upon the twin pillars of innovation and ethics. In this reborn civilization, renewable energy—solar, wind, and geothermal—flows as naturally as rivers and winds, and its implementation harmonizes with the environment. Biotechnology reshapes food security by introducing resilient crops that flourish in adverse conditions while respecting ecological boundaries. Artificial intelligence has become a benevolent force, aiding in resource management, urban planning, and disaster mitigation. Yet, this reliance on technology requires safeguards to prevent exploitation and preserve human dignity.

Education: Cultivating the Architects of Progress

A civilization rooted in sustainability prioritizes education as its most vital tool. The curricula extend beyond traditional academics to include critical thinking, ethics, and adaptability. Students are taught to approach problems with interdisciplinary strategies, blending the logic of science with the creativity of art and the wisdom of philosophy. Imagine an education system where a biologist collaborates with a historian to explore climate change's impact on ancient societies, producing insights that shape future policies. Such education ensures that every individual becomes a steward of progress, armed with knowledge and empathy.

Resourcefulness: The Virtue of Sustainable Living

The architects of this new dawn understand that progress is not about abundance but about resourcefulness. Every resource—material, intellectual, and emotional—is utilized with precision and purpose. Recycling and upcycling replace wasteful consumption. Circular economies thrive, where one industry's byproduct becomes another's raw material. Such ingenuity transforms scarcity into opportunity, fostering innovation born of necessity.

Unity and Ethical Leadership

Progress demands visionaries capable of uniting fractured societies under shared goals. Leaders of this future are philosophers as much as strategists, weaving narratives that inspire collective action while embodying accountability and foresight. They guide humanity through the labyrinth of progress, balancing ambition with caution, unity with individuality. Examples of such leadership abound in history: Mahatma Gandhi's philosophy of self-reliance and equity, or Eleanor Roosevelt's vision of human rights as pillars for enduring societal growth.

A Call to Harmonize with Nature

Progress that ignores the natural world is no progress at all. Ecological balance must be central to every innovation. Reforestation projects regenerate lost ecosystems; urban centers evolve into green cities with vertical farms and carbon-neutral designs. The air hums with renewal, the soil breathes life, and humanity exists not as a conqueror of nature but as its harmonious partner. The symphony of coexistence becomes the ultimate melody of progress.

Emotional and Cultural Sustainability

Cultural heritage and emotional well-being are threads interwoven into this future's fabric. Storytelling, art, and music become conduits for resilience, reminding society of its roots while offering hope for the future. Community rituals celebrate achievements, fostering unity and a collective sense of purpose. These emotional pillars transform individuals into a society that transcends mere survival to thrive in meaning and connection.

Conclusion

The pillars of progress are not monuments to fleeting glory but enduring testaments to humanity's capacity for renewal and growth. This is a narrative of how future generations, armed with the knowledge and lessons of history, can rise from the ashes of catastrophic incidents. With unity, foresight, and resilience, we can craft a civilization where sustainability is not an aspiration but a foundation. Let us be the architects of this vision, building a future that stands unshaken by time, its pillars reflecting not only the strength of our will but the boundless possibilities of our shared humanity. In this post-apocalyptic narrative infused with hope, the call for a new beginning resonates—a symphony of renewal that promises an era of peace, innovation, and unwavering determination for a new generation.

III. Beyond Utopia: Navigating the Labyrinth

The idyllic vision of a utopia might shimmer on the horizon, but the architects of a new dawn understand that the path toward it is rarely a straight line. Theirs is a journey through a labyrinth, a complex network of unforeseen challenges and obstacles. Scarcity of resources, political instability, and technological disruptions—these are the shadows lurking within the labyrinth, ever-present threats that could derail their progress.

Introduction: The Paradox of Perfection

Utopia, an idea as old as philosophy itself, promises a society of unbroken harmony and boundless prosperity. Yet, this vision carries within it an inherent paradox: the pursuit of perfection often uncovers the imperfections of human ambition. History has repeatedly shown that attempts to craft flawless societies can lead to unintended consequences, from the social inequalities of industrial revolutions to the environmental degradation of rapid modernization. It is within this labyrinth of aspirations and contradictions that humanity must tread carefully.

Lessons from History: The Unintended Costs of Idealism

The labyrinth is not a modern construct. Consider the collapse of the Mayan civilization, where overexploitation of resources and political fragmentation unraveled centuries of progress. Or the Industrial Revolution, which transformed societies but introduced social stratification and environmental consequences that persist to this day. These cautionary tales reveal a truth often overlooked: the pursuit of utopia must be tempered by humility, foresight, and adaptability.

Navigating Complexities: The Role of Critical Thinking

In the labyrinth of progress, critical thinking becomes the compass guiding humanity through its twists and turns. This discipline, a fusion of logic and creativity, enables societies to analyze problems and devise innovative solutions. Imagine a generation trained not only to solve immediate challenges but to anticipate ripple effects—to foresee how technological advancements might affect social structures or how economic growth might strain ecological systems. Critical thinking transforms the labyrinth from a confounding maze into a navigable journey.

Adapting to Scarcity: A Virtue Born of Necessity

Scarcity—of resources, time, or stability—is an ever-present shadow within the labyrinth. Yet, history teaches that scarcity often sparks ingenuity. The Apollo 13 mission, a story of survival amidst the void of space, demonstrates how resourcefulness can turn crisis into triumph. In this future, architects of progress will rely on resource optimization, harnessing technologies like 3D printing and decentralized energy grids to create solutions tailored to localized challenges. Scarcity is not a barrier but a forge, shaping resilience and creativity.

Balancing Innovation and Ethics

The labyrinth is not without moral quandaries. The pursuit of innovation, while necessary, often collides with ethical boundaries. Artificial intelligence, for example, holds the potential to revolutionize governance and healthcare, yet its misuse could entrench inequality or erode privacy. Navigating these dilemmas requires a philosophical lens, ensuring progress aligns with humanity's core values. This balance transforms technology into a tool of empowerment rather than an instrument of exploitation.

Leadership in the Labyrinth: Visionaries and Navigators

Every labyrinth requires guides—visionaries who see the broader map and navigators who illuminate the immediate path. These leaders must embody both audacity and humility, steering society through uncertainty while remaining grounded in ethical principles. Figures like Nelson Mandela, who united a fractured nation, or Elon Musk, whose ambition seeks to redefine interplanetary existence, exemplify leadership that balances vision with pragmatism. Such leaders inspire societies to venture deeper into the labyrinth without losing sight of their moral compass.

Cultural and Emotional Resilience: The Beacons of Hope

In the face of the labyrinth's challenges, cultural and emotional resilience act as guiding lights. Art, music, and storytelling remind humanity of its shared journey, offering solace and inspiration. Following the devastation of Hurricane Katrina, New Orleans' jazz and communal celebrations symbolized a city's determination to reclaim its identity. Such cultural anchors ensure that societies do not merely endure adversity but emerge enriched by their struggles.

Practical Frameworks: Mapping the Labyrinth

Navigating the labyrinth requires tangible strategies. These include fostering interdisciplinary collaborations, leveraging grassroots innovation, and creating adaptive policies that evolve with changing circumstances. Imagine a city designed not as a static structure but as a living organism, its infrastructure responsive to environmental changes and its governance informed by real-time data. These frameworks transform the labyrinth into a dynamic system that empowers progress rather than impedes it.

Conclusion

The labyrinth is not a trap but an opportunity—a journey that tests humanity's ingenuity, resilience, and moral clarity. Beyond its twists and shadows lies not a perfect utopia but a society capable of embracing imperfection and transforming challenges into catalysts for growth. Future generations, armed with knowledge and guided by empathy, can navigate this labyrinth and craft a world that harmonizes progress with purpose. Let this journey inspire a relentless pursuit of innovation and a steadfast commitment to the ideals that illuminate our shared path forward.

IV. The Architect Within: Building Your Legacy

The Architect Within: Building Your Legacy

The grand narrative of civilization rising from the ashes concludes, but the embers of inspiration still glow. We've explored the blueprints for a new dawn, the challenges that lie within the labyrinth, and the unwavering spirit of the architects who navigate it. Yet, a crucial question remains – how does this grand narrative translate to our own lives?

Introduction: Becoming the Architect

In the vast symphony of human progress, every individual holds the potential to play a defining note. The architects we've encountered—the survivors, the visionaries, the leaders—are not distant figures but reflections of the potential within each of us. The qualities that define a resilient civilization—critical thinking, creativity, and ethical behavior—are not just societal aspirations; they are personal imperatives. Each choice we make, each act of discipline or creativity, contributes to a legacy that shapes not only our lives but the lives of generations to come.

A Historical Lens: Legacies That Resonate

History abounds with individuals who forged legacies that transcended time. Consider the quiet resolve of Harriet Tubman, whose courage as an abolitionist carved pathways to freedom, or the pioneering ingenuity of Nikola Tesla, whose visions of energy and technology continue to illuminate our world. These figures remind us that building a legacy is not about grandeur but persistence—an accumulation of intentional acts that ripple outward into society. Their stories underscore the importance of personal discipline and resilience in crafting a meaningful contribution to the broader tapestry of humanity.

The Foundations of a Personal Legacy

Every legacy begins with an unwavering commitment to personal growth. The architect within us is forged through reflection, learning, and action. Like an intricate mosaic, legacies are composed of small but deliberate decisions—decisions rooted in authenticity and guided by purpose. Imagine an individual who dedicates themselves to environmental advocacy, planting trees not for their own shade but for future generations to enjoy. This simple, repeated action creates a profound impact that outlives the architect.

The Interplay of Individual and Collective Impact

No legacy is built in isolation. The architect's work is inherently intertwined with the collective efforts of a community. Consider the grassroots movements of the 20th century that transformed societal norms, from civil rights to environmental conservation.

These movements began with individuals who dared to act but gained momentum through collective action. The architect within each of us is both a solitary creator and a vital collaborator, contributing our unique talents to a shared vision.

Technology as a Tool for Legacy

In an age of unprecedented technological advancement, the tools at our disposal amplify the reach and resonance of our legacies. Social media platforms allow voices to echo across continents, while advancements in renewable energy and biotechnology enable solutions to challenges once deemed insurmountable. However, these tools must be wielded with intentionality. The architect within us must navigate the ethical labyrinth of technology, ensuring that innovation serves humanity rather than undermines it.

The Role of Emotional Resilience

Building a legacy is not without its trials. The journey demands emotional resilience and the ability to withstand setbacks and adapt to unforeseen challenges. Viktor Frankl's philosophy of finding meaning even in suffering reminds us that adversity can forge strength and clarity of purpose. Emotional resilience transforms obstacles into opportunities, shaping a legacy defined not by ease but by perseverance and integrity.

Cultural and Artistic Expressions of Legacy

Legacy is not confined to grand achievements or technological breakthroughs. It also resides in the cultural and artistic expressions that inspire and connect us. Consider the enduring works of Maya Angelou or the timeless music of Beethoven, which continue to touch lives across generations. Through art, storytelling, and music, the architect within us weaves a legacy that transcends temporal boundaries, uniting people through shared experiences and emotions.

A Practical Framework: Laying the Stones of Your Legacy

1. **Reflection**: Identify your core values and aspirations. What legacy do you wish to leave?

2. **Education**: Equip yourself with the knowledge and skills necessary to achieve your goals.

3. **Action**: Take consistent, intentional steps toward your vision, however small they may seem.

4. **Collaboration**: Engage with others who share your purpose, amplifying your impact through collective effort.

5. **Resilience**: Embrace setbacks as opportunities to learn and grow, maintaining focus on your ultimate vision.

6. **Ethics**: Navigate decisions with integrity, ensuring your actions align with both personal and societal well-being.

Conclusion

The architect within each of us holds the power to shape not only personal destiny but the contours of a brighter future for all. By embracing discipline, fostering creativity, and committing to purposeful action, we contribute to a legacy that resonates far beyond our individual lives. Let us rise as architects of progress, building structures of hope and innovation that stand unshaken by time. Together, as stewards of this shared journey, we can weave a future where our legacies illuminate paths for generations to come.

Conclusion: From Ashes to Ascendance: Crafting the Symphony of Tomorrow

The flames of destruction have subsided, leaving a canvas upon which a new future must be painted. This is not the work of a singular hero or a fleeting moment of triumph—it is a symphony of efforts, a tapestry woven by countless hands and hearts. Each act of resilience, every spark of innovation, contributes to a greater whole. Together, we rise from the ashes, not as echoes of what was lost but as creators of what is to come.

Let this chapter be a reminder that the greatest stories are not born of comfort but of struggle and perseverance. From the ruins of the past, we craft a vision for tomorrow—a world resilient, harmonious, and boundless in its possibilities. As you journey through these pages, may you find not only the blueprint for a new dawn but also the inspiration to become its architect. This is our story, and it begins now.

THE VANGUARD OF A NEW ORDER: THE ATTRIBUTES OF A CIVILIZED NATION SYSTEM

ᏮᏮᏮ

I magine a nation that stands as a beacon of progress, compassion, and innovation—a society where every citizen is empowered to dream, grow, and contribute to a brighter future. This is not a utopian vision; it is a call to action, a blueprint for constructing a truly civilized nation system.

This chapter invites you to embark on a journey of transformation, exploring the attributes that define a thriving society. From the foundations of ethical governance to the heights of human potential, from harmonious economic structures to environmental stewardship, this is a vision of a nation that harmonizes ambition with integrity, progress with justice, and individuality with a collective purpose.

Let this chapter ignite your imagination, challenge your perceptions, and inspire your actions. Together, we will explore how a society can transcend its limitations, weave its diverse strengths into a tapestry of unity, and compose a symphony of shared prosperity that resonates for generations to come.

I. The Foundations of a Civilized Nation System

1. Synthesis of Sovereign Forces: A Symphony of Individual Potential

We've ventured through the labyrinth, witnessed the rise of a new dawn, and uncovered the immense potential within each of us to be the architects of a brighter future. Now, our focus shifts outward toward the **societal structures** that have the power to cultivate and amplify this potential. Here, the disciplined mind takes on a new dimension: the **concept of a civilized nation system**, a framework designed to harmonize individual liberty with collective progress.

Governance as the Conductor of the Grand Symphony

Imagine a world where governance transcends the narrow confines of control and evolves into a **conductor of a grand symphony**. In this symphony, every citizen contributes their unique strengths, weaving their talents into a vibrant tapestry of progress. This vision is impossible under systems that stifle individuality or prioritize conformity. A truly civilized nation system embraces **individual liberty** and the relentless pursuit of talent, allowing every voice to enrich the collective melody.

Much like a conductor drawing out the unique brilliance of each musician to create a powerful and cohesive performance, governance in a civilized nation system aligns its citizens' diverse contributions into a symphony of purpose. It values the singularity of each person's melody, fostering a society that is both harmonious and dynamic.

The Science of Collaboration: Insights from Complex Systems

Science offers compelling insights through complex systems theory. Just as an ant colony thrives through the coordinated efforts of individual ants, a society flourishes when its citizens are empowered to contribute their unique talents to shared goals. In this model:

- **Diversity becomes a strength** as varied skills and perspectives are channeled toward collective progress.
- Individuals are not constrained by rigid structures but encouraged to **pursue their passions** and contribute their best to society.

This system doesn't stifle potential; it **cultivates it**, creating an environment where every citizen plays an indispensable role in the nation's success.

Technology as a Facilitator of Human Potential

Fast forward to a future shaped by **remarkable technological advancements**. Imagine a world where sophisticated AI systems are not tools of control but **facilitators of human potential**:

- AI identifies hidden talents and strengths within individuals, connecting them with opportunities that align with their capabilities.
- Citizens thrive in an environment where **personal growth and societal progress** are intertwined, creating a dynamic and innovative society.

Further, **virtual reality and AI breakthroughs** eliminate barriers of geography and access:

- A musician in a remote village collaborates with a world-renowned composer, creating art that transcends borders.

- A budding scientist uses virtual laboratories to conduct groundbreaking research that benefits humanity as a whole.

This vision of a **civilized nation system** transforms limitations into opportunities, unlocking the **latent brilliance** within every individual.

Dismantling Hierarchies: Breaking the Chains of Birthright

A truly civilized nation dismantles the **rigid hierarchies of the past**, ensuring that talent and innovation are no longer stifled by circumstance or birthright.

Imagine:

- A peasant with a gift for engineering, designing structures that redefine urban living.
- An artisan with a scientific mind developing tools that transform industries.

This isn't just about **social justice**; it's about unlocking a **wellspring of creativity and innovation**. By empowering every citizen to contribute their unique verse to the symphony, the resulting melody becomes richer, more vibrant, and profoundly transformative.

Rising from Crisis: Collaboration as the New Foundation

History shows that **crisis can forge new orders**. In the aftermath of devastation, survival depends on the collective strength of individuals. A **civilized nation system**:

- Facilitates the exchange of skills and expertise, ensuring that everyone has a role in rebuilding society.
- Empowers citizens to contribute their talents, fostering a sense of ownership and purpose.

This is more than a **pragmatic necessity**; it is a testament to the resilience and ingenuity of the human spirit. When individuals feel valued and empowered, their contributions create a **symphony of rebuilding**, a force that drives progress and hope.

Empowerment and Fulfillment: The Psychological Foundation of Progress

Human beings are social creatures, thriving when they feel valued and connected to a larger purpose. A civilized nation system fosters this by:

- Creating an environment where every individual can contribute their unique gifts.
- Tapping into the human desire for **autonomy, competence, and purpose**.

When individuals feel empowered to use their talents, they experience a profound sense of fulfillment. This intrinsic motivation leads to:

- A more engaged and productive citizenry.
- A society where innovation and collaboration flourish.

The resulting symphony is not a monotonous drone but a **vibrant tapestry** woven from the diverse melodies of empowered individuals. This is the **collective power of the human spirit**, unleashed to its fullest potential.

Conclusion: The Song of a Truly Civilized Nation

By celebrating individual potential and facilitating collaboration, a civilized nation system becomes the **conductor of a grand symphony**. It empowers citizens to contribute their talents, creating a society that thrives on:

- **Innovation**: Embracing creativity and new ideas to solve challenges and advance progress.
- **Progress**: Building a future that uplifts every member of society.
- **The collective spirit of humanity**: Where unity and diversity coexist in harmony.

This symphony isn't merely a metaphor; it is the **song of a truly civilized nation**, a testament to the boundless potential of a society that values and empowers every individual. Together, its citizens compose a melody that resonates far beyond their time, ensuring a legacy of progress, hope, and shared achievement for generations to come.

2. The Equilibrium of Governance: A Symphony of Checks and Balances

A grand symphony requires not only a skilled conductor but also a solid foundation—a **bedrock of justice**. In a truly civilized nation system, governance transcends mere control, becoming the **embodiment of a just and equitable society**. Here, the balance between individual liberty and collective well-being forms the harmonic structure upon which a thriving civilization is built.

Justice as the Bedrock of Progress

Imagine a future where ideals like justice and equality are not distant aspirations but the **very bricks and mortar of a thriving nation**. In this society:

- The **rule of law** and commitment to fairness safeguard the freedoms of every individual.
- Each citizen finds their voice within a larger chorus, contributing to the symphony of progress.

This equilibrium ensures that the collective strength of society upholds individual rights, creating a space where:

- **Unique talents flourish**: Every citizen is empowered to contribute their distinct melody.
- **Equality of opportunity prevails**: Success is determined by effort and ability, not by privilege or circumstance.

This harmonious balance does not demand a **monotonous chorus** where every note is the same. Instead, it celebrates the diversity of melodies, ensuring that each instrument plays its part in a beautifully orchestrated performance.

Governance as a Conductor: Facilitating Harmony, Not Control

A civilized nation walks a tightrope between the needs of the individual and the collective. The **conductor of governance** ensures this balance by:

- Safeguarding individual liberties while promoting the collective good.
- Facilitating an environment where every citizen has a **stake in the nation's success**.

Imagine a government that:

- **Empowers its citizens** to develop their unique talents.
- Protects their rights while maintaining the harmony of the whole.

This vision transforms governance into an **art of facilitation**, where the role of the state is not to dictate but to empower, allowing every voice to be heard and every contribution to be valued.

Technology as a Guardian of Justice

Fast forward to a future where **technology becomes a powerful tool** for safeguarding this delicate balance.

Imagine:

- **AI-powered systems** monitoring for corruption and ensuring the impartial application of laws.
- Technology fostering a **sense of trust** between the citizens and their leaders, ensuring that governance is fair and transparent.

However, technology is a **double-edged sword**. In the hands of unchecked power, it could lead to government overreach. A truly civilized nation mitigates this risk through:

- **Robust checks and balances**: Ensuring no single entity wields unchecked authority.
- An **independent judiciary**: Protecting citizens' rights and acting as a bulwark against tyranny.
- **Civic engagement**: Allowing citizens to shape policies and hold leaders accountable.

This system ensures that the conductor remains a **facilitator of harmony**, not a tyrant dictating every note.

The Consent of the Governed: Leadership Through Trust

In a civilized nation, leaders rule not by fiat but through **the consent of the governed**. A strong and equitable legal system ensures:

- The **protection of all citizens**, from the noble bard to the artisan with hidden potential.
- A **sense of security and stability**, empowering individuals to pursue their aspirations without fear.

Imagine governance as a **benevolent patron**:

- Providing clear laws (the "sheet music") for citizens to follow.
- Ensuring that the tools and resources (the "instruments") are accessible to all.
- Creating an environment where everyone feels safe to express their unique voice within the symphony.

This model transforms leadership into an **act of service**, where the well-being of citizens becomes the ultimate goal.

Rebuilding Harmony From Crisis

The scars of crisis remind us of the importance of **social contracts** in forging a new order. In the aftermath of catastrophe:

- Citizens recognize the need for a strong central authority to maintain **order and security**.
- However, this authority is tempered by **checks and balances**, preventing the rise of despotism.

Imagine a society where survivors rebuild not only their infrastructure but also the **trust and collaboration** that bind them together. This **social contract**:

- Ensures that governance remains a facilitator, not a dictator.
- Empowers citizens to contribute their skills to rebuilding the symphony of society.

Security as the Foundation for Creativity and Progress

Psychology teaches that security fosters progress. When individuals feel:

- Their rights are protected,
- Laws are applied fairly, and
- Their contributions are valued,

They are more likely to **take risks, innovate, and create**. This sense of security:

- Encourages citizens to **experiment with new ideas** and **push boundaries**.
- Creates a richer and more dynamic performance, where the symphony of progress becomes a continuous crescendo.

Trust: The Cornerstone of Harmony

Trust is the **foundation of societal harmony**. When citizens feel their voices resonate in the halls of power:

- They develop a **sense of belonging** and **collective purpose**.
- They unite in pursuit of common aspirations, weaving a **bond of fellowship**.

This trust transforms a collection of individuals into a cohesive community, ready to face challenges and seize opportunities together.

Conclusion: Governance as the Heart of a Civilized Nation

A truly civilized nation understands that **progress is a symphony**—a delicate balance of individual liberty and collective responsibility. By fostering:

- **Justice and equity**: Ensuring every citizen's rights are upheld.
- **Checks and balances**: Safeguarding against tyranny while empowering individuals.
- **Trust and collaboration**: Uniting citizens in a shared purpose.

This nation transforms governance into an art form, where the conductor brings together the diverse talents of its people to create a harmonious and thriving society.

This symphony is not merely an ideal; it is the **heartbeat of progress**, resonating with hope, innovation, and shared achievement. As each citizen contributes their unique melody, the resulting harmony becomes a testament to the **power of justice, trust, and collaboration**, ensuring a brighter future for all.

3. Spectrum-Wide Empowerment: A Rising Tide Lifts All Boats

The symphony of a civilized nation thrives on the **unique melodies** of its citizens, but what happens when the instruments themselves are out of reach for many? A truly civilized nation system understands that **opportunity should not be a privilege** for the select few; it is the **birthright of all**. Here, the vision of a civilized nation takes a pivotal step toward inclusivity by **dismantling barriers** that limit potential. This system doesn't aim to create a monotonous chorus but celebrates the **rich tapestry of human potential** woven from the diverse talents and experiences of its people.

The Power of Equal Opportunity: Unlocking a Well of Potential

Science reveals the transformative power of equal opportunity in building strong societies. A hallmark of a civilized nation is its commitment to providing a **level playing field**:

- **Quality education and healthcare** become accessible to all, enabling citizens to achieve their potential.
- This creates a **ripple effect**, fostering upward mobility and innovation across all sectors of society.

Imagine a society where:

- A talented young artist from a remote village accesses the same resources as a child in a bustling metropolis.

- A farmer's child with a knack for science is equipped to explore their potential alongside urban peers.

This commitment to **equity and opportunity** doesn't just lead to fairness; it **unlocks a wellspring of creativity and innovation** that benefits everyone. A society built on such principles becomes a **cradle of discovery and progress**, where every individual feels empowered to contribute.

Technology as the Bridge: Connecting Potential with Opportunity

Fast forward to a future powered by **technological advancements**. In this world:

- **AI-powered mentors** guide individuals toward their goals, tailoring education to their unique strengths.
- **Virtual reality platforms** offer world-class learning experiences, bridging the gap between remote locations and global opportunities.

For instance:

- A child in a rural village participates in an interactive simulation, mastering engineering concepts once inaccessible to them.
- A citizen in need of access to cutting-edge medical treatment, not limited by income or location.

Technology becomes the bridge that connects untapped potential with opportunity, ensuring that:

- Every voice is heard in the **symphony of progress**.
- No talent is left undiscovered due to geographic, economic, or social limitations.

Greatness from Anywhere: Cultivating Hidden Talent

A **just and equitable society** understands that **greatness can emerge from anywhere**. In such a nation:

- A blacksmith's apprentice with a thirst for knowledge rises to become an innovator in engineering.
- A farmhand with a talent for strategy becomes a leader in agricultural technology.

This is not just about **social justice**—it's about ensuring the **Symphony of Progress has access to all its instruments**. A civilized nation:

- Recognizes untapped potential in every corner of society.
- Provides the tools and education necessary for individuals to **rise above their circumstances** and contribute their unique talents to the collective good.

By ensuring that no citizen is excluded from opportunity, the nation creates a system where **diverse perspectives and abilities enrich the entire society**.

Rising from Crisis: Cooperation as a Foundation for Growth

The aftermath of crises often reveals the importance of **cooperation and collective effort**. In a society rebuilding from the ground up:

- Every individual, from the doctor to the mechanic, plays a critical role in reconstruction.
- A **strong social safety net** ensures that citizens have access to education and training, enabling them to contribute to the rebuilding process.

This spirit of cooperation:

- Recognizes that the **rising tide of opportunity lifts all boats**.
- Encourages citizens to share their skills and work together, ensuring that every member of society contributes to the **symphony of rebuilding**.

Empowerment Breeds Progress: The Psychology of Motivation

Psychology teaches us that when individuals feel they have:

- The **agency to act**, and
- The **resources to succeed**,

They experience a surge of **motivation and creativity**. This translates to:

- A citizenry actively engaged in their personal pursuits.
- A society invested in the collective good, creating a **harmonious performance fueled by shared purpose**.

When empowered individuals come together:

- Their contributions form a tapestry of innovation and collaboration.
- The symphony they create is not a collection of isolated notes but a **thriving, dynamic masterpiece** driven by the collective potential of an empowered populace.

Conclusion: A Symphony of Empowerment

By fostering a system that **dismantles barriers** and **empowers every citizen**, a civilized nation creates a **rising tide that lifts all boats**. This system ensures that:

- **Diversity** becomes the foundation of strength, enriching society with varied talents and perspectives.

- **Innovation** thrives in an environment where every individual has the opportunity to contribute.
- **The human spirit flourishes**, unencumbered by limitations, creating a society defined by progress and hope.

In this symphony of empowerment:

- Every individual contributes their unique melody to the grand composition of progress.
- The resulting harmony is a **testament to the boundless potential** of a society that values inclusivity and opportunity.

This is the essence of a truly civilized nation—a place where the talents of all its citizens converge, creating a brighter future that thrives on the **diversity, creativity, and boundless spirit of humanity**.

II. Cultivating Human Potential

1. The Alchemy of Inspiration and Recognition: A Symphony of Motivation

In the futuristic tapestry of a thriving civilization, the driving force isn't technology or infrastructure alone—it is **motivation**, the indomitable fire that propels individuals to dream, create, and contribute. Imagine a society where this motivation is not manipulated through fear or scarcity but fostered by **recognition, inspiration, and purpose**.

This isn't a world of rigid hierarchies or mindless drones following orders. Instead, it's a place where every individual feels a connection to their role and a sense of ownership in the larger mission. This society operates on the principle that **human potential flourishes in the presence of acknowledgment and encouragement**.

The Energy of Motivation: A Catalyst for Brilliance

Imagine a civilization where **motivation isn't a carrot or a stick—** it's a **self-sustaining force** born from purpose and the desire to contribute.

- **Science offers a roadmap**, revealing that intrinsic motivation—the kind that comes from within—is the most powerful driver of creativity and productivity.
- Effective systems of governance, organizations, and communities in this futuristic world cultivate **environments where individuals feel valued** and connected to a higher purpose.

In this context:

- Recognition programs **celebrate accomplishments** and fuel ambition.
- Opportunities for growth and collaboration foster a sense of shared purpose, empowering every citizen to rise to their potential.

Picture a society where individuals understand the profound importance of their contributions. The engineer sees how their innovation powers clean energy systems; the artist realizes their creation inspires communities to dream bigger. This interconnectedness ignites a civilization-wide **symbiosis of motivation and contribution**.

A Culture of Innovation: Recognizing Sparks of Creativity

A thriving nation isn't built on static success—it thrives on **continuous innovation**. Imagine a society where:

- **Recognition isn't limited to achievements alone** but also celebrates the **spark of creativity** that leads to breakthroughs.

- Citizens are encouraged to experiment, take risks, and push boundaries, knowing that their failures are stepping stones to collective progress.

This futuristic system:

- Rewards individuals not only for **final triumphs** but also for their bold attempts and creative explorations.
- Fosters an **ecosystem of ingenuity** where new ideas are welcomed, and collaboration multiplies the impact of individual brilliance.

For instance:

- A young scientist exploring renewable energy receives funding and recognition for an unconventional idea.
- A tech developer experimenting with AI receives mentorship to refine their vision.

Such systems **unleash a floodgate of potential**, ensuring progress is not stagnant but an ever-expanding horizon of possibilities.

Transforming Challenges Into Purpose: Rising From the Ashes

In times of crisis, this motivation becomes a **force of regeneration**. Imagine a post-catastrophe society where rebuilding isn't just a necessity—it's a **shared mission** fueled by purpose.

- A **strong and trusted government** recognizes and rewards the efforts of citizens, big and small, creating a collective spirit of responsibility.
- From the farmer rebuilding food systems to the programmer restoring communication networks, **every individual plays a vital role** in the revival of civilization.

This collective purpose ensures that the society rising from the ashes is not only rebuilt but **stronger, more united, and more innovative** than before.

The Science of Recognition: Fostering Engagement and Innovation

Psychology teaches us that when people feel their contributions are valued:

- They are more engaged, innovative, and productive.
- They experience **fulfillment and intrinsic motivation,** driving them to strive not just for personal achievement but for collective progress.

In this society:

- Citizens receive not just material rewards but also an **acknowledgment of their efforts**, fostering a deep sense of pride and belonging.
- Recognition strengthens **social bonds,** creating a culture where collaboration and mutual respect thrive.

Imagine a future where:

- A young designer receives national acclaim for their sustainable architecture.
- A group of scientists is celebrated for developing technology that eradicates disease.

These moments of recognition create a ripple effect, inspiring others to uncover their hidden potential and contribute to the **shared mission of progress**.

Collaboration and Cohesion: A Unified Purpose

Recognition isn't just about individual accomplishments; it's about **building community and fostering unity**. In a society where every voice matters:

- Collaboration becomes second nature, with individuals from diverse backgrounds harmonizing their efforts toward shared goals.
- Success is seen not as a solitary victory but as a **collective triumph**.

Imagine a world where:

- A roboticist partners with an artist to create interactive installations that inspire education and innovation.
- A biologist collaborates with a software engineer to develop AI tools that revolutionize healthcare.

These collaborative efforts weave a **tapestry of interdependence**, where every contribution enhances the collective good.

A Vision of Continuous Improvement: The Thrill of Growth

In this civilization, recognition and motivation create a **culture of perpetual improvement**. Every citizen:

- Strives to **refine their skills**, inspired by the acknowledgment of their progress.
- Experiments with new ideas, knowing their efforts will be valued, regardless of outcome.

This leads to a **dynamic society**:

- Where failure is viewed as a stepping stone to innovation.
- Where the drive for improvement fuels a **continuous crescendo of progress**.

Conclusion: The Dawn of a Thriving Civilization

A truly civilized nation system transforms motivation from a fleeting spark into a **sustained flame**. By fostering a culture of **purpose, recognition, and innovation**, it creates a society where:

- Individuals are not only engaged and productive but also **inspired and fulfilled**.
- Collaboration and recognition amplify the impact of individual efforts, creating a **harmonious ecosystem of progress**.

This civilization isn't just about surviving—it's about **thriving**. It understands that the key to unlocking its future lies in the **alchemy of inspiration and recognition**, transforming every citizen into an **architect of a brighter dawn**.

2. The Democratic Forge of Talent: A Symphony of Strengths

Imagine a society that transcends the constraints of the past—a dynamic civilization where the potential of every citizen is realized, celebrated, and woven into a vibrant tapestry of collective progress. In this advanced nation, talent is not hoarded by a select few; it is a **universal asset** cultivated and utilized to create a **harmonious system of progress and innovation**. Here, no individual's contribution is too small, and every skill adds to the brilliance of the whole.

This is the essence of a **civilized nation system**—a **democratic forge of talent**, where every citizen's abilities are nurtured and empowered to shape a future filled with unbounded potential.

Every Contribution Counts: Unlocking the Power of Diverse Skills

Gone are the days of homogeneous societies where sameness stifled creativity. In a truly civilized nation:

- The **blacksmith's dedication**, the **farmer's precision**, and the **scientist's imagination** are equally valued.
- A diverse pool of talent fuels innovation, ensuring that every citizen contributes a **distinct melody** to the composition of progress.

Science highlights the transformative power of diversity in fostering innovation. A civilized nation:

- Builds systems that **identify and develop unique skills**, ensuring that everyone, regardless of background, has an opportunity to thrive.
- Leverages **advanced AI** not as a replacement for human ingenuity but as a tool for matching individual strengths with societal needs.

Imagine a future where:

- AI-driven systems identify the hidden potential of a young artist and connect them with opportunities to revolutionize digital storytelling.
- A farmer's problem-solving ability is harnessed to develop sustainable food systems that combat global hunger.

Even in the aftermath of global crises, the **spirit of cooperation reigns**. Education and training programs ensure that:

- **Every citizen becomes an architect of recovery**, contributing their talents to rebuild and innovate.
- **Communities thrive on collaboration**, recognizing that every individual has a role in shaping the future.

The Craft of Service Innovation: Ingenuity in Action

Innovation is not confined to laboratories or think tanks—it is a cornerstone of everyday life in this futuristic society. A civilized nation fosters a **culture of excellence** where individuals are inspired to push the boundaries of what's possible.

This advanced society:

- Prioritizes **quality education**, robust healthcare, and strong social safety nets as the foundation of progress.
- Incentivizes creativity and experimentation, ensuring that **service innovation is rewarded** across all levels.

Imagine:

- A mechanic in a technologically advanced outpost devising a renewable energy solution for their community.
- A teacher reimagining education through virtual reality, ensuring no child is left behind in the digital age.

These contributions are not just acknowledged but celebrated. Recognition instills a **sense of accomplishment and purpose**, driving individuals to aim higher. This relentless pursuit of excellence:

- Fuels continuous improvement and sparks new waves of **discovery and progress**.
- Creates an environment where **ingenuity is an honor, not a burden**, and individuals take pride in refining their craft.

Shared Success: A Unified Vision for the Future

The cornerstone of this civilization is its **commitment to collective ownership and shared success**.

Imagine:

- Communities pool resources, collaborate on projects and celebrate achievements as collective victories.
- A system where the **benefits of innovation** are distributed equitably, ensuring everyone has a stake in the future.

This creates a society where:

- Individuals feel part of a **larger purpose**, motivated to contribute their best efforts for the common good.
- Citizens experience **collective well-being**, knowing their contributions are valued and impactful.

This **spirit of unity** extends beyond crisis recovery, embedding itself in the fabric of the nation:

- Economic opportunity is distributed fairly, allowing individuals to take risks and **pursue groundbreaking ideas without fear of failure**.
- Social safety nets act as platforms for innovation, empowering citizens to explore their potential.

Lifelong Learning: Adapting and Evolving

In this advanced civilization, learning is not confined to classrooms but is a **lifelong journey of discovery**. The nation recognizes that:

- **Knowledge evolves**, and individuals must grow alongside it.
- Advanced AI systems enable **personalized learning**, tailoring experiences to individual strengths and aspirations.

This culture of lifelong learning:

- Empower citizens to **adapt to a rapidly changing world**.
- Prepares them to tackle the challenges and opportunities of the future with confidence and creativity.

Imagine a society where:

- An artisan learns new techniques through immersive simulations, keeping traditional crafts alive in a modern context.

- A scientist collaborates with a historian to develop interdisciplinary solutions that solve present challenges while honoring the past.

This **continuous evolution of skills and knowledge** ensures that citizens remain resilient, resourceful, and ready to contribute to the **ever-changing landscape of progress**.

The Harmony of Shared Purpose: A Collective Symphony

At its heart, the **democratic forge of talent** is about creating a society where:

- Every citizen is **cherished and motivated** to share their unique abilities.

- The varied talents of individuals unite to form a **harmonious symphony of progress**.

In this civilization:

- A musician's craft inspires innovation in acoustics.

- A farmer's expertise in sustainable practices contributes to ecological preservation.

- A programmer's ingenuity ensures ethical advancements in artificial intelligence.

Together, these contributions weave a **tapestry of advancement** that resonates far beyond national borders, inspiring other societies to embrace **collaboration, inclusivity, and shared purpose**.

Conclusion: The Blueprint for a Flourishing Future

The **democratic forge of talent** transcends mere productivity—it aspires to cultivate a society where:

- **Innovation and collaboration** are natural extensions of shared purpose.
- **Economic opportunity** uplifts everyone, ensuring progress benefits all citizens.
- The **boundless potential of humanity** is unleashed, driving a future defined by creativity, equity, and achievement.

This civilization is not built on a foundation of privilege but on the belief that **each individual holds the key to collective progress**. By empowering citizens to discover, refine, and share their talents, the nation creates a legacy of **innovation, unity, and hope**.

In this **architectural marvel of progress**, every citizen is a builder, every contribution is a cornerstone, and every dream adds to the **magnificent structure of a brighter tomorrow**.

3. The Crucible of Visionary Thought: Cultivating the Architects of Progress

Imagine a civilization not as a static collection of individuals but as a **vibrant nexus of visionary thought**, where ideas are forged like precious alloys in the crucible of innovation. This is not a place where knowledge is passively absorbed but an arena where **bold visions are refined into the tools and technologies** that shape a brighter future. A truly advanced society creates an environment that equips its citizens not only with knowledge but with the **fire and focus to turn ideas into reality**, making every individual an architect of progress.

The Garden of Visionaries: Where Dreams Take Root

Great civilizations do not bloom by accident. They are cultivated from **seeds of ambition, purpose, and insight**, planted in fertile soil, and nurtured with care. A futuristic society fosters these qualities in its citizens, creating a **generation of dreamers and**

doers who see not only the possibility of a better tomorrow but also their role in building it.

- **Science underscores** the importance of education that goes beyond rote memorization. A society focused on progress cultivates:

  o **Critical thinking**: Encouraging individuals to question, analyze, and innovate.
  o **Problem-solving skills**: Equipping citizens to tackle complex challenges.
  o **An entrepreneurial spirit**: Inspiring bold steps toward the unknown.

This is a society where the farmer, driven by a vision of sustainability, invents irrigation systems that reshape agriculture, and the artist uses virtual reality to reimagine how stories are told. By instilling a **thirst for knowledge and curiosity**, this civilization empowers everyone to contribute their unique perspectives to the collective good.

In a world increasingly tested by crises, **visionary leadership** becomes indispensable. A society rooted in visionary thought:

- Nurtures **resilience and ingenuity**, enabling its citizens to rebuild stronger and more sustainably.
- Fosters an environment where individuals feel **empowered to pursue their ideas**, knowing they have the tools to make an impact.

When people feel that their ideas matter, they experience a profound sense of **purpose and agency**, fueling a collective effort to shape a better future.

The Markers of Advancement: The Building Blocks of Progress

Visions alone cannot transform the world—they must be **tempered with determination, imagination, and action**. A truly civilized nation creates systems that:

- **Celebrate intellectual curiosity** while emphasizing the importance of dedication and perseverance.
- Inspire citizens to push the **boundaries of human knowledge**, ensuring that no dream remains confined to the realm of possibility.

In a future defined by rapid technological advancements:

- Adaptability becomes a cornerstone of survival. Citizens are encouraged to approach challenges with creativity and enthusiasm, ensuring society doesn't merely react to change but **actively shapes its trajectory**.
- Grand ideas are matched with robust systems of **planning and execution**, ensuring that sparks of imagination are transformed into **flames of achievement**.

For instance:

- A scientist's breakthrough in energy storage technology is swiftly translated into global solutions for renewable energy.
- A community initiative to combat water scarcity is scaled into a national program, saving countless lives.

This ability to translate vision into reality is what defines a society's **capacity for progress**.

Collaborative Optimism: A Vision Shared and Realized

Crises test the resilience of any society, but a **spirit of optimism and collaboration** transforms adversity into opportunity. In such moments:

- **Communities unite** around shared visions, blending talents to rebuild and innovate.
- Collaboration between diverse disciplines results in breakthroughs that no single group could achieve alone.

Imagine:

- A doctor, inspired by the vision of a healthier future, collaborates with an engineer to design groundbreaking sanitation systems.
- An architect works with environmental scientists to rebuild communities devastated by natural disasters using sustainable materials and techniques.

This **collective action** ensures that the embers of hope are fanned into a roaring flame, propelling the nation toward a brighter tomorrow.

Celebrating the Journey: From Spark to Symphony

In this advanced society, progress is celebrated not just for its outcomes but for the **effort, imagination, and collaboration** that make it possible. Every spark of innovation, every bold attempt, and every unwavering act of dedication is recognized and woven into the **narrative of shared success**.

When individuals feel that:

- Their ideas are valued,
- Their enthusiasm is contagious, and
- Their contributions are essential to the collective mission,

They experience a profound sense of **empowerment and belonging**. This intrinsic motivation inspires citizens to reach beyond their limits, creating a culture where innovation is both a personal journey and a collective triumph.

A Civilization Defined by Visionary Thought

The measure of a society is not just in its infrastructure or technology but in the **crucible of visionary thought** that burns within its people. A truly civilized nation:

- Fosters an environment where **dreams are nurtured**, and every citizen sees themselves as an architect of progress.
- Translates ideas into actions and solutions, creating a **tapestry of innovation** that benefits all.

This is a world where individuals are not merely observers of change but **active participants in shaping the future**. By cultivating visionary thought, the nation ensures that:

- Every citizen's potential is unleashed.
- Every challenge becomes an opportunity.
- Every innovation serves as a step toward a brighter, more equitable future.

Conclusion: Architects of a Brighter Future

A society built on visionary thought is one that thrives not on the backs of a few but on the **collective genius of all**. It is a place where:

- Dreams take root in fertile soil and grow into towering achievements.
- Innovation and resilience become the foundation of progress.
- Collaboration turns individual aspirations into collective triumphs.

This is the **true essence of a civilized nation**—a dynamic and thriving entity where every citizen is both a dreamer and a builder, creating a future that is brighter, bolder, and boundless in its possibilities. It is a world where visionary thought becomes the **keystone of civilization**, ensuring that progress is not only achieved but sustained, illuminating the path for generations to come.

4. Illuminating the Gems: Unearthing and Polishing Leaders for a Brighter Tomorrow

In a truly advanced civilization, progress is not measured solely by technological marvels or economic strength, but by the leaders, **it nurtures**—individuals who guide with vision, inspire with purpose, and elevate society as a whole. Imagine a society not dominated by the harsh glare of competition but bathed in the **warm spotlight of talent cultivation**, where leadership is a **shared responsibility** built on mentorship, creativity, and collaboration. Here, leaders are not figureheads but **architects of a brighter tomorrow**, empowered to steer humanity into uncharted realms of possibility.

The Hunt for Pioneers: Cultivating Tomorrow's Guiding Lights

Great leaders are not born by chance; they are **discovered, nurtured, and empowered**. A futuristic society understands that:

- **Identifying potential** is only the first step. Actual progress requires actively cultivating a **pipeline of leaders** who are prepared to face the complexities of an evolving world.
- This isn't left to chance. Imagine a **network of talent scouts** embedded in educational institutions, corporations, and communities, working to identify individuals with exceptional qualities of **vision, empathy, and determination**.

Science reveals that strong leadership pipelines are the backbone of thriving economies. A futuristic nation:

- Fosters policies that encourage **leadership development programs** in both private and public sectors.
- Ensures that mentorship is not just a tradition but a **systematic effort**, where seasoned leaders pass on their wisdom and experience to the next generation.

In a world shaped by complexity, **strategic thinking and problem-solving** become indispensable. Programs designed to:

- **Identify exceptional cognitive abilities** to ensure that society has leaders capable of navigating a future filled with **unforeseen challenges and opportunities**.
- Empower individuals with the **tools to lead**, fostering resilience, adaptability, and vision.

Imagine:

- A young innovator mentored by an elder statesperson, learning not just the mechanics of leadership but the values and ethics that sustain a thriving society.
- Leadership summits that combine the wisdom of history with the insights of cutting-edge technology, creating a **fusion of tradition and innovation**.

This commitment to leadership development ensures that the **flames of progress are never extinguished**, even in the most challenging times.

The Drive for Distinction: Igniting a Passion for Excellence

True leadership emerges not from privilege but from **excellence and initiative**. A truly civilized nation fosters a **culture of distinction** where individuals are encouraged to:

- Push their boundaries and discover their unique potential.
- Celebrate not just outcomes but the **creativity and effort** that fuel progress.

Science confirms that high-performance cultures thrive on **recognition and reward systems**. In this futuristic society:

- Performance-based programs incentivize **dedication, ingenuity, and collaboration**.
- Citizens are motivated not by the promise of status but by the joy of **contributing to a collective vision**.

Imagine a system where:

- Risk-taking is encouraged, and unconventional ideas are celebrated, paving the way for **groundbreaking solutions**.
- Leaders inspire through their **commitment to innovation and inclusivity**, ensuring that every voice is heard and valued.

From the blacksmiths honing their craft to the engineers designing spacecraft, this **spirit of excellence** permeates every layer of society, creating a **culture where every contribution matters**.

Collaboration as a Catalyst: Harnessing the Power of Many

The **scars of crisis** remind us that progress is never a solitary endeavor—it is a **collective journey**. A futuristic society harnesses the power of collaboration by:

- Fostering a **spirit of collective brainstorming**, where diverse perspectives come together to tackle complex challenges.
- Encouraging cross-disciplinary partnerships, uniting scientists, artists, technologists, and educators in pursuit of shared goals.

Imagine:

- A community rebuilding after a natural disaster, where architects and environmental scientists collaborate to create sustainable housing.
- A global summit where leaders from every field pool their expertise to address climate change, ensuring a resilient future for all.

This culture of collaboration transforms obstacles into opportunities, creating a **society that thrives on unity and shared purpose**.

Recognition and Empowerment: Unlocking Human Potential

Psychology teaches us that when individuals feel recognized and valued:

- They are more likely to **push their limits**, striving for excellence.
- Their sense of purpose and engagement fuels a **virtuous cycle of progress**.

A futuristic nation ensures that:

- **Achievements, big and small**, are celebrated as stepping stones in the journey of progress.
- Systems of recognition foster a **sense of community and shared responsibility**, where every citizen feels empowered to contribute.

This isn't about creating a world of isolated successes but about weaving a **tapestry of collective brilliance**, where every effort enhances the whole.

A Legacy of Leadership: Lighting the Path Forward

Leadership in this advanced civilization is not about **singular brilliance** but about **cultivating collective potential**. A nation that invests in its leaders ensures:

- **Sustainability of progress**, as each generation builds on the achievements of the last.
- A culture where leaders are **mentors and collaborators**, not just decision-makers.

Imagine a world where:

- Leadership summits bring together thinkers, innovators, and dreamers to chart the course for humanity's next great chapter.
- The torch of leadership is passed seamlessly from one visionary to the next, ensuring continuity and growth.

Conclusion: Illuminating the Future Together

A genuinely civilized nation understands that its **greatest resource is its people**. By identifying potential, fostering excellence, and encouraging collaboration, it creates a society where:

- Every citizen has the opportunity to **lead in their own way**, contributing their unique talents to the collective good.
- Leadership is not confined to a select few but is a **shared responsibility**, ensuring that progress is inclusive and sustainable.

This is the essence of a **future-ready civilization**—a place where leaders are not rulers but **architects of possibility**, guiding society toward a horizon of infinite potential. Together, they illuminate the path forward, ensuring that every step is a stride toward a brighter, more equitable tomorrow.

III. Building Economic and Social Harmony

1. The Collective Enterprise: A Shared Prosperity

Imagine a civilization that transcends the narrow confines of a winner-take-all economy, embracing instead a **shared vision of prosperity**. Here, wealth is not a gilded cage reserved for the privileged few but a **collective enterprise** where every citizen contributes their talents and reaps the rewards of progress. This isn't simply about financial security—it's about weaving a **vibrant tapestry of economic participation**, where every thread strengthens the social and economic fabric of the nation.

In this futuristic society, prosperity becomes a **shared endeavor**, where opportunity is not rationed but cultivated, and every individual has a stake in the nation's progress.

The Mosaic of Investment: Building Wealth Together

True prosperity begins with **access and inclusion**. A civilized nation goes beyond traditional employment models, fostering a **mosaic of investment** where individuals are not just workers but **stakeholders** in the future.

- Imagine a baker investing in a **local tech start-up**, sharing in its success.
- Envision an engineer owning shares in the company where they innovate, creating a direct link between their contributions and the organization's growth.

In this society:

- **Micro-investment platforms** empower citizens to invest in ventures ranging from small, local businesses to transformative global enterprises.
- **Collective ownership models** replace systems of concentrated wealth, ensuring a more equitable distribution of opportunity and reward.

As automation reshapes traditional labor markets, a civilized nation:

- Recognizes the shift and implements policies that empower individuals to become **entrepreneurs and innovators**.
- Provides **access to capital** and investment opportunities, allowing citizens to shape the future economy.

This creates a system where:

- Everyone has the tools to **build wealth and thrive**.
- Prosperity is no longer confined to an elite minority but is a **shared experience** that uplifts the entire nation.

Resilience Through Cooperation: Revitalizing Communities

In times of crisis, the true strength of a society lies in its ability to **rebuild together**. A civilized nation fosters:

- **Micro-loans and community investment pools**, enabling individuals to recover from personal setbacks while contributing to the larger economy.
- **Collaboration among artisans, small business owners, and professionals**, ensuring that communities rebuild with resilience and innovation.

Imagine:

- A craftsman pooling resources with other local creators to launch a shared marketplace.

- A community rebuilding its infrastructure through cooperative investment in sustainable technologies.

When citizens feel that they have a **personal stake** in the economic success of their communities, they are:

- **Motivated to innovate and contribute**.
- Empowered by a sense of **ownership and agency**, knowing their efforts drive both personal and collective progress.

The Tapestry of Economic Participation: A Web of Opportunity

In this advanced society, economic participation becomes a **woven tapestry**, where every citizen plays a vital role in the nation's prosperity.

Diversity is the cornerstone of this thriving economy:

- From the aspiring entrepreneur to the corporate leader, everyone has **equal access to resources and opportunities**.
- Policies encourage **entrepreneurship and small business creation**, fueling innovation and competition.

In this society:

- Cutting-edge technologies are not monopolized by corporations but made accessible to **small businesses and start-ups**.
- **Legal protections** ensure that artisans, freelancers, and small business owners can thrive, regardless of their background.

This fosters a spirit of **ingenuity and fairness**, creating an economic system where:

- **Greatness emerges from anywhere**, not just from established institutions.

- Citizens feel **empowered to shape their own destinies**, knowing that success is attainable through talent and effort.

Entrepreneurship and Innovation: A Path to Economic Resilience

The **scars of crisis** reveal the importance of adaptability. A civilized nation:

- Encourages individuals to **take control of their economic destinies** by fostering entrepreneurship.
- Implements systems that reward **risk-taking and creativity**, ensuring that citizens feel supported in their endeavors.

Imagine:

- A society where start-ups thrive in the aftermath of economic downturns, revitalizing local economies with fresh ideas.
- Communities united by a shared vision, creating jobs and opportunities that rebuild more vigorous and more innovative ecosystems.

This **spirit of entrepreneurial resilience** ensures that the economy is not just repaired but **reborn, infused with innovation and creativity**.

Shared Prosperity: An Economy for All

A genuinely civilized nation understands that progress must be **inclusive**. Economic opportunity is not a privilege but a **right**, ensuring that:

- Every citizen has the chance to **contribute and benefit**.
- Effective social safety nets **encourage innovation**, allowing individuals to explore bold ideas without fear of failure.

Imagine:

- A musician refining their craft without the constant worry of financial instability.
- A researcher pursuing groundbreaking scientific advancements, knowing their efforts are supported by a fair and equitable system.

In this society, progress is not a **zero-sum game**. Instead, it is a **rising tide** that lifts all boats, fostering an environment where innovation and collaboration create **endless opportunities**.

Conclusion: A Collective Enterprise of Hope and Progress

A nation's true wealth is not measured by its GDP but by the **spirit of collective enterprise** that animates its citizens. In this advanced society:

- **Every voice matters**, and every contribution strengthens the whole.
- Prosperity is shared, ensuring that no one is left behind in the march of progress.

This is a world where:

- Investment is not just financial but **personal**, empowering citizens to shape their own futures.
- Participation is celebrated, creating a society where **diverse talents** converge to form an economic system that thrives on fairness, opportunity, and innovation.

The **collective enterprise** is not just an economic model—it is a **manifestation of hope and unity**, a promise that the future is brighter when **everyone has a stake in its success**. In this civilization, progress is a shared journey, and prosperity is a **symphony of collaboration**, resonating with opportunity, resilience, and boundless possibility.

2. The Liquidity of Progress: A Symphony of Opportunity in a Dynamic Marketplace

Imagine a civilization where economic progress is not a stagnant pool but a **thriving marketplace**, a fluid ecosystem where opportunity flows freely and innovation flourishes. Here, wealth is not hoarded but circulated, fueling creativity, growth, and empowerment. This is not merely an economic system—it is a **liquid symphony of progress**, where every citizen has a role, every investment contributes, and every idea finds fertile ground to grow.

In this advanced society, the marketplace is **dynamic and adaptable**, designed to evolve with the changing tides of technology and human ambition. **Economic liquidity** becomes the cornerstone of prosperity, ensuring that progress reaches every corner of the nation.

The Flux of Ownership: Ensuring Constant Motion

A thriving economy depends on its ability to **adapt and evolve**, much like a river that sustains life by continually flowing. A civilized nation fosters this fluidity by creating a **dynamic investment environment** where:

- **Shares and investments are traded seamlessly**, allowing individuals to adjust their portfolios with ease.
- Capital flows to its most productive uses, ensuring that innovation and growth are never stifled.

Science confirms that a well-functioning stock market is the heartbeat of a strong economy. A futuristic society:

- Ensures **transparency, fairness, and efficiency**, protecting investors while providing businesses with the resources needed to innovate.

- Implements regulations that promote **adaptability**, allowing capital to flow to emerging industries and groundbreaking ideas.

Imagine a system where:

- A biotech start-up developing life-saving treatments easily attracts investments from individuals across the nation.
- An AI-driven marketplace ensures that **every dollar invested maximizes societal benefit**, connecting resources with innovation in real-time.

This perpetual motion keeps the economy vibrant, creating an **ecosystem of opportunity** that empowers individuals and fuels societal progress.

Stability in Crisis: Confidence Through Fair Systems

In moments of crisis, access to capital becomes a lifeline. A truly advanced civilization:

- Creates systems that facilitate the **transfer of ownership**, ensuring that businesses can adapt and thrive in challenging conditions.
- Encourages **community-based investment initiatives**, enabling citizens to pool resources and rebuild local economies.

When citizens feel:

- That their investments are **secure and impactful**, and
- That the market operates with **integrity and fairness**,

They experience a sense of **confidence and ownership**, becoming active participants in the collective journey of progress.

The Accessibility of Prosperity: A Marketplace for All

A civilized nation understands that economic liquidity must be paired with **inclusivity**. A dynamic market is not a privilege for the elite; it is a **platform for everyone** to participate and benefit. This inclusivity:

- Broadens the base of ownership, democratizing wealth and opportunity.
- Empower individuals from all walks of life to contribute to and share in the growth of the economy.

Science highlights that inclusive participation strengthens economic systems. In this society:

- **Micro-investment platforms** enable small investors to participate in ventures, from local businesses to global innovations.
- Crowdfunding becomes a cornerstone of progress, allowing communities to directly support projects that align with their values and needs.

Imagine a world where:

- A teacher invests in renewable energy start-ups, contributing to a greener future.
- A mechanic's savings fund is a robotics company, which in turn develops tools that enhance productivity in workshops worldwide.

This **distributed prosperity** creates a marketplace where **every voice matters**, fostering a sense of shared ownership and collective progress.

Collaboration and Community: Economic Revitalization Through Unity

The power of a community-driven economy lies in its ability to **harness collective resources**. In times of upheaval, this spirit of collaboration becomes even more vital. A civilized nation:

- Encourages **community investment pools**, where citizens unite to fund local projects, revitalizing neighborhoods and fostering economic growth.
- Implements policies that incentivize **cooperative ventures**, ensuring that communities thrive together rather than in isolation.

Imagine:

- A rural town pooling resources to create a sustainable agriculture initiative that feeds the region and generates income.
- Urban communities funding shared housing projects that provide affordable and eco-friendly living spaces.

This **shared investment model** doesn't just rebuild economies— it strengthens social bonds, creating a society where success is a **collective achievement**.

The Role of Technology: Connecting Potential with Progress

In this advanced marketplace, technology serves as the **bridge between opportunity and action**. AI-powered systems:

- Democratize access to investments, ensuring that even small contributors can make impactful choices.
- Provide **real-time insights**, enabling investors to make informed decisions that align with their values and aspirations.

Virtual reality platforms allow citizens to:

- Explore potential investments with immersive experiences, understanding their impact before committing resources.
- Collaborate with like-minded individuals across the globe, pooling resources to support groundbreaking initiatives.

This fusion of technology and inclusivity creates a **marketplace where progress is accessible to all**, ensuring that every idea, talent, and resource is utilized to its fullest potential.

The Symphony of Opportunity: Progress for Every Citizen

When individuals feel they have:

- A **stake in the economy**,
- **Control over their investments**, and
- A sense of **agency in shaping their futures**,

They are inspired to contribute with passion and purpose. This sense of belonging transforms the marketplace into a **living symphony**, where every citizen plays a role in creating a harmonious and prosperous society.

Conclusion: A Flowing Future of Shared Progress

A genuinely civilized nation is not defined by stagnant wealth or exclusive markets but by the **liquidity of progress** that flows through its veins. In this society:

- Participation is encouraged, ensuring that every citizen has a role in shaping the future.
- Capital is accessible, providing the resources needed to innovate and thrive.
- Prosperity is shared, creating an economic landscape that uplifts all.

This **dynamic marketplace** is more than an economic model—it is a testament to the power of **collaboration, adaptability, and inclusivity**. It ensures that the **music of progress** reaches every corner of society, creating a future filled with opportunity, innovation, and hope.

The **liquidity of progress** is the lifeblood of this advanced civilization—a flow that connects individuals, ideas, and industries in an unending symphony of success. Together, they compose a masterpiece that resonates across generations, proving that the **greatest wealth lies in the collective potential of humanity**.

3. The Axis of Financial Autonomy: A Balancing Act for Progress

Imagine a society that masterfully walks the tightrope between **dynamic innovation** and **unshakable stability**—a place where the **axis of financial autonomy** finds perfect harmony. In this advanced civilization, a well-functioning economic system enables resources to flow seamlessly into large corporations, the **engines of progress** that drive technological breakthroughs, infrastructure development, and global influence. Yet, with great power comes great responsibility; these corporations are held accountable to not just shareholders but the entire community.

This is a future where financial autonomy becomes the cornerstone of a **thriving and equitable society**, ensuring that the economic framework serves both innovation and the collective good.

The Pillars of Empowered Possession: Ownership with Responsibility

A genuinely civilized nation doesn't merely concentrate wealth—it **empowers ownership** with responsibility, transforming corporations into **catalysts of progress**. In this system:

- The stock market evolves into a bustling **marketplace of ideas and innovation**, enabling companies to reinvest in growth and job creation.
- Businesses operate not only for profit but also for the **collective well-being**, ensuring sustainable and ethical practices.

Science confirms that a competitive private sector is a pillar of economic vitality. A futuristic society:

- Fosters policies that encourage **investment in innovation-heavy industries**, ensuring corporations remain at the forefront of global progress.
- Implements robust regulations to guarantee that businesses prioritize the **well-being of stakeholders**, from workers to the environment.

Imagine a system where:

- Corporations are accountable to **independent oversight bodies** that monitor ethical practices.
- Investments flow into technologies that not only generate profit but also **uplift society**, such as renewable energy, advanced healthcare, and equitable education platforms.

This framework ensures that corporations are not just powerhouses of wealth but **stewards of progress**, driving economic growth while safeguarding the planet and its people.

Innovation Meets Responsibility: A Balance of Power

In the future, powered by rapid technological advancement, large corporations will often be in charge of research and development. However, unchecked power can lead to inequities and exploitation. A civilized nation mitigates these risks by:

- Promoting **good corporate governance**, ensuring transparency and ethical behavior.
- Creating mechanisms that encourage **long-term investments** over short-term profits, fostering sustainable innovation.

This balance of power transforms corporations into:

- **Collaborative partners** that align their goals with societal priorities.
- **Engines of progress** that fuel discovery while contributing to the greater good.

In the aftermath of crises, these corporations become **critical lifelines**, helping rebuild infrastructure, revitalize economies, and provide essential goods. Through **public-private partnerships**, governments and corporations work together to:

- Mobilize resources efficiently.
- Address urgent societal challenges, such as climate resilience and equitable healthcare.

The Constancy Amidst Change: Building Resilient Systems

Economic stability is the backbone of innovation. A genuinely advanced society:

- Ensures that corporations are **resilient in the face of economic volatility**, safeguarding jobs and investments during downturns.
- Encourages businesses to **diversify revenue streams** and maintain healthy cash reserves, creating financial buffers against unforeseen challenges.

Imagine:

- A multinational corporation using its resources to develop localized solutions, such as disaster relief technologies or sustainable agriculture practices.

- Governments implementing **regulations that incentivize R&D**, ensuring companies remain adaptable and competitive in a rapidly evolving global marketplace.

In this framework:

- Even the most powerful institutions are prepared for the unexpected, with access to credit and resources to maintain operations.

- Corporations play a **stabilizing role**, providing continuity and hope in times of uncertainty.

Disaster Preparedness: Corporations as Lifelines

The scars of crises highlight the need for **disaster-ready economies**. A futuristic nation implements systems that:

- Ensure corporations can **continue operating** during disruptions, maintaining the flow of goods, services, and jobs.

- Incentivize businesses to **invest in resilience technologies**, from climate-proof infrastructure to AI-driven supply chain management.

For example:

- A tech company develops decentralized energy grids to maintain power in disaster-stricken areas.

- A pharmaceutical giant accelerates the distribution of life-saving medicines during a pandemic.

These efforts transform corporations into **pillars of stability**, providing not just resources but also hope and confidence in the nation's ability to rebuild.

Empowerment and Accountability: A Harmonious Axis

When businesses operate with both **autonomy and accountability**, they become engines of:

- **Innovation**, driving advancements that benefit society.
- **Community well-being**, fostering trust and shared purpose.

A society that fosters this balance:

- Empower corporate leaders to **take calculated risks** and invest in visionary projects.
- Holds these leaders accountable through transparent governance systems, ensuring that profits align with societal progress.

Conclusion: The Bridge Between Progress and Equity

A civilized nation is not a slave to market whims or corporate power; it is a **harmonious system** where financial autonomy and accountability work in tandem. This balance:

- Enables corporations to act as **catalysts of innovation and growth**.
- Ensures that economic prosperity uplifts not just shareholders but the entire community.

The **axis of financial autonomy** becomes a **bridge** between the economic engine and societal needs, creating a system where:

- Progress is inclusive, driven by collaboration between governments, corporations, and citizens.
- Stability fosters confidence, empowering individuals and businesses alike to invest in a shared future.

This is a society where economic power is wielded not as a weapon but as a tool for collective progress. As corporations innovate and expand, they do so with the knowledge that their success is intrinsically tied to the well-being of the people and the planet.

The result is a civilization defined by **shared prosperity, resilience, and hope**, a world where the **axis of financial autonomy** spins steadily, ensuring that innovation and stability remain in perfect harmony for generations to come.

4. The Tapestry of Toil: Weaving a Brighter Future, Thread by Thread

Imagine a society where success is not built on **segregated roles or hierarchies** but on a **vibrant, interconnected tapestry of collaboration and innovation**. In this world, the boundaries between leaders and workers blur, replaced by a **shared purpose** and a collective drive toward prosperity. This is a civilization where every individual's contribution is a vital thread woven together to form a strong and resilient fabric of progress.

This **tapestry of toil** is not merely a metaphor for work—it is the foundation of a society that thrives on unity, shared ownership, and a collective vision of a brighter future.

The Fusion of Investment and Work: When Effort Becomes Ownership

In this advanced civilization, **work transcends mere labor**—it becomes a form of **investment** in one's own future. Every individual, from the frontline innovator to the visionary CEO, is empowered to:

- **Invest directly in their workplace**, transforming a paycheck into a stake in the company's success.
- Share in the rewards of their collective effort, creating a powerful incentive for productivity and innovation.

Science underscores the transformative power of **performance-based rewards**. A genuinely civilized nation:

- Fosters policies that encourage **profit-sharing programs** and **Employee Stock Ownership Plans (ESOPs)**, aligning the interests of employees with those of shareholders.
- Cultivates a workforce where every individual feels **a sense of ownership**, breaking down the barriers between labor and management.

Imagine a workplace where:

- A designer feels as much responsibility for the company's success as the executive team, knowing their **efforts directly impact their personal stake**.
- A production team innovates not because they are told to but because they are **motivated by shared goals** and tangible rewards.

This fusion of investment and labor fosters an environment of **collaboration, pride, and shared achievement**, turning every worker into a co-creator of prosperity.

Worker Cooperatives: Collaboration in Times of Crisis

Crises reveal the power of **shared ownership and responsibility**. A civilized nation recognizes this and:

- Implements systems that encourage **worker cooperatives**, where employees co-own and manage enterprises.
- Empower communities to rebuild industries with a sense of **collective purpose**.

Imagine:

- A factory devastated by an economic downturn was restructured as a worker-owned cooperative where employees controlled production and shared in the profits.
- A rebuilding effort after a natural disaster, where co-owned businesses emerge as resilient economic engines for their communities.

This system ensures that everyone, regardless of their role, has a **stake in the enterprise's success,** fostering an enduring spirit of **cooperation and resilience**.

The Harmony of Direction and Execution: Breaking Down Barriers

In this futuristic society, the rigid distinctions between leaders and workers dissolve, replaced by a **unified culture of collaboration and respect**. Here:

- Management and labor share the same goals, creating a workplace where **every idea is valued,** regardless of rank.
- Flat organizational structures and team-based initiatives replace traditional hierarchies, fostering an environment where creativity thrives.

Science highlights the importance of **collaboration in achieving organizational success**. A civilized nation:

- Encourages companies to **cross-train employees,** ensuring adaptability and a well-rounded workforce.
- Promotes **knowledge-sharing programs** that empower individuals at every level to contribute their insights.

Imagine a future where:

- An engineer mentors a new hire while simultaneously learning from their fresh perspective.

- A mechanic's innovative idea for improving efficiency is celebrated and implemented, regardless of their position in the company.

This **egalitarian approach** fosters a sense of belonging and connection, motivating individuals to **collaborate for the greater good**.

A Culture of Mutual Respect: Building Unity Through Shared Purpose

The strength of this society lies in its commitment to **mutual respect and shared purpose**. Just as a master artisan values the apprentice's fresh ideas, a civilized nation:

- Creates systems that emphasize **collaboration across all levels**, ensuring that every voice is heard.
- Encourages a culture where **success is a collective achievement**, not an individual pursuit.

The scars of crises serve as powerful reminders of the need for **shared sacrifice**. In this advanced civilization:

- Profit-sharing and incentive programs ensure that **everyone benefits** from the team's efforts.
- Adversity strengthens the bonds of the workforce, inspiring individuals to work for the **betterment of the entire community**.

Psychology teaches that when individuals feel they are part of a **unified team**, they:

- Experience a sense of **belonging and purpose**.
- Are more likely to innovate, take initiative, and excel in their roles.

This unity transforms workplaces into **hubs of creativity and innovation**, where the lines between direction and execution blur, and every contribution becomes indispensable.

The Tapestry of Shared Success: A Collective Vision

A genuinely advanced society understands that progress is not built on the efforts of a few but on the **combined strengths of all**. By weaving individual contributions into a **tapestry of shared success**, this civilization:

- Fosters a culture of **continuous learning**, where education and skill-building are lifelong pursuits.
- Creates social safety nets that support individuals as they take risks and **explore new ideas**.

Imagine:

- Advanced AI systems tailoring educational programs to help workers refine their skills and adapt to new challenges.
- Social programs enabling artisans, innovators, and professionals to **collaborate across disciplines**, driving innovation in every sector.

This commitment to **lifelong learning and shared success** ensures that progress is inclusive, sustainable, and enduring.

Conclusion: A Future Woven Together

A genuinely civilized nation isn't built on the separation of classes or hierarchies—it thrives on the **unified efforts of co-owners and collaborators**. By fostering:

- **Shared ownership** that motivates individuals to take pride in their work,
- **Harmonious collaboration** that blurs traditional boundaries, and

- **Mutual respect and shared purpose** that inspires creativity and innovation,

This society creates a **tapestry of toil** where every thread strengthens the whole. The result is a future where prosperity is not just shared but **amplified**, where every individual feels empowered to contribute their talents to a greater cause.

This vibrant tapestry, woven thread by thread through the combined efforts of all its citizens, ensures a world filled with **shared prosperity, collective achievement, and boundless possibility**. Together, they craft a brighter dawn—**a future where unity, innovation, and progress intertwine** to create a legacy that inspires generations.[1]

---

[1] **Implementing these policies and systems can vary depending on the economic context. Here are some general steps and considerations:**

1. **Assess the current economic situation:** Evaluate the nation's economic health, labor market dynamics, and existing policies.
2. **Identify opportunities for reform:** Identify areas where employee ownership and participation can be implemented or strengthened.
3. **Develop a comprehensive plan:** Create a detailed plan outlining the specific policies and programs to be implemented.
4. **Engage stakeholders:** Involve businesses, labor unions, government officials, and other relevant stakeholders in the development and implementation of the plan.
5. **Provide education and training:** Educate employees, managers, and policymakers about the benefits of employee ownership and participation.
6. **Address potential challenges:** Anticipate and address potential obstacles, such as financial constraints, resistance to change, or lack of employee interest.
7. **Monitor and evaluate:** Track the progress of the implementation and make adjustments as needed.

Examples of successful implementation:

- **Mondragon Corporation in Spain:** This cooperative conglomerate has demonstrated the effectiveness of employee ownership in creating a thriving economy and improving the lives of its members.
- **John Lewis Partnership in the UK:** This employee-owned department store chain has a long history of success and has been a model for other employee-owned businesses.

By carefully considering these factors and following a well-planned approach, nations can successfully implement policies and systems that foster a culture of shared ownership and participation, leading to a more equitable and prosperous future for all.

IV. Forging Aspirational Growth

1. Unity as the Cradle of Opportunity: A Rising Tide Lifts All Boats

In the grand design of a thriving civilization, unity is not merely a virtue—it is the **cradle of opportunity**, the foundation upon which progress and innovation flourish. A nation's collective potential is akin to a vast ocean, deep and boundless, capable of lifting every individual to new heights. However, this ocean is not born of isolated efforts; it is formed when **social and individual powers converge**, creating an environment where every citizen has the tools to succeed and contribute.

This is the essence of a **civilized nation system**: a society that harmonizes the aspirations of individuals with the collective good, forging a future where **shared purpose fuels personal and societal growth**.

Synergy Between Society and the Individual: Cultivating Opportunity

Imagine a society where unity is not a burden but an **engine of empowerment**, creating a synergy between **individual ambition and collective strength**. Here:

- A **trusted government** acts not as a dictator but as a **wise facilitator**, providing the infrastructure and support needed for every citizen to pursue their unique path.
- Talents are nurtured, and individuality is celebrated, allowing creativity and innovation to flourish.

This is a civilization where:

- **Infrastructure fuels growth**: Roads, communication networks, and digital platforms connect individuals to opportunities and resources.
- **Institutions foster empowerment**: Schools, research centers, and entrepreneurial hubs provide the tools for success.

Psychology reveals that humans are most motivated when they feel their contributions matter. In this society, individuals experience a profound sense of **purpose and belonging**, knowing their efforts enhance the whole. This fuels an **ecosystem of opportunity** where personal growth aligns seamlessly with societal progress.

A Future Powered by Collective Intelligence

Fast forward to a world shaped by **remarkable advancements** in collective intelligence:

- **Vast databases** store information on individual skills, aspirations, and interests, enabling governments to connect citizens with tailored opportunities.
- AI-powered systems act as **mentors and matchmakers**, ensuring every person finds their place in the grand design of progress.

Imagine:

- A scholar with a vision for sustainable agriculture is paired with an engineer capable of creating innovative irrigation systems.
- A budding artist gains access to cutting-edge tools through a digital platform, allowing them to collaborate with peers across the globe.

In this society:

- **Resources are democratized**, eliminating barriers of geography, income, or privilege.

- Individual contributions fuel collective progress, ensuring that every citizen's unique abilities are leveraged to advance the nation.

This creates a **dynamic and inclusive system**, where the aspirations of individuals ignite the collective imagination, driving the civilization forward.

Strength Through Unity: The Power of Collaboration

A genuinely civilized nation understands that its strength lies in **unity, not division**. It harnesses the power of collaboration to:

- Merge **individual ingenuity with shared knowledge**, creating a fertile ground for innovation.
- Ensure that **everyone has a role**, from the artisan to the scientist, from the dreamer to the builder.

Imagine a society where:

- A blacksmith's resourcefulness combines with a scientist's expertise to create sustainable technologies.
- A small farming community adopts advanced irrigation systems designed by urban innovators, increasing yields and reducing waste.

This **synergy of talents and perspectives** enriches the entire system, fostering a culture where **collective prosperity is both the goal and the reward**.

Rebuilding From Crisis: A Community of Shared Purpose

The ashes of global catastrophe often serve as the forge for **new orders built on collective strength**. In the wake of disaster:

- Citizens recognize that their **individual well-being is intertwined with the health of their community**.

- Governments facilitate **collaboration and resource-sharing**, ensuring that no one is left behind.

Imagine:

- A mechanic repairing vital machinery in exchange for food and shelter.
- A teacher sharing knowledge to rebuild an educational system, ensuring the next generation is prepared for a brighter future.

This collaborative spirit:

- **Reinforces social bonds**, creating a society that thrives on mutual support.
- Unlocks a wellspring of creativity and resilience, enabling communities not only to survive **but thrive**.

The Psychology of Unity: Purpose and Belonging

Psychology teaches us that humans are social creatures driven by a desire for **connection and contribution**. A civilized nation:

- Recognizes this innate need and creates opportunities for **collaborative endeavors**.
- Fosters a culture where every individual feels their efforts are **recognized and valued**.

In this society:

- Working together on shared goals builds a sense of **belonging and fulfillment**.
- Citizens are more likely to innovate, experiment, and push boundaries, knowing their contributions benefit the larger whole.

This **intrinsic motivation** transforms communities into dynamic ecosystems of growth and progress, where **unity fuels individual ambition**.

Conclusion: A Rising Tide for All

Unity is not just a principle; it is the **foundation of opportunity**, the fertile ground where individual potential meets collective progress. In this advanced civilization:

- **Social and individual power merge**, creating a boundless ocean of opportunity.
- **Collaboration becomes second nature**, enabling communities to achieve what individuals alone cannot.
- **Innovation thrives** as citizens work together to build a brighter future.

This is a society where:

- Every individual is empowered to **pursue their dreams**, knowing their success contributes to the greater good.
- The **rising tide of unity** lifts all boats, ensuring that no one is left behind in the journey toward progress.

The cradle of opportunity is not a static entity—it is a **dynamic force** constantly adapting and evolving to meet the needs of its citizens. In this **civilization of unity**, the music of progress resonates across every corner, creating a world of shared prosperity, boundless creativity, and enduring hope.

2. The Symphony of Self: Composing a Future of Shared Success

Imagine a civilization where the economy isn't merely a mechanism for profits but a **harmonious symphony**, where each individual's contributions compose the **melody of collective progress**. In this society, people are not passive workers—they are **active co-creators** empowered by a sense of ownership and purpose. This isn't about assigning tasks; it's about cultivating **agency and pride** within every member of the workforce.

This **symphony of self** is a testament to the power of **individual motivation** and **collective endeavor**, creating a society where work becomes a platform for personal growth and societal transformation.

The Currency of Personal Endeavor: Turning Work into Investment

In this advanced society, work is not just labor; it is an **investment in one's own future**. Every individual, from the CEO to the frontline innovator, has the opportunity to:

- **Own a stake in the enterprise** they help build, transforming a paycheck into a symbol of shared success.
- Feel a direct connection between their efforts and the growth of their organization, fostering a powerful incentive for **productivity and creativity**.

Science confirms that a highly engaged workforce drives innovation and resilience. A genuinely civilized nation:

- Implements **employee ownership programs**, such as profit-sharing and stock options, aligning individual success with organizational progress.
- Encourages a culture where workers feel their efforts directly contribute to the **greater good**.

Imagine a workplace where:

- A production worker feels the same pride and responsibility for the company's success as its executives.

- Profit-sharing ensures that the team innovating a new product shares in the financial rewards of its success.

This system **blurs the lines between employee and entrepreneur**, fostering a workforce driven by **shared ambition and mutual benefit**.

Worker Cooperatives: Resilience Through Shared Ownership

In times of uncertainty, **collaborative models of ownership** become vital. A civilized nation empowers its citizens through:

- **Worker cooperatives**, where employees co-own and co-manage enterprises, ensuring that every voice contributes to decision-making.
- Systems that **distribute responsibility and reward**, creating a culture of shared accountability and collective prosperity.

Imagine:

- A local business transitioning to worker ownership after a crisis, uniting employees in rebuilding efforts.
- A cooperative tech start-up where developers, marketers, and support staff all share in the success of their innovations.

These models create not just economic stability but **a profound sense of community**, where success is celebrated as a shared achievement.

The Labyrinth of Self-Progression: A Journey of Continuous Growth

In this future-forward society, personal growth is not an afterthought—it is the cornerstone of progress. Here:

- Work becomes more than a job—it is a **pathway to self-discovery and mastery**, motivating individuals to excel and innovate.
- **Lifelong learning** is a societal norm, empowering citizens to adapt to change and seize emerging opportunities.

Science underscores the importance of skill development in driving economic resilience. A civilized nation:

- Fosters policies that mandate **ongoing training and development**, ensuring every worker has the tools to thrive.
- Builds systems of **apprenticeships and mentorships**, preserving knowledge and passing it to future generations.

Imagine a society where:

- Advanced AI tailors education to individual strengths, enabling workers to refine their skills with precision and efficiency.
- Master artisans train a new generation, blending tradition with cutting-edge techniques to create groundbreaking innovations.

This **labyrinth of self-progression** ensures that no citizen is left behind, creating a workforce that is dynamic, motivated, and future-ready.

Resilience Through Continuous Learning: Adapting to Change

Rapid technological advancements demand a **resilient and adaptable workforce**. A civilized nation anticipates these changes by:

- Providing universal access to **educational resources**, enabling citizens to upskill and reskill as industries evolve.

- Promoting a culture where **knowledge-sharing and collaboration** become second nature, ensuring collective growth.

Imagine:

- A factory worker learns advanced programming skills through company-sponsored training, transitioning seamlessly into robotics design.
- A community initiative brings together retirees with specialized knowledge and young innovators eager to learn, creating a pipeline of expertise.

This culture of **continuous learning** transforms challenges into opportunities, fostering a society that thrives on **adaptability and ingenuity**.

Empowerment Through Recognition: Valuing Every Contribution

Psychology teaches that when individuals feel their contributions are recognized:

- They experience a sense of **ownership and agency**, driving them to excel.
- Their engagement and creativity flourish, benefiting both the individual and society.

A genuinely civilized nation:

- Celebrates achievements, big and small, creating a culture where **recognition fuels motivation**.
- Empowers individuals to see themselves not as cogs in a machine but as **builders of their own destinies**.

Imagine:

- An employee's innovative idea revolutionizes an industry, and they are celebrated as a pioneer, inspiring others to dream boldly.
- Teams that achieve milestones are recognized publicly, reinforcing a sense of pride and belonging.

This system fosters a workforce that is **energized, innovative, and deeply committed** to collective success.

Finland as a Model: Empowering Through Lifelong Learning

To illustrate these principles, consider **Finland**, a nation renowned for its commitment to education and personal development:

- By prioritizing high-quality education and lifelong learning, Finland has created a culture of **empowered individuals** who take pride in shaping their futures.
- Its emphasis on collaboration and skill development has fostered a workforce that is both **highly skilled and deeply motivated**, driving innovation and economic growth.

This model demonstrates the **transformative power of investing in people**, a principle that lies at the heart of the symphony of self.

Conclusion: A Symphony of Shared Success

A thriving economy is not built on a foundation of disconnected workers but on a **harmonious symphony of owners and learners**. By fostering:

- **Shared ownership** that empowers individuals to invest in their futures,
- **Continuous learning** that adapts to a changing world, and
- **Recognition and growth** that fuel intrinsic motivation,

A civilized nation creates a workforce that is the driving force behind its success. This **symphony of self**, composed of individual efforts and collective ambition, ensures a future where prosperity and opportunity are shared by all.

Together, the citizens of this society compose a **melody of innovation and progress**, proving that the greatest wealth lies in the empowerment of people. This symphony resonates not just as an economic system but as a **vision for humanity's boundless potential**, securing a future defined by **creativity, resilience, and shared achievement**.

3. The Ascendancy of Aspirations: Scaling the Summit of Potential

Imagine a society where the path to success is not a preordained road limited to a privileged few but a **mountain of limitless potential** waiting to be climbed by anyone with ambition and determination. Here, **talent and effort become the sturdy ropes** that propel individuals upward, and the summit offers breathtaking vistas of achievement available to all. This society is not about simply filling jobs—it is about creating a **meritocratic journey** where dedication, innovation, and skill illuminate the way to a **more prosperous and equitable future**.

The Ladder of Meritocratic Rise: Climbing the Rungs of Success[2]

Actual progress lies in empowering individuals to **rise based on their merit and contribution**, not their background or connections. In this advanced civilization:

---

[2] **To ensure a truly meritocratic system, it's essential to:**
- **Promote diversity and inclusion:** Create a workplace culture where everyone feels valued and has equal opportunities for advancement.

- **Everyone has the opportunity to ascend**, with success determined by skill, effort, and resilience.
- Ambition is fueled by a clear, transparent system that **rewards excellence** and provides equal access to opportunities.

Science highlights that strong economies thrive on mobile, adaptable workforces. A civilized nation:

- Fosters **transparent promotion systems** that clearly outline paths to advancement.
- Invests in **employee training and development**, ensuring that every citizen has the skills to climb the ladder of success.

Imagine a society where:

- Scholarships and lifelong learning programs ensure that individuals from all walks of life have access to **world-class education**.
- A talented coder from a rural village works alongside engineers in urban innovation hubs, contributing to breakthroughs in artificial intelligence.

This commitment to **continuous learning** transforms the pursuit of knowledge into a **thrilling climb**, with every rung on the ladder revealing new vistas of opportunity.

- **Provide mentorship and support:** Offer mentorship programs and support services to help individuals from disadvantaged backgrounds overcome barriers and achieve their goals.
- **Measure performance objectively:** Use fair and transparent performance metrics to evaluate employees and ensure that promotions are based on merit, not on personal connections or biases.
- **Address biases:** Be aware of unconscious bias.

Overcoming Challenges: Addressing Barriers to Progress

Creating a meritocratic society is not without challenges, but a truly civilized nation confronts these head-on, ensuring fairness and inclusivity at every step. Common barriers include:

- **Bias and discrimination** can undermine the fairness of advancement systems.
- **Limited access to education and training**, which leaves talent untapped.
- **Resistance to change**, often arising from entrenched systems or traditional mindsets.

To overcome these challenges, a civilized nation implements:

1. **Diversity and inclusion initiatives**: Promoting equity in all sectors.
2. **Accessible education and training programs**: Ensuring opportunities for all citizens to develop their potential.
3. **A culture of meritocracy**: Rewarding individuals based on their achievements and skills, regardless of their origins.
4. **Transparent feedback systems**: Allowing individuals to understand and improve their performance.

By addressing these barriers, society unlocks a **broader pool of talent**, enriching its workforce with diverse ideas and perspectives and paving the way for innovation and progress.

The Demise of Stagnation: Breaking Through Barriers

In a truly meritocratic civilization, no one is held back by circumstances of birth or environment. This society:

- Actively dismantles **structural barriers**, ensuring that every citizen has the chance to rise.
- Recognizes that **talent can emerge from anywhere**, fostering policies that cultivate and celebrate diverse abilities.

Science emphasizes that economies thrive on the **diversity of their workforce**. A civilized nation:

- Encourages **cross-cultural exchange** and **interdisciplinary collaboration**, allowing varied perspectives to converge into groundbreaking solutions.
- Creates systems that connect **individual potential to societal challenges**, fostering innovation that benefits all.

Imagine:

- A young farmer developing precision agriculture techniques through collaboration with urban technologists.
- Apprenticeships that empower individuals from underserved communities to master advanced manufacturing skills, fueling economic growth.

This commitment to **breaking barriers** ensures that the **mountain of potential is scalable by all**, enriching the nation with a tapestry of innovation and progress.

Hope and Resilience: Inclusivity as a Catalyst for Growth

In times of crisis, inclusivity becomes a **critical pillar of recovery**. A civilized nation:

- Implements **skills retraining programs**, ensuring that workers in declining industries transition smoothly into emerging fields.
- Fosters a spirit of **collective responsibility**, where every citizen contributes to rebuilding and strengthening the nation.

Imagine:

- A community devastated by economic collapse transforms itself into a hub of renewable energy innovation through collaborative retraining programs.

- A former coal miner becomes a leader in green energy technology, inspired by opportunities provided through government initiatives.

Psychology reveals that when individuals feel **unlimited by their circumstances** and empowered to pursue their aspirations, they experience profound **hope and optimism**. This intrinsic motivation:

- Fuels creativity and engagement.
- Propels the nation toward a **future brimming with possibility**.

Inspiration Through Action: A Society of Mentors and Masters

In a civilization committed to **ascending aspirations**, every individual has the chance to:

- Learn from experienced mentors who pass down knowledge and skills, creating a **continuous cycle of improvement**.
- Aspire to become a master of their craft, inspiring others to pursue their own journeys of excellence.

Imagine:

- Guilds where artisans, scientists, and technologists collaborate, ensuring that expertise is preserved and innovation flourishes.
- Master-apprentice relationships that combine **tradition and technology**, creating a workforce that is both skilled and adaptive.

This system fosters a **culture of mentorship**, where every citizen feels supported in their journey to greatness.

Conclusion: Scaling the Summit of Potential

A truly civilized nation understands that **true prosperity is not built on rigid hierarchies** but on the **merit, effort, and collaboration of its people**. By fostering:

- A **meritocratic system** that rewards skill and dedication,
- A commitment to **breaking barriers** that hold individuals back and
- A culture of **hope, inclusivity, and mentorship**,

The nation empowers its citizens to become **architects of their own destinies** and the driving force behind societal progress. As individuals climb the **mountain of potential**, their combined efforts create a **tapestry of shared achievement**, ensuring a future filled with **opportunity, innovation, and boundless possibility**.

This ascent is not just about reaching the summit—it's about transforming the journey itself into a **symbol of collective growth**, proving that the **greatest heights are achieved together**. By scaling this summit, society crafts a brighter dawn, a future where **every aspiration fuels a collective symphony of success**.

4. Embarking on the Odyssey of Potential: A Journey of Self-Discovery and Societal Ascendancy

Imagine a civilization not just defined by prosperity but alive with the **vibrancy of individual journeys**, where each citizen embarks on a **lifelong odyssey of self-discovery and mastery**. In this society, personal ambition and societal progress are not competing forces but **interwoven paths**, forging a world where every individual's growth contributes to the **collective ascension of humanity**.

This is a nation that understands true prosperity flows not from hoarded wealth or isolated success but from the **empowerment of individuals** to realize their unique potential, creating a **network of innovation and progress** that uplifts all.

The Empowerment Through Enlightenment: Unlocking Potential Through Education

In this advanced society, education is not a linear system but a **thrilling expedition of exploration and growth**. Here:

- Citizens embark on a **lifelong quest to uncover and refine their talents**, supported by cutting-edge tools and immersive learning experiences.
- Education becomes a **force of empowerment**, leveling the playing field and ensuring everyone has the resources needed to succeed.

Science confirms that strong economies thrive on skilled and adaptable workforces. A civilized nation:

- Ensures **universal access to quality education and training**, regardless of background or socioeconomic status.
- Fosters policies that prioritize **lifelong learning and continuous reskilling**, equipping citizens to adapt to rapidly evolving technologies.

Imagine:

- AI-driven platforms that personalize learning, enabling a young inventor to master advanced robotics or an artist to refine their craft in virtual studios.
- Apprenticeships where experienced professionals mentor the next generation, ensuring that **knowledge and innovation flow seamlessly** between eras.

In a world shaped by automation and artificial intelligence, **adaptability becomes the cornerstone of survival**. This society ensures that no citizen is left behind, creating a population that is **resilient, resourceful, and ever-evolving**.

The Nexus of Growth and Relations: A System That Benefits All

Prosperity in this society is not the product of isolated ambition but the result of a **thriving network of interconnected contributions**. This economic framework:

- Empower individuals to **grow and innovate** while fostering a culture where their success enriches the entire community.
- Aligns **personal development with societal progress**, creating an ecosystem where growth is mutual and enduring.

Science underscores the importance of human capital development in driving economic innovation. A futuristic civilization:

- Encourages businesses to **invest in their workforce**, recognizing that training and development are not costs but strategic investments in collective success.
- Breaks down silos by promoting **cross-disciplinary collaboration**, enabling engineers, artists, scientists, and economists to tackle complex challenges together.

Imagine:

- A team of environmental scientists and engineers partnering with economists and urban planners to design sustainable, inclusive cities.
- Biologists collaborating with technologists to develop AI-powered solutions for global health crises.

This **spirit of collaboration** unleashes a richness of perspectives, fostering an economy that thrives on **diversity, creativity, and interconnectedness**.

Shared Prosperity: Building a Resilient and Inclusive Economy

Actual progress is measured not by the wealth of a few but by the **shared prosperity of all**. A civilized nation:

- Creates systems that **ensure fair wages and economic opportunity**, fostering a sense of collective responsibility and ownership.
- Rewards **hard work and innovation**, ensuring that those who contribute to societal progress feel valued and motivated.

Imagine:

- Guilds that support artisans, ensuring they are well-compensated and their crafts preserved for future generations.
- Social safety nets that empower individuals to **take risks and explore new ventures**, driving innovation without fear of failure.

The scars of crises reveal the importance of **shared sacrifice and mutual support**. In this society:

- Communities rebuild stronger, united by a shared purpose.
- Citizens are inspired to contribute their knowledge, skills, and ingenuity, propelling their society toward a **brighter, more equitable future**.

The Psychology of Empowerment: Purpose and Fulfillment

Psychology teaches us that humans thrive when they feel **valued, empowered, and connected**. A society that fosters a culture of growth and collaboration:

- Creates opportunities for individuals to **pursue their passions**, knowing their contributions matter.
- Instills a sense of **agency and belonging**, inspiring citizens to go beyond what they thought possible.

In this civilization:

- Every citizen feels that their **unique talents are recognized**, driving them to achieve personal excellence.
- Collective progress becomes a **shared mission**, weaving a tapestry of purpose and fulfillment that defines the national ethos.

A Vision for the Future: The Symphony of Self-Discovery

In this society, the journey of personal growth is not a solitary endeavor but a **collective odyssey**. By empowering individuals to reach their full potential:

- The nation creates a workforce that is **motivated, innovative, and resilient**.
- Communities become hubs of creativity and progress, ensuring that **no talent is wasted**.

This is not just a vision of prosperity—it is a vision of **shared humanity**, where the success of one becomes the success of all. As citizens embark on their personal journeys, their combined efforts propel society toward a future defined by **opportunity, unity, and boundless possibility**.

Conclusion: A Civilization Defined by Collaboration and Aspiration

A truly civilized nation understands that its greatest wealth lies in the **untapped potential of its people**. By:

- Cultivating a system of **education and empowerment** that inspires lifelong learning,
- Creating an economy that rewards **collaboration and contribution**, and
- Fostering a culture of **shared prosperity and purpose**,

The nation sets the stage for a **symphony of progress**, where every citizen plays a vital role in shaping the future.

As individuals embark on their **personal Odysseys of self-discovery**, their collective journey transforms society into a **living masterpiece** of innovation, resilience, and hope. This is the **brighter dawn of humanity**, a future where ambition and collaboration illuminate the path forward for generations to come.

V. The Flourishing Future

1. The Symphony of Progress: A Composition of Coordinated Systems

Imagine a civilization not as a static framework of isolated entities but as a **living symphony**, where governance, economy, education, infrastructure, and social systems weave together to create a masterpiece of progress. In this advanced society, no system operates in isolation; each plays its part in a **harmonious composition** that propels humanity toward a future brimming with opportunity and innovation.

This **symphony of progress** is not just about functionality—it is a **vision of unity**, where the interplay of systems creates a world where individuals thrive, communities prosper, and humanity ascends to its full potential.

The Convergence of Rule and Wealth: A Virtuous Cycle of Growth

At the heart of this symphony lies a powerful synergy: the **convergence of governance and economic systems**. A truly civilized nation understands that:

- Progress stems not from the isolated power of any single entity but from the **synergistic relationship** between its systems.

- Wise governance fuels economic growth, and economic growth provides the resources for governance to **address societal needs** effectively.

Science underscores the importance of collaboration between governments and private sectors in fostering sustainable development. A futuristic society:

- Implements **public-private partnerships**, uniting the innovation of businesses with the oversight of governance to address challenges such as climate change, infrastructure development, and equitable access to technology.

- Utilizes **scientific evidence and data-driven policies** to make decisions that not only solve immediate problems but also **secure the well-being of future generations**.

Imagine:

- A government collaborating with private tech firms to create an AI-driven system for equitable resource distribution.

- An economic engine that thrives on sustainability, ensuring profits are reinvested into **education, healthcare, and environmental protection**.

This **virtuous cycle** creates a society where every citizen feels the impact of progress, fostering a sense of **shared purpose and collective responsibility**.

Leadership and Social Cohesion: Building Trust and Unity

A flourishing nation thrives on **leadership that inspires and unites**:

- Wise leaders ensure that the wealth of the nation is **shared equitably**, fostering trust and unity.

- Governance is **responsive to the needs of its citizens**, creating systems that amplify voices and address concerns.

Psychology teaches that when individuals feel their government is acting in their best interests, they experience:

- A sense of **security and hope**, motivating them to invest their energy in building a better future.

- Enhanced **social cohesion**, as trust in leadership strengthens communal bonds.

Imagine a society where:

- Citizens are active participants in shaping policies, ensuring that decisions reflect **collective aspirations**.

- Governance adapts to emerging challenges, ensuring a resilient and united population ready to face the future together.

The Rhythm of a Civilized Existence: Creating a Flourishing Society

In this symphony of progress, the rhythm of a flourishing society is composed of **coordinated systems working in harmony**. These systems ensure:

- **Education empowers citizens**, equipping them with the skills to innovate and lead.

- **Healthcare guarantees well-being**, creating a foundation for productivity and happiness.

- **Infrastructure connects communities**, enabling growth and collaboration.

- **Social safety nets provide stability**, ensuring that no one is left behind.

Science emphasizes that nations prioritizing human well-being enjoy more substantial and more innovative economies. A civilized nation:

- Invests in **quality healthcare, affordable housing, and accessible education**, creating an environment where citizens can thrive.

- Anticipates challenges and implements **resilient infrastructure and social programs** to ensure adaptability and continuous progress.

Imagine:

- A healthcare system powered by AI, providing personalized care to every citizen.

- Infrastructure that integrates sustainability, such as solar-powered smart cities connected by hyper-efficient transportation networks.

These elements create a **thriving society** where innovation and well-being are woven into the fabric of everyday life.

Sustainability and Stewardship: Progress Without Compromise

Actual progress is sustainable, ensuring that advancements today do not come at the expense of future generations. A genuinely civilized nation:

- Balances **economic development with environmental stewardship**, fostering a culture of responsibility.

- Implements systems that prioritize **renewable energy, circular economies, and social equity**, ensuring long-term prosperity.

Imagine:

- Industries that minimize waste by embracing **circular manufacturing**, turning byproducts into valuable resources.

- Policies that protect natural ecosystems while promoting **green technology**, creating a future where nature and progress coexist harmoniously.

Psychology reveals that when individuals feel they live in a society that values sustainability, they experience the following:

- A sense of **well-being and fulfillment**, knowing their efforts contribute to a brighter future.

- Motivation to innovate, as sustainability challenges spark creativity and collaboration.

A Tapestry of Contributions: Thriving Through Unity

The strength of this civilization lies in its ability to harness the **unique contributions of its citizens**. In this thriving society:

- Communities work together, pooling resources and talents to achieve **shared success**.

- Individuals feel empowered to **explore their passions and skills**, knowing their contributions are valued.

Imagine:

- A rural artist collaborates with urban engineers to design culturally inspired, sustainable architecture.

- Communities come together to rebuild after natural disasters, pooling knowledge and resources to create stronger, more resilient neighborhoods.

This spirit of **unity and collaboration** transforms society into a **tapestry of interconnected progress**, where every citizen plays an essential role.

Conclusion: A Symphony That Resonates Across Generations

A truly civilized nation understands that progress is not a **solitary melody** but a **grand symphony**, where every system, every individual, and every innovation contributes to a harmonious whole. By:

- Ensuring that governance and economy work in synergy,

- Prioritizing sustainability and human well-being, and

- Empowering communities to thrive together,

This nation composes a masterpiece of progress that resonates across generations. It is a society where individuals flourish, communities thrive, and humanity reaches its full potential.

As the final notes of this symphony fade, they leave behind not just a legacy of wealth or power but a **living testament to the boundless potential of unity, innovation, and shared purpose**. This is the **flourishing future** envisioned by the **Architects of a Future Dawn**—a future where the music of progress never ceases, creating a world of hope, harmony, and endless possibility.

2. The Flourishing of Humanity: A Symphony of Liberty and Contribution

The most significant hallmark of a truly advanced civilization is not its technological marvels or its economic might but its **unwavering commitment to personal liberty and collective contribution**. Imagine a society where individual freedom is not just a right but a **cornerstone principle**, empowering every citizen to **pursue their dreams and define their destiny**. This freedom becomes the spark that ignites innovation, creativity, and collaboration, weaving a **vibrant tapestry of human potential**.

In this enlightened society, liberty and contribution are not opposing forces but **intertwined threads** that form the foundation of a thriving and equitable future.

The Apex of Personal Sovereignty: Unleashing Human Potential

Actual progress begins with **unleashing the potential of the individual**. A civilized nation:

- Goes beyond safeguarding basic rights to **cultivate environments** where every citizen can pursue life on their own terms.

- Celebrates the **freedom to dream, innovate, and achieve**, understanding that individual aspirations drive societal advancement.

Science underscores that thriving economies are built on **free market systems** that encourage entrepreneurship and competition. In this society:

- Policies foster **unrestricted exploration of ideas**, allowing inventors, creators, and entrepreneurs to challenge norms and chart new courses.

- Freedom to innovate leads to **breakthroughs that benefit all**, from scientific discoveries to cultural revolutions.

Imagine a world where:

- A young inventor develops life-saving medical technology because they have the freedom to explore their ideas without interference.

- A rural artist uses advanced digital platforms to share their work globally, inspiring a new wave of creativity.

This commitment to **personal sovereignty** unlocks a reservoir of ingenuity and ambition, enabling every individual to contribute their unique talents to a **collective vision of progress**.

Resilience Through Freedom: Empowering Ownership and Agency

The scars of crises remind us of the importance of **individual agency**. In a truly civilized nation:

- Systems are designed to empower individuals to make their own choices and **contribute in ways that align with their passions and strengths**.

- Every citizen becomes an **active participant** in shaping their collective future, fostering a sense of ownership and responsibility.

Psychology reveals that when people feel empowered to make their own decisions:

- They experience a profound sense of **autonomy and intrinsic motivation**.

- This motivation drives them to **excel in their endeavors** and contribute meaningfully to society.

Imagine:

- A citizen-run innovation hub where diverse thinkers collaborate to solve global challenges.

- A society where individuals don't just work for a living but engage in pursuits that align with their personal and professional aspirations.

This culture of **personal freedom** creates a nation where individuals are **not cogs in a machine** but **architects of their own futures**.

The Tribute to Contribution: A Meritocratic Tapestry

Freedom alone is not enough—it must be paired with a system that **values and rewards contribution**. A truly civilized nation:

- Fosters a **meritocratic culture**, ensuring that individuals are recognized and rewarded for their **skills, talents, and efforts**.

- Celebrates the **achievements of all citizens**, creating a culture of pride and accomplishment.

Science confirms that meritocracy fuels innovation and excellence. In this society:

- Contributions are woven into a **tapestry of progress**, where collaboration amplifies individual effort.

- Programs encourage **cooperation over competition**, uniting citizens in shared missions.

Imagine:

- An engineer's breakthroughs in renewable energy are celebrated alongside the farmer who implements these technologies to revolutionize agriculture.

- A student receives national recognition for designing a low-cost solution to urban housing challenges.

This **culture of recognition and reward** motivates individuals to pursue excellence, knowing their efforts will be valued and their contributions celebrated.

Shared Prosperity: The Foundation of Collective Responsibility

The scars of crisis underscore the importance of **shared prosperity**. In a world where success is equitably distributed:

- Systems ensure that everyone benefits from the collective effort, fostering **social cohesion and mutual support**.

- Citizens are motivated not only by personal gain but by a **sense of shared responsibility** for their community's success.

Imagine:

- A healthcare system where profits from innovative treatments are reinvested into making care accessible to all.

- Cooperative businesses where workers share in both decision-making and profits, creating a **more equitable and motivated workforce**.

This commitment to **shared prosperity** ensures that progress uplifts every member of society, creating a foundation for **enduring stability and growth**.

A Symphony of Liberty and Contribution

A thriving society is not an orchestra of competing instruments but a **harmonious symphony** where every voice contributes to the melody of progress. This symphony is built on:

- **Personal sovereignty**, empowering individuals to pursue their passions and unlock their potential.

- **Meritocracy**, rewarding contributions that propel society forward.

- **Shared prosperity**, creating an equitable foundation for collective success.

In this society:

- A scientist's innovation in clean energy is celebrated alongside a teacher's role in shaping future leaders.

- The artist, the entrepreneur, and the environmentalist work in unison, each playing a vital role in a **shared vision of progress**.

This **delicate balance between liberty and contribution** ensures that individuals flourish while strengthening the fabric of society.

Conclusion: Humanity Flourishing in Harmony

A truly civilized nation understands that its greatest strength lies in the **synergy between individual liberty and collective responsibility**. By fostering:

- A culture of **personal freedom and creativity**,

- Systems that **reward and recognize contributions**, and

- A commitment to **equity and shared prosperity**,

The nation creates a society that thrives on **hope, innovation, and collaboration**.

This is not just a vision of progress—it is a testament to the **boundless potential of humanity**. As every individual contributes their unique melody to the symphony, the resulting harmony becomes a beacon of inspiration, illuminating the path toward a future defined by **freedom, contribution, and collective flourishing**.

This symphony of liberty and contribution is the heartbeat of a thriving civilization, proving that when humanity works together, the **music of progress never ceases**, leaving behind a legacy of hope, unity, and boundless possibility.

3. The Symphony of Progress: A Continuous Crescendo of Change

Imagine a nation not as a static structure but as a **living, breathing entity in perpetual motion**, a vibrant **symphony of progress**. In this civilization, progress is not about clinging to traditions or fearing the unknown; it is about **embracing change as an opportunity** to evolve, adapt, and overcome. This society understands that true advancement lies in its ability to grow, guided by **individual creativity, collective ingenuity, and resilient adaptability**.

This **continuous crescendo of progress** ensures that every citizen becomes a note in the grand symphony, contributing to a future that resonates with innovation, collaboration, and boundless potential.

The Momentum of Innovation: Building on Success

In this society, change is not a threat—it is the **driving force of innovation**. A genuinely civilized nation fosters a culture where:

- Experimentation is celebrated, and **new ideas are the building blocks** of a better tomorrow.

- Success is not a destination but a **stepping stone**, a foundation for further exploration and discovery.

Science confirms that research and development are the engines of societal progress. A futuristic nation:

- Prioritizes **entrepreneurship and innovation**, ensuring citizens have the resources to explore, create, and transform.

- Balances **learning from the past** with bold steps toward the future, ensuring every experiment builds on the wisdom of previous generations.

Imagine:

- Laboratories where scientists, artists, and engineers collaborate on renewable energy breakthroughs.

- Start-ups supported by policies that reward **calculated risk-taking**, fostering a culture of fearless creativity.

This momentum ensures the nation is not just surviving but **thriving in constant motion**, with each success fueling the next wave of progress.

The Experimentation of Self: A Petri Dish for Progress

True progress begins with the individual. In this advanced civilization:

- Personal innovation becomes a **catalyst for societal advancement**. Citizens are encouraged to experiment with new ideas, knowing their successes and lessons learned contribute to collective growth.

- **Lifelong learning** is a societal norm, empowering individuals to continuously refine their skills and expand their horizons.

Science emphasizes the importance of personal growth in driving societal innovation. A civilized nation:

- Encourages citizens to **step outside their comfort zones**, exploring uncharted territories of knowledge and skill.

- Fosters a culture where ideas are **shared, refined, and adopted**, ensuring collective progress.

Imagine:

- A teacher integrating virtual reality into classrooms, revolutionizing education.

- An artisan experimenting with AI tools to create futuristic designs that blend tradition with modernity.

This spirit of experimentation transforms every citizen into a **pioneer**, unlocking a wellspring of creativity that propels society forward.

Adaptability as a Keystone: A System in Perpetual Motion

A truly civilized nation is **not rigid but agile**, designed to adapt and evolve with the changing tides of technology, culture, and global challenges. Here:

- Governance is not static but **responsive**, ensuring policies evolve to meet emerging needs.

- Institutions embrace a culture of **flexibility and innovation**, enabling society to anticipate challenges and seize opportunities.

Science informs us that evidence-based decision-making is essential in navigating a complex world. A forward-thinking nation:

- Relies on **data and analysis** to shape policies that serve the greater good.

- Implements **scenario planning and long-term strategies**, ensuring readiness for unforeseen changes.

Imagine:

- A society where governments use predictive AI to allocate resources effectively, preventing crises before they arise.

- Communities empowered with tools to adapt to environmental changes, ensuring resilience in the face of natural disasters.

This perpetual motion creates a **resilient society** capable of weathering storms and flourishing in uncertainty.

Progress Rooted in Resilience: Learning From Crisis

The scars of crisis serve as powerful reminders of the importance of **adaptability and innovation**. A truly advanced society:

- Learns from past mistakes, using them as **stepping stones to greater heights**.

- Implements systems that encourage **collaboration across disciplines**, ensuring diverse perspectives drive solutions.

Imagine:

- A nation rebuilding after a global catastrophe, where engineers, biologists, and economists unite to design sustainable infrastructure.

- Citizens pooling knowledge and resources to address food scarcity with innovative agricultural techniques.

Psychology teaches that when individuals feel their society is resilient and responsive, they:

- Experience a sense of **security and hope**, motivating them to contribute their talents.

- Become active participants in **shaping a better future**, knowing their efforts are valued.

This spirit of resilience ensures that crises become opportunities for **reinvention and growth**, creating a society that thrives no matter the challenge.

A Society of Active Participants: Shaping the Future Together

In this dynamic civilization:

- Citizens are not passive observers but **active architects** of progress, empowered to innovate, experiment, and collaborate.

- Individual efforts are celebrated and woven into a **collective tapestry of advancement**.

Imagine:

- A mechanic contributing to a nationwide project on sustainable transportation.

- A programmer using their skills to design community-driven apps that address local challenges.

This culture of **shared responsibility and opportunity** transforms society into a living organism where every member plays a vital role in **shaping the future**.

Conclusion: A Continuous Crescendo of Change

A truly civilized nation is not defined by rigid traditions or static systems but by its **ability to adapt, evolve, and grow**. By fostering:

- A culture of **momentum and innovation** that builds on success.

- Systems that **encourage experimentation and creativity.**

- Policies that ensure **adaptability and resilience.**

The nation creates a **symphony of progress** that resonates across generations.

This is not merely a vision of survival—it is a blueprint for **flourishing in perpetual motion**, ensuring that every citizen has the opportunity to **dream, innovate, and contribute**. As the symphony crescendos, it leaves behind a legacy of hope, collaboration, and boundless possibility, proving that the **greatest harmonies are those composed together**.

This ongoing journey of progress ensures a future where humanity thrives as **pioneers of possibility**, charting a course toward a brighter dawn and a world of **endless opportunity**.

VI. THE AXIS OF ETHICAL FOUNDATIONS

A truly civilized nation is built on a strong ethical framework that permeates every aspect of society, ensuring fairness, justice, and trust.

1. The Pillar of Trust: Building Transparent Institutions

In the heart of every truly advanced civilization lies a **pillar of trust**, a cornerstone that supports fairness, justice, and collective prosperity. Trust is not merely a moral ideal; it is the **lifeblood of a thriving society**, permeating every aspect of governance, commerce, and interpersonal relationships. Imagine a nation where **transparency is the norm**, not the exception—a society where citizens feel confident that every decision, policy, and action aligns with the **greater good**.

This **foundation of trust** transforms governance into a collaborative partnership between institutions and citizens, fostering unity, innovation, and resilience.

Trustworthy Governance: The Backbone of Societal Confidence

Trust is the currency of governance, and a nation that prioritizes ethical leadership builds an unshakable bond with its citizens. In such a society:

- Leaders exemplify **honesty, accountability, and fairness**, setting a standard that inspires citizens to actively participate in shaping their future.

- Institutions operate with **transparency**, ensuring every action is open to scrutiny and aligned with societal values.

Science underscores that transparency reduces corruption and enhances institutional efficiency. A truly civilized nation:

- Implements **public audits, accessible records, and open communication channels** to ensure governance is visible and accountable.

- Promotes **data transparency**, empowering citizens to monitor progress in areas such as economic development, environmental sustainability, and social equity.

Imagine:

- A government where citizens can access real-time dashboards tracking public spending and project progress.

- Leaders who regularly engage with citizens through open forums, discussing challenges and solutions with honesty and humility.

This **culture of openness** fosters a sense of security and confidence, motivating citizens to contribute their talents and ideas to the collective good.

Policies Ensuring Transparency in Public and Private Sectors

Transparency must extend beyond governance to every corner of society. A civilized nation:

- Enforces **public disclosure laws**, requiring governments and corporations to share information about budgets, operations, and decision-making processes.

- Provides **whistleblower protections**, encouraging individuals to expose unethical practices without fear of retaliation.

- Leverages **technology platforms** to make information accessible, enabling citizens to stay informed and hold institutions accountable.

Imagine:

- A corporate transparency portal where consumers can review the environmental and social impact of businesses.

- A blockchain-based system that ensures every government transaction is traceable and verifiable, eliminating corruption and inefficiency.

Science fiction envisions societies where technology guarantees absolute transparency, fostering trust and fairness. While this may seem idealistic, a truly advanced nation strives toward this vision, embracing innovations that empower citizens and promote accountability.

Mechanisms for Accountability and Responsiveness

Trust is not a static value; it must be **nurtured and reinforced** through robust systems of accountability and responsiveness. In a truly civilized society:

1. **Independent Oversight Bodies** monitor government actions, ensuring adherence to ethical standards and fair practices.

2. **Public Participation Channels** enable citizens to voice concerns, propose solutions, and participate in decision-making processes.

3. **Feedback-Responsive Institutions** adopt policies and practices based on citizen input, ensuring governance evolves to meet societal needs.

Imagine:

- A community-driven app that allows citizens to submit feedback on public services, with real-time updates on how their concerns are being addressed.

- Independent panels reviewing major policies, ensuring decisions are ethical, equitable, and aligned with long-term societal goals.

The **scars of crises** remind us of the importance of trust during adversity. When citizens believe in their institutions:

- They comply with emergency measures, trusting that these actions are for the collective good.

- They collaborate with authorities to overcome challenges, creating a **united front against adversity**.

- They invest in rebuilding, confident that their efforts will contribute to a brighter future.

Psychology reveals that trust fosters a sense of security and belonging. Citizens who trust their leaders are more likely to:

- Engage actively in civic life.

- Innovate and collaborate for the collective benefit.

- Demonstrate resilience in the face of challenges.

Conclusion: Trust as the Bedrock of Civilization

The **pillar of trust** is not just a foundation—it is the invisible thread that weaves society into a cohesive and thriving tapestry. A nation that prioritizes trust:

- Ensures citizens feel **confident in their leaders and institutions**, fostering unity and engagement.

- Embeds **ethical practices** into every facet of governance and commerce, creating a culture of accountability and fairness.

- Operates as a collaborative organism, where citizens and institutions work together to **build a future defined by equity and opportunity**.

This **feedback loop of trust** creates a thriving ecosystem where transparency and accountability inspire confidence, and confidence fuels progress. As trust flourishes, it becomes the **lifeblood of civilization**, ensuring that society operates with resilience, unity, and a shared sense of purpose.

In this future, trust is not merely a value—it is the **axis upon which a flourishing world turns**, proving that the greatest societies are built not on force or fear but on the **enduring strength of mutual confidence and collaboration**.

2. The Moral Compass: Guiding Ethical Progress

Imagine a nation not only defined by its technological and economic achievements but also by the principles that guide its every step. In this society, progress is not a blind pursuit but a deliberate journey, aligned with values of **integrity, responsibility, and justice**. The **moral compass** serves as the guiding force, ensuring that every innovation, policy, and advancement enhances the **well-being of humanity**.

In this civilization, ethics is not a constraint—it is the **foundation of progress**, transforming ambition into purpose and innovation into a **force for good**.

Ethical Guidelines for Technological Advancement

The rapid pace of technological innovation offers unprecedented opportunities, but it also raises profound ethical questions. A truly advanced nation confronts these challenges by embedding ethics into the core of its innovation ecosystem.

Some of the critical questions include:

- How do we balance **privacy and autonomy** with the immense power of artificial intelligence?

- How do we ensure automation **elevates society** without marginalizing vulnerable populations?

- How do we wield tools like genetic engineering and advanced medicine **responsibly and equitably**?

To navigate these challenges, a civilized nation:

1. **Establishes ethical frameworks** for emerging technologies, ensuring fairness, transparency, and accountability in their development and deployment.

2. **Creates independent ethics councils** to evaluate the societal impact of technological advancements and propose safeguards.

3. **Encourages public discourse** on the implications of innovation, empowering citizens to shape the trajectory of progress.

Science underscores the dangers of unregulated technological growth, from widening inequalities to unforeseen risks. A forward-thinking nation:

- Embeds ethics into every stage of innovation, ensuring technology serves as a tool for **uplifting humanity**, not exacerbating divisions.

- Leverages technology to **enhance equality**, such as AI systems designed to eliminate bias or digital platforms that democratize education and opportunity.

Imagine:

- An AI-powered healthcare system that prioritizes equitable access, ensuring breakthroughs benefit patients in underserved communities as much as urban hubs.

- Genetic engineering policies that prioritize ethical considerations, ensuring advancements cure diseases without creating harmful inequalities.

This approach ensures that progress is **inclusive, responsible, and aligned with the values of justice and humanity**.

The Role of Education in Instilling Ethical Values

Ethics begins with education. A truly civilized nation recognizes that cultivating integrity, responsibility, and justice starts with empowering its citizens to navigate complex moral dilemmas.

In this society:

- **Early education** instills empathy, fairness, and respect as foundational values, creating a strong moral compass from a young age.

- **Higher education** incorporates ethics into STEM fields, law, business, and public policy programs, ensuring that future leaders and innovators prioritize societal well-being.

- **Lifelong learning** opportunities, such as public seminars and workshops, keep citizens informed about evolving ethical challenges in a rapidly changing world.

Psychology teaches that values instilled early are reinforced throughout life, creating citizens who approach their endeavors with a deep sense of integrity. By embedding ethics into education, a civilized nation:

- Empower individuals to balance personal ambition with societal impact.

- Fosters leaders and innovators who **prioritize responsibility over short-term gain**.

Imagine:

- A robotics engineer designing systems that prioritize safety and fairness, informed by ethical training.

- A business leader who leverages AI responsibly, ensuring transparency in decision-making and protecting user privacy.

By aligning education with ethical values, this society ensures that **progress enhances human dignity**, creating a culture where integrity is not aspirational—it is the standard.

Balancing Progress With the Moral Imperative of Fairness

Progress without fairness is **empty**. A truly advanced nation understands that innovation must be accompanied by justice, ensuring that advancements uplift everyone, not just a privileged few.

To achieve this balance, a civilized nation:

1. **Regulates access** to critical advancements, such as healthcare, green technology, and digital tools, ensuring inclusivity.

2. **Closes gaps** in education, healthcare, and technological access, ensuring no one is left behind.

3. **Promotes equity in opportunity**, creating policies that level the playing field and allow everyone to contribute to and benefit from progress.

History teaches that unchecked progress can lead to exploitation, inequality, and harm. A truly civilized society:

*   Learns from these lessons, prioritizing **responsible innovation** over reckless advancement.

*   Crafts systems that emphasize **collaboration, inclusivity, and equity**, ensuring progress becomes a shared journey.

Imagine:

*   A green energy revolution that prioritizes rural and underserved areas, bringing clean power to the most vulnerable communities.

*   A digital platform that provides free educational resources to bridge global disparities in learning.

Science fiction often explores dystopian futures where progress runs unchecked, creating stark inequalities. These cautionary tales serve as reminders that ethical foresight is essential to building a just and inclusive future.

Conclusion: A Society Guided by Ethics

A truly civilized nation is not measured by how far it advances but by how **responsibly it wields its progress**. By embracing its moral compass, this society ensures that:

- Innovation serves humanity, uplifting lives, and advancing dignity.

- Education instills values of integrity, fostering generations of ethical leaders and innovators.

- Justice remains at the heart of progress, ensuring that no one is excluded from its benefits.

This ethical framework transforms progress into a **beacon of hope**, illuminating a future where greatness and goodness are inseparable. By embedding ethics into the foundation of its advancement, a nation creates a **legacy of meaningful progress**, proving that humanity's greatest achievements are not measured in technological milestones but in the **depth of its responsibility and compassion**.

A society guided by its **moral compass** builds a world where innovation is not just a tool for success but a **testament to the enduring power of justice, integrity, and the human spirit**.

3. The Justice Symphony: Equal Access to Legal and Social Protections

Imagine a society where justice is not a privilege for the powerful but a **universal right** accessible to all, regardless of wealth, status, or background. In this advanced civilization, the **justice system operates as a symphony**, harmonizing fairness, equality, and compassion to create a foundation of trust and opportunity. By prioritizing **equal access to legal and social protections**, this society ensures that no one is left behind, building a nation defined by dignity, safety, and unity.

This **justice symphony** resonates as a unifying melody, fostering societal cohesion and empowering every citizen to contribute to the greater good.

Creating a Judicial System Accessible to All

True justice begins with **accessibility**. A civilized nation ensures that its judicial system is:

- **Transparent**: Open and understandable to all.

- **Fair**: Free from bias or undue influence.

- **Accessible**: Within reach of every citizen, regardless of their circumstances.

To achieve this, the nation:

1. **Eliminates financial barriers**:

   o Provides **free or low-cost legal representation** for those unable to afford it, ensuring that economic disparities do not hinder access to justice.

   o Implements **subsidized court fees** and streamlined processes to reduce financial burdens.

2. **Decentralizes legal services**:

   o Establishes **community-based legal aid centers**, especially in rural and underserved areas, ensuring that no one is isolated from essential services.

   o Deploys mobile legal units to reach remote populations, bridging gaps in accessibility.

3. **Leverages technology**:

   ○ Creates **online platforms** for legal advice, public record access, and dispute resolution, simplifying bureaucratic processes.

   ○ Incorporates AI-driven tools to provide **real-time updates on case progress**, reducing delays and increasing transparency.

Science reveals that equitable judicial systems reduce crime, foster social trust, and promote economic stability.

Imagine:

- A single parent accessing free legal aid to resolve housing disputes without fear of financial strain.

- Rural communities using digital platforms to resolve conflicts and access vital legal resources.

This commitment to accessibility ensures that **justice is not delayed, denied, or distorted**, making fairness a cornerstone of governance.

Policies to Eliminate Systemic Inequities and Promote Restorative Justice

Justice is not just about punishment—it is about **transformation**. A truly civilized nation implements policies that address the root causes of harm and inequality, fostering a culture of **healing and reconciliation**.

Key approaches include:

1. **Anti-discrimination laws**:

   ○ Protect individuals from bias in employment, housing, education, and public services.

o   Establish strict penalties for discriminatory practices, ensuring accountability.

2. **Restorative justice programs**:

    o   Focus on **victim-offender mediation**, community service, and rehabilitation over incarceration for non-violent offenses.

    o   Empower communities to participate in resolving disputes, fostering accountability and healing.

3. **Equity-driven reforms**:

    o   Address systemic inequities by eliminating discriminatory practices in the judiciary and law enforcement.

    o   Ensure fair representation in legal institutions, reflecting the diversity of the population.

Psychology underscores that punitive systems often exacerbate resentment and recidivism, while restorative approaches:

- Foster **healing and accountability**, reducing repeat offenses.

- Reinforce community bonds by promoting **understanding and reconciliation**.

Imagine:

- A young offender participating in a community service program that teaches them responsibility while repairing the harm caused.

- A court system prioritizing rehabilitation, turning lives around, and reducing the social cost of incarceration.

This transformative approach ensures that justice is not merely about enforcing laws but about **building a fairer, more compassionate society**.

The Interplay of Justice, Equality, and Societal Harmony

Justice and equality are the twin pillars upon which **societal harmony** is built. When citizens feel that laws are fair and applied equally:

- They trust institutions and engage actively in civic life.

- They contribute to collective progress, knowing their rights and responsibilities are respected.

This harmony is cultivated through the following:

1. **Balancing rights and responsibilities**:

   o Every citizen enjoys equal protection under the law while fulfilling their obligations to society.

2. **Promoting social justice**:

   o Addressing structural **inequalities** in education, healthcare, and housing to break cycles of poverty and exclusion.

3. **Fostering community-led initiatives**:

   o Empower local groups to design and implement justice reforms, ensuring solutions reflect the diverse needs of the population.

The **scars of history** remind us that unchecked inequality breeds discord while fairness and justice foster unity.

Imagine:

- A society where marginalized communities are actively involved in shaping policies that impact their lives.

- Programs that rebuild trust between law enforcement and citizens, creating partnerships based on mutual respect.

This **interplay of justice and equality** transforms society into a cohesive entity, where fairness becomes the bridge to a brighter, more united future.

Conclusion: Justice as the Melody of a Civilized Society

The **justice symphony** of a truly advanced nation resonates with the harmonious notes of fairness, equality, and compassion. By:

- Creating a judicial system that is transparent and accessible to all,

- Eliminating systemic inequities and promoting restorative justice, and

- Balancing rights, responsibilities, and social harmony,

The nation ensures that **every citizen is protected, empowered, and heard**. This symphony builds:

- **Trust in institutions**, strengthening societal bonds.

- **Social cohesion**, enabling communities to flourish together.

- **Shared progress**, where dignity and equality guide every step forward.

In this symphony, justice is not a solitary note—it is the **unifying melody** that harmonizes the diverse voices of society into a powerful testament to humanity's potential for fairness, empathy, and collective success. The **justice symphony** becomes a legacy, proving that when fairness prevails, society not only survives but **thrives in harmony and hope**.

VII. EMBRACING CULTURAL RICHNESS

A civilized nation celebrates diversity and leverages cultural richness as a source of strength and creativity.

1. The Kaleidoscope of Diversity: Unity in Differences

Imagine a nation that views diversity not as a challenge but as a **reservoir of strength and creativity**. In this enlightened society, the **kaleidoscope of diversity** celebrates the unique perspectives, traditions, and histories that each citizen brings to the collective table. Unity is not forged from sameness but emerges from the **rich interplay of differences**, creating a culture of inclusion, mutual respect, and shared progress.

This vision transforms diversity into a **living masterpiece**, where every thread of identity weaves a tapestry of **unity and innovation**.

Policies That Promote Inclusivity and Representation

A truly civilized nation ensures that every voice is **heard, valued, and represented**. Inclusivity is not merely an ideal but a **cornerstone of governance, business, education, and culture**. To achieve this, the nation implements robust policies, including:

1. **Inclusive Representation**:
   - Leadership roles in government, business, and institutions reflect the **diverse population** they serve.

- o Diverse voices are prioritized in decision-making, ensuring that policies resonate with the realities of all communities.

2. **Anti-Discrimination Policies**:

- o Protections are enacted against bias based on **race, ethnicity, gender, language, religion, or disability**.

- o Strong enforcement mechanisms ensure that equality is more than a promise—it is a **guaranteed right**.

3. **Equitable Opportunities**:

- o Programs empower marginalized communities by ensuring **equal access to education, healthcare, and employment**.

- o Scholarships, mentorships, and grants target underserved groups, leveling the playing field for all.

Science underscores that diverse teams excel at problem-solving, creativity, and decision-making. A civilized nation embraces this insight, recognizing that inclusivity is not just a **moral imperative** but a **strategic advantage**, fostering stronger institutions and more dynamic societies.

Imagine:

- A government where representatives of all cultural backgrounds collaborate to shape policies that resonate across the nation.

- Corporations that prioritize diversity, creating teams whose varied perspectives drive innovation and growth.

This commitment to inclusivity creates a society where **no one is left behind**, ensuring every citizen has the opportunity to contribute and thrive.

Recognizing and Valuing Cultural, Linguistic, and Historical Diversity

The fabric of a nation's identity is woven from the **threads of its people's stories, languages, and traditions**. A civilized nation treasures this richness, seeing it as a source of inspiration and pride. To preserve and celebrate cultural diversity, the nation invests in:

1. **Preserving Cultural Heritage**:

    o   Museums, archives, and cultural festivals honor traditions and histories, ensuring they are passed to future generations.

    o   Local artisans, storytellers, and cultural custodians are supported, preserving their invaluable contributions to the national narrative.

2. **Promoting Multilingualism**:

    o   Education systems embrace linguistic diversity, encouraging citizens to **celebrate and connect across cultures**.

    o   Language preservation initiatives protect endangered dialects, ensuring that no voice fades from the cultural symphony.

3. **Honoring Shared History**:

    o   Historical narratives reflect the **contributions and struggles of all groups**, fostering a sense of belonging and pride.

    o   Public spaces, art, and media celebrate diversity, ensuring representation in the nation's storytelling.

Psychology reveals that individuals who feel their identities are respected are more likely to engage positively with their communities.

Imagine:

- A school curriculum that teaches students the stories of all cultural groups, fostering **empathy and global awareness**.

- Cities that honor their multicultural roots through vibrant festivals and art that reflects the **richness of their diversity**.

By recognizing and valuing its cultural wealth, a nation strengthens its **social fabric**, creating unity rooted in respect and mutual appreciation.

Encouraging Intercultural Dialogue to Foster Unity and Understanding

True unity arises when individuals and communities learn to **appreciate and understand each other's perspectives**. A civilized nation nurtures this understanding through:

1. **Community Programs**:

    o **Neighborhood festivals, dialogue forums, and interfaith events** encourage cultural exchange and foster connections.

    o Initiatives that bring together individuals from different backgrounds to **collaborate on shared goals**.

2. **Educational Curricula**:

    o Schools incorporate lessons about the **history, traditions, and perspectives of diverse cultures**, teaching students to value differences as strengths.

    o   Students participate in intercultural activities that build **empathy and global citizenship**.

3. International Partnerships:

    o   Exchanges and collaborations bridge cultural divides, creating opportunities for **global understanding**.

    o   Cultural diplomacy initiatives promote **dialogue and shared creativity** on an international scale.

History reminds us that misunderstanding and prejudice weaken societies while collaboration and openness build bridges.

Imagine:

- Communities coming together for dialogue events that transform former divisions into newfound partnerships.

- International cultural exchanges that inspire solutions to global challenges through the **fusion of diverse ideas**.

Science fiction often envisions futures where diverse civilizations collaborate to achieve common goals, highlighting the transformative power of understanding. A truly civilized nation brings this vision to life, turning diversity into a **source of unity and strength**.

Conclusion: A Symphony of Diversity

The **kaleidoscope of diversity** is a defining hallmark of a truly civilized nation. By:

- **Promoting inclusivity** and ensuring representation across all sectors,

- **Valuing cultural, linguistic, and historical richness**, and

- **Fostering intercultural dialogue** to build understanding and unity,

The nation creates a society where differences are not divisions but **opportunities for connection and growth**.

This symphony of diversity:

- Builds a foundation of **mutual respect and shared purpose**.

- Unlocks the **creative and innovative potential** of a richly diverse citizenry.

- Proves that true strength lies in the **beauty of our differences and the unity of our aspirations**.

In this symphony, every voice contributes to a **vibrant and harmonious composition**, a testament to humanity's ability to **flourish together**. By embracing cultural richness, a nation doesn't just celebrate its past—it charts a future of boundless creativity, inclusion, and shared success.

2. The Artistic Tapestry: Cultivating Creative Expression

Imagine a civilization where artistic expression is the **heartbeat of progress**, weaving together threads of tradition and innovation to create a vibrant cultural tapestry. In this society, creativity is not an afterthought or a luxury—it is a **vital force** that connects communities, inspires generations and drives transformation.

Art becomes a **universal language**, a bridge between the past and the future, and a **celebration of the human spirit**, fostering unity, understanding, and innovation.

Investments in Arts, Literature, and Cultural Heritage

A truly advanced nation recognizes that **investing in the arts** is not merely an act of cultural preservation but an investment in its **soul and future**. Prioritizing creative expression nurtures a society where imagination fuels both innovation and identity.

1. **Funding and Grants**:

   o Financial support for artists, writers, filmmakers, and cultural organizations enables them to **thrive and innovate**.

   o Grants for community art projects foster local engagement, transforming neighborhoods into **vibrant cultural hubs**.

2. **Public Art Initiatives**:

   o Murals, sculptures, and performance art are integrated into **public spaces**, making creativity accessible to all and inspiring daily life.

   o Interactive installations invite citizens to **participate in the creative process**, breaking down barriers between creators and audiences.

3. **Preservation of Cultural Heritage**:

   o Historical landmarks, manuscripts, and traditional crafts are carefully protected, ensuring they endure as **anchors of identity** for future generations.

   o Digital archives safeguard intangible cultural assets, such as oral histories and endangered languages, for the benefit of all.

Science reveals that exposure to art enhances cognitive abilities, emotional intelligence, and problem-solving skills.

Imagine:

- Schools with vibrant murals that tell stories of resilience and progress, inspiring students to dream boldly.

- Communities revitalized by public art projects that honor local histories while envisioning a brighter future.

By investing in arts, literature, and cultural heritage, the nation builds a **society where creativity becomes the lifeblood of education, governance, and public life**.

Support Systems for Artists and Creatives

Artists are the **visionaries and storytellers** of a society, reflecting its struggles, hopes, and aspirations. A civilized nation recognizes its indispensable role and creates systems to support its work and well-being.

1. **Professional Resources**:

   o Mentorship programs pair emerging artists with established creators, ensuring the **transfer of knowledge and inspiration** across generations.

   o Workshops and access to materials empower creators to refine their craft and **push the boundaries of innovation**.

2. **Economic Stability**:

   o Fair compensation models ensure that artists can focus on their work without the strain of financial insecurity.

   o Healthcare and retirement benefits provide a safety net, recognizing artists as essential contributors to societal progress.

3. **Diversity in the Arts**:

- o Inclusive programs amplify the voices of underrepresented groups, ensuring that the **full spectrum of experiences** is reflected in the nation's cultural narrative.

- o Festivals and platforms celebrate diverse artistic expressions, fostering a more prosperous and more inclusive cultural identity.

History reminds us that art is a powerful catalyst for healing and unity.

Imagine:

- Post-crisis murals that transform scars into symbols of resilience.

- Songs and performances that bring divided communities together, fostering understanding and hope.

By supporting its artists, a nation **elevates creativity as a cornerstone of its progress**, ensuring that every story finds its place in the cultural tapestry.

Art as a Bridge Between Tradition and Innovation

Art thrives on the **dynamic interplay** between tradition and innovation. A truly civilized nation fosters this synergy, encouraging creators to honor their heritage while exploring **new frontiers of expression**.

1. **Interdisciplinary Collaborations**:

- o Scientists, technologists, and artists collaborate to produce works that **inspire and educate**, such as interactive exhibits on climate change or immersive virtual reality histories.

○ Public and private sectors partner to fund **boundary-pushing projects** that merge creativity with technology.

2. **Fusion of Mediums**:

○ Traditional crafts are revitalized through digital tools, creating works like **3D-printed sculptures** inspired by ancient designs or augmented reality experiences that bring historical events to life.

○ Artists experiment with AI and robotics, blending tradition with modernity to **challenge perceptions and expand horizons**.

3. **Cultural Festivals**:

○ Celebrations showcase **artistic traditions alongside contemporary innovations**, bridging generational and cultural divides.

○ Events invite participants to engage in both heritage crafts and cutting-edge art, fostering a deeper appreciation of the **past, present, and future**.

Science fiction often depicts futures where art transcends language and cultural barriers, uniting disparate societies.

Imagine:

- A global art installation that uses holographic technology to share cultural expressions from every corner of the world.

- Festivals where AI-generated music harmonizes with traditional instruments, symbolizing the fusion of history and innovation.

This vision transforms art into a **universal language**, connecting people across time and space.

Conclusion: A Canvas for Progress

The **artistic tapestry** of a truly civilized nation is a testament to its vibrancy, vision, and humanity. By:

- Investing in arts, literature, and cultural heritage,

- Supporting artists as vital contributors to societal progress and

- Fostering a dynamic interplay between tradition and innovation,

The nation builds a **culture that values creativity as a cornerstone of progress**. In this society:

- Individuals are empowered to **express their unique perspectives**, enriching the collective narrative.

- Art becomes a bridge between the **past and the future**, inspiring both continuity and transformation.

This civilization proves that **art is not merely aesthetic—it is essential**, a catalyst for unity, understanding, and progress. The artistic tapestry is not just a reflection of a nation's identity—it is the **canvas upon which its future is painted**, weaving a story of beauty, resilience, and boundless possibility.

3. The Global Citizenry: Fostering International Collaboration

Imagine a society where **boundaries become bridges**, connecting nations in shared challenges and collective aspirations. In this visionary civilization, citizens are not only proud of their unique cultural heritage but also embrace their role as **global citizens**, actively contributing to a world defined by cooperation, understanding, and mutual progress. Through collaborations in science, technology, and culture, this nation fosters a **rich tapestry** of **global ties**, ensuring that progress transcends borders and humanity thrives together.

This vision transforms the world into a **network of interconnected innovations and cultures** united by a shared belief in the **power of collaboration**.

Programs Encouraging International Cooperation

A genuinely advanced nation recognizes that **global challenges demand collective solutions**. Whether combating climate change, advancing medical breakthroughs, or exploring the cosmos, collaboration is the key to unlocking humanity's full potential. To this end, the nation implements programs designed to foster international cooperation:

1. **Scientific Exchanges**:

   o   Researchers, scientists, and innovators collaborate across borders on pressing issues, pooling expertise and resources to address challenges like **pandemics**, **renewable energy**, and **sustainable agriculture**.

   o   Joint research initiatives create networks of knowledge that advance science for the **global good**.

2. **Cultural Partnerships**:

   o   International festivals, exhibitions, and artistic exchanges celebrate the **diversity of human expression**, promoting understanding and connection through shared creativity.

   o   Artists and performers from different cultures collaborate on projects that **transcend language and tradition**, creating universal narratives of hope and resilience.

3. **Technological Alliances**:

- o Partnerships between nations drive the development of cutting-edge technologies, such as **AI-powered solutions**, **space exploration**, and **green innovations**.

- o Open-source platforms enable nations to share advancements, ensuring that technology serves humanity as a whole.

Science underscores that diverse perspectives fuel innovation while collective resources accelerate breakthroughs.

Imagine:

- A global team of researchers developing renewable energy solutions to combat climate change.

- Cultural festivals where traditions from every corner of the globe inspire new forms of art and connection.

These programs create a world where **nations collaborate rather than compete**, transforming shared challenges into **opportunities for progress**.

Strengthening Global Ties While Preserving National Identity

In fostering global collaboration, a truly civilized nation does not sacrifice its unique cultural heritage. Instead, it strikes a balance, ensuring that:

- **National identity is enriched**, not diluted, through global interaction.

- Indigenous traditions, languages, and histories are celebrated and protected, even as citizens engage with international ideas and practices.

- Citizens become **ambassadors of their culture**, sharing their heritage on the global stage while learning from others.

Psychology reveals that individuals with strong cultural grounding are better equipped to engage with diverse communities. A forward-thinking nation nurtures this balance by:

- Promoting cultural pride alongside **global awareness**, ensuring citizens feel both rooted and open to the world.

- Designing policies that safeguard cultural heritage while embracing **international collaboration**.

Imagine:

- A multilingual education system that teaches children both their native language and global languages, equipping them to connect across cultures.

- Global summits where nations showcase their unique traditions while collaborating on shared goals.

By weaving **national identity into global collaboration**, the nation creates a society where **diversity becomes a strength**, fostering innovation, connection, and shared purpose.

Preparing Citizens for Participation in a Global Society

Thriving in an interconnected world requires citizens to possess the **skills and mindset of global participants**. A truly advanced nation prepares its citizens by fostering education and experiences that emphasize global engagement.

1. **Education for Global Awareness**:

   o Curricula incorporate **international history, global challenges, and cultural understanding**, giving students a nuanced perspective on the world.

o   Lessons emphasize the interconnectedness of humanity, inspiring students to think globally while acting locally.

2. Language Programs:

o   Schools promote **multilingualism**, enabling citizens to communicate across cultures and build meaningful connections.

o   Language exchange initiatives connect students and professionals from different countries, fostering empathy and collaboration.

3. Opportunities for International Experience:

o   Exchange programs, internships, and collaborative projects abroad provide firsthand experience of global interconnectedness.

o   Virtual platforms connect students and professionals with peers worldwide, enabling **borderless collaboration**.

History reminds us that misunderstanding and division fuel conflict while understanding and cooperation cultivate peace.

Imagine:

•   A generation of young leaders fluent in multiple languages, collaborating across continents to address global crises.

•   Virtual classrooms where students from different countries solve problems together, learning from each other's perspectives.

By preparing its citizens for global participation, the nation **cultivates empathy, dialogue, and shared responsibility**, ensuring that its people are not only leaders of their country but also stewards of the world.

Conclusion: A World of Shared Horizons

The **global citizenry** of a truly civilized nation is a testament to the power of collaboration, empathy, and mutual respect. By:

- Fostering **international cooperation** in science, technology, and culture,

- Strengthening **global ties while celebrating national identity**, and

- Preparing citizens for participation in a **global society,**

The nation builds a world where **boundaries dissolve into bridges**, enabling progress that transcends borders.

This vision creates:

- **Bridges of understanding**, connecting cultures and ideas.

- **Ambassadors of unity** who celebrate their unique identities while striving for shared global goals.

- A society that thrives in a world where challenges and opportunities are universal, proving that **progress is best achieved together**.

In this vision of global citizenry, the world becomes a **mosaic of cultures and innovations**, united by the belief that humanity's greatest achievements are born from collaboration. This is not just a nation's triumph—it is a collective step toward a **brighter future for all of humanity**.

VIII. ADVANCING ENVIRONMENTAL RESILIENCE

Imagine a civilization where progress is not achieved at the expense of the planet but in **harmony with the natural world**. In this enlightened society, sustainability is not an afterthought—it is the **foundation of every decision**, ensuring that economic growth, environmental conservation, and human well-being coexist seamlessly.

This vision transforms sustainability into a **core principle**, a guiding force that secures both the planet's health and humanity's future.

1. The Green Framework: Sustainability as a Core Principle

In this **civilized society**, environmental resilience is a cornerstone of governance. A nation's prosperity is seen as inseparable from the health of its ecosystems, leading to policies that harmonize economic ambition with ecological responsibility.

1. **Green Urban Planning**:

   o Cities are designed with **green spaces, sustainable architecture, and efficient public transport**, reducing carbon footprints and enhancing quality of life.

   o Vertical gardens and rooftop solar panels adorn urban skylines, transforming cities into **living, breathing ecosystems**.

2. **Sustainable Industry Regulations**:

   o Laws enforce **reduced emissions, conservation of natural resources**, and **waste minimization**, ensuring industries operate responsibly.

   o Incentives reward businesses that adopt **circular economies**, turning waste into resources.

3. **Environmental Impact Assessments**:

- ○ Major projects undergo rigorous evaluations to mitigate harm to **biodiversity, water systems, and air quality**.

- ○ Communities are engaged in discussions about local projects, ensuring **transparency and accountability**.

Science underscores that sustainable practices are essential for combating climate change, preserving biodiversity, and ensuring long-term resource availability.

Imagine:

- Cities that act as carbon sinks, offsetting emissions through intelligent design and renewable infrastructure.

- Policies that make every new development a **model of environmental harmony**, creating urban areas that work *with* nature, not against it.

This **green framework** becomes a beacon of progress, proving that **economic growth and environmental conservation can coexist** in perfect balance.

Investments in Renewable Energy, Sustainable Agriculture, and Green Technologies

Progress is achieved through **action**, and a truly advanced nation leads by investing in sustainability. These investments transform the economy, creating **innovation hubs** that drive progress while safeguarding the planet.

1. **Renewable Energy**:

    - ○ Solar, wind, hydroelectric, and geothermal power replace fossil fuels, reducing greenhouse gas emissions and paving the way for a **carbon-neutral future**.

    - ○ Smart grids ensure efficient energy distribution, bringing clean power to even the most remote areas.

2. **Sustainable Agriculture**:

   o   Practices like **crop rotation, organic farming,** and **regenerative techniques** protect soil health, conserve water, and increase food security.

   o   Urban farming initiatives turn rooftops and vertical spaces into productive ecosystems, feeding communities sustainably.

3. **Green Technologies**:

   o   Innovations like **carbon capture, biodegradable materials**, and **energy-efficient systems** revolutionize industries, addressing global environmental challenges.

   o   Advanced recycling systems ensure that waste becomes a resource, fostering a circular economy.

Science fiction often imagines worlds where green technologies restore the planet and redefine progress. A civilized nation brings this vision to life by championing innovation and creating a foundation for a sustainable and **prosperous future**.

Imagine:

- Fields of solar panels stretching across deserts, turning arid lands into **energy havens**.

- Biodegradable packaging replacing plastic, erasing waste while preserving ecosystems.

These investments ensure a **green economy** where technology and nature collaborate to secure humanity's survival and success.

Educating Citizens on Ecological Responsibility

Environmental resilience begins with **individual action**, and a truly civilized nation empowers its citizens to become **stewards of the**

environment. Through education and community engagement, the nation fosters a culture of ecological responsibility.

1. **Eco-Literacy in Schools**:

    o   From an early age, students learn about **biodiversity, climate change, and sustainable living**, equipping them with the tools to protect the planet.

    o   Interactive lessons, such as **school gardens and conservation projects**, inspire hands-on learning and foster a love for nature.

2. **Community Programs**:

    o   Workshops on **recycling, energy conservation, and water management** empower citizens to adopt sustainable habits.

    o   Local initiatives, such as tree-planting drives and clean-up campaigns, create **collective momentum for environmental preservation**.

3. **Incentives for Green Behavior**:

    o   Tax benefits reward eco-friendly homes, renewable energy adoption, and sustainable business practices.

    o   Discounts for using public transport and cycling infrastructure encourage citizens to reduce their carbon footprints.

Psychology reveals that people are more likely to adopt sustainable habits when they understand their impact and feel their contributions matter.

Imagine:

- A city where every citizen participates in an annual "Green Day," planting trees and learning about sustainable practices.

- Incentive programs that reward households for **achieving energy efficiency**, transforming sustainability into a **shared mission**.

By fostering a **sense of collective responsibility**, the nation ensures that every individual becomes a contributor to **planetary preservation**.

Conclusion: A Blueprint for Sustainability

The **green framework** of a truly advanced nation is more than a policy—it is a **commitment to the future**. By:

- Balancing **economic growth with environmental conservation**,

- Investing in **renewable energy, sustainable agriculture, and green technologies**, and

- Educating citizens on **ecological responsibility**,

The nation builds:

- A **sustainable economy** that thrives while safeguarding natural resources.

- A culture of **environmental stewardship**, where citizens are inspired to protect the planet for future generations.

- A **legacy of resilience**, ensuring a thriving world for centuries to come.

In this society, sustainability is not just a goal—it is a **way of life**, a testament to the nation's vision and its dedication to **harmonizing progress with nature**. This **blueprint for sustainability** serves as an inspiration for other nations, proving that a better world is possible when humanity works **with the planet, not against it**.

As humanity stands on the cusp of a new dawn, the **green framework** becomes the foundation of a world where progress and preservation are no longer in conflict but are **united in purpose and potential**.

2. The Blueprint for Resilience: Preparing for Environmental Challenges

Imagine a society not only thriving in harmony with nature but also **empowered to adapt and respond** to the challenges of an ever-changing environment. In this **civilized nation**, resilience is not a passive defense—it is an active strategy, a **blueprint for preparedness and adaptation** that ensures the safety and sustainability of its people and ecosystems.

This vision transforms resilience into a way of life, preparing the nation to **weather adversity and emerge stronger**.

Proactive Measures for Disaster Preparedness and Climate Adaptation

A truly advanced nation understands that **environmental challenges are inevitable**, from rising seas to intensifying storms. By taking **proactive measures**, it minimizes risks and protects both its citizens and its natural heritage.

Key strategies include:

1. **Comprehensive Disaster Planning**:
   o National and local emergency systems are developed to address **floods, wildfires, hurricanes**, and other crises.

o Regular drills and simulations empower communities with **knowledge and readiness**, ensuring swift action when disaster strikes.

2. **Climate Adaptation Strategies**:

o **Flood defenses**, such as levees and wetlands restoration, safeguard vulnerable areas.

o **Drought-resistant crops** and **heat-resistant urban designs** mitigate the impacts of changing weather patterns, ensuring food security and livable cities.

3. **Early Warning Systems**:

o Advanced technologies, such as **satellite monitoring** and **AI-driven analytics**, predict natural disasters with precision, enabling **timely evacuations** and resource allocation.

o Public alerts, delivered through mobile apps and community networks, ensure **real-time communication** during crises.

Science underscores that preparedness saves lives and resources. A forward-thinking nation:

- Aligns policies with **scientific research**, ensuring robust and data-driven plans.

- Prioritizes **anticipation of overreaction,** creating systems that protect communities before crises occur.

Imagine:

- Coastal cities shielded by green barriers of mangroves and artificial reefs, buffering against rising seas.

- Communities notified days ahead of extreme weather, ensuring **orderly evacuations** and resource distribution.

This proactive approach ensures that a nation is not just **reacting to challenges** but leading the way in **climate resilience**.

Strengthening Infrastructure to Withstand Natural and Environmental Crises

Infrastructure is the **backbone of resilience**, and a truly civilized nation designs systems that endure and adapt to the **realities of a changing climate**. These investments create a foundation for safety, connectivity, and progress, even in the face of adversity.

1. **Resilient Urban Design**:

   o Cities feature **green roofs, permeable pavements**, and natural flood barriers, reducing the impact of extreme weather.

   o Urban planning incorporates **tree-lined streets and reflective materials**, mitigating heat islands and enhancing air quality.

2. **Energy Security**:

   o Diversified energy grids integrate **renewable sources** like solar, wind, and geothermal, ensuring uninterrupted power during crises.

   o Microgrids enable communities to **operate independently**, reducing vulnerabilities to centralized grid failures.

3. **Smart Infrastructure**:

   o Bridges, roads, and buildings are equipped with **sensors and real-time monitoring**, detecting vulnerabilities and preventing catastrophic failures.

o   AI systems predict maintenance needs, ensuring that critical infrastructure remains **functional and secure**.

The scars of past disasters remind us that **robust infrastructure saves lives** and accelerates recovery.

Imagine:

- Bridges that adjust to rising waters, maintaining vital connections between communities.

- Energy grids that remain operational during storms, powering hospitals and shelters when they are needed most.

By investing in resilient infrastructure, a nation ensures that its systems are **built to endure**, safeguarding its people and their future.

Encouraging Community-Driven Initiatives for Local Sustainability

Resilience begins **at the community level**, where empowered citizens take an active role in sustainability and preparedness. A truly advanced nation fosters **local leadership and collective action**, creating a shared sense of responsibility.

1. **Neighborhood Action Plans**:

    o   Communities form **disaster response teams** equipped with resources like food banks, medical supplies, and temporary shelters.

    o   Localized response plans ensure **swift and effective action** during emergencies.

2. **Grassroots Environmental Projects**:

    o   Residents participate in restoring wetlands, planting trees, and managing waste, enhancing local ecosystems.

○ Urban gardens and community composting programs provide **sustainable food sources** while reducing environmental impact.

3. **Collaborative Funding Models**:

○ Grants and incentives support small-scale sustainability projects, such as **solar installations** and water conservation systems.

○ Crowdsourced funding empowers neighborhoods to implement **innovative, community-driven solutions**.

Psychology reveals that individuals feel more secure and engaged when they are part of collective efforts.

Imagine:

• A neighborhood organizing a tree-planting day that strengthens community bonds while improving local air quality.

• Citizens collaborating to install rainwater harvesting systems, reducing reliance on centralized water supplies.

By fostering a **sense of ownership and responsibility**, a nation ensures that resilience is not just a **policy directive** but a **shared mission**.

Conclusion: A Foundation for Resilience

The **blueprint for resilience** is more than a plan—it is a **testament to a nation's foresight and commitment** to its citizens and the planet. By:

• Implementing **proactive measures** for disaster preparedness and climate adaptation,

- Strengthening **infrastructure to withstand environmental crises**, and

- Encouraging **community-driven sustainability initiatives**,

The nation builds:

- A society that is **prepared for the unpredictable**, minimizing damage and accelerating recovery.

- Systems that are **sustainable, adaptable, and enduring**, ensuring safety and progress in the face of adversity.

- Communities that are **empowered and engaged**, working together to safeguard their future.

In this society, resilience is not a reaction—it is a **way of life**, an ongoing effort to create a sustainable, secure, and thriving world. This **foundation for resilience** ensures that the nation not only survives but flourishes, proving that humanity's strength lies in its ability to **adapt, innovate, and unite**.

As the **Architects of a Future Dawn**, this vision sets a precedent for how civilizations can prepare for the unknown while preserving the hope and promise of a **better tomorrow**.

3. The Intergenerational Compact: Preserving Resources for the Future

Imagine a nation where every decision reflects a profound commitment to future generations—a society that measures progress not solely by the achievements of today but by the **legacy it secures for tomorrow**. In this visionary civilization, the **intergenerational compact** ensures that natural resources are conserved, youth are empowered as environmental stewards and long-term strategies prioritize **ecological harmony and resilience**.

This compact is more than an agreement—it is a **moral imperative**, a pledge to leave the Earth not just as it was but better **for those yet to come**.

Strategies for Conserving Natural Resources for Future Generations

Natural resources are finite, and a truly advanced nation recognizes its responsibility to **safeguard them**. Conservation is not a reaction to scarcity; it is a deliberate strategy to ensure that the planet's treasures endure.

Key strategies include:

1. **Sustainable Resource Management**:

   o   Policies regulate the use of **water, forests, and minerals**, ensuring resources are replenished and ecosystems preserved.

   o   Quotas and incentives encourage industries to adopt **sustainable practices**, balancing economic development with environmental health.

2. **Protected Areas and Biodiversity Hotspots**:

   o   National parks, marine sanctuaries, and wildlife reserves are expanded to shield **vulnerable ecosystems from exploitation**.

   o   Local communities are engaged as **guardians of biodiversity**, blending traditional knowledge with modern conservation methods.

3. **Circular Economy Models**:

   o   Recycling, upcycling, and resource efficiency become societal norms, reducing waste and **extending the lifecycle of materials**.

○ Products are designed for durability and reuse, fostering a **circular flow of resources**.

Science confirms that sustainable resource management mitigates climate change and maintains biodiversity.

Imagine:

- Vast tracts of forests are preserved as **carbon sinks**, balancing human activity with nature's rhythms.

- Circular economies where waste is transformed into resources, creating a society that thrives on **efficiency and innovation**.

This commitment ensures that future generations inherit a planet rich in **life, beauty, and opportunity**.

Empowering Youth to Become Stewards of Environmental Progress

The future is written by the next generation, and a truly civilized nation invests in their **education, empowerment, and engagement**. By cultivating a sense of **ownership and purpose**, youth become the **torchbearers of environmental progress**.

1. **Environmental Education**:

   ○ Sustainability and conservation are integrated into school curricula, teaching students to **understand and protect the planet**.

   ○ Interactive programs, such as nature expeditions and eco-projects, inspire **hands-on learning** and foster a love for the natural world.

2. **Youth Leadership Programs**:

- o Platforms enable young people to **advocate for** environmental **causes**, innovate solutions, and lead community initiatives.

- o Youth-driven councils collaborate with policymakers, ensuring that their **voices shape the nation's ecological future**.

3. **Mentorship from Environmental Leaders**:

- o Young activists and innovators are paired with **scientists, advocates, and policymakers**, gaining guidance and inspiration.

- o Programs amplify the contributions of youth-led initiatives, showcasing their impact on a **global stage**.

History reminds us that youth-driven movements have often been the catalyst for profound change.

Imagine:

- A student-led project restoring wetlands that double as a flood defense for their community.

- Young innovators designing solar-powered solutions that bring energy to remote areas.

By empowering the next generation, a nation secures a future where **leadership and responsibility thrive**, ensuring that progress continues to build on the foundation of **sustainability and justice**.

Long-Term Planning to Ensure Ecological Harmony and Resilience

A truly civilized nation understands that short-term gains must never come at the expense of the planet's future. Long-term planning becomes the **keystone of resilience**, ensuring that economic growth, societal well-being, and environmental preservation remain in balance.

1. **National Sustainability Frameworks:**

   o Comprehensive strategies integrate **conservation, energy efficiency, and pollution reduction** into every sector.

   o Policies incentivize businesses to adopt **green practices**, creating a sustainable economy that **aligns with nature's limits**.

2. **Climate Adaptation Roadmaps:**

   o Long-term plans address challenges like rising sea levels, extreme weather, and resource scarcity.

   o Cities are redesigned with **adaptive infrastructure** capable of withstanding environmental stressors.

3. **Interdisciplinary Collaboration:**

   o Scientists, policymakers, engineers, and communities work together to create **holistic solutions** that balance development with ecological stability.

   o Innovation hubs foster ideas that harmonize progress with sustainability, from **biodegradable materials** to **self-healing ecosystems**.

Science fiction often imagines futures where humanity thrives by aligning innovation with nature. A truly civilized nation turns these visions into reality, creating systems that sustain both **the planet and its people**.

Imagine:

- A city where every building is energy-positive, producing more power than it consumes.

- Coastal defenses that blend **mangrove forests with engineering marvels**, protecting communities while enhancing biodiversity.

This commitment to long-term planning ensures that the nation becomes a **model of ecological harmony**, proving that progress and preservation are not opposing forces but **partners in prosperity**.

Conclusion: A Legacy of Stewardship

The **intergenerational compact** is more than a strategy—it is a testament to a nation's commitment to the future. By:

- **Conserving natural resources** through sustainable practices,

- **Empowering youth** as stewards of progress, and

- **Engaging in long-term planning** to ensure ecological harmony,

The nation builds:

- A **sustainable future** where ecosystems and humanity flourish together.

- A generation of leaders equipped to address **emerging environmental challenges**.

- A society united by a shared commitment to leave the planet **better than it was found**.

In this vision, each generation becomes both the **beneficiary and guardian** of the Earth's treasures. Together, they weave a narrative of progress rooted in **responsibility and hope**, ensuring that the promise of tomorrow is fulfilled for all.

As the **Architects of a Future Dawn**, this nation stands as a beacon of what humanity can achieve when it chooses to thrive **in harmony with nature**. It leaves behind not only a thriving planet but also a legacy of **resilience, unity, and inspiration**, proving that the greatest measure of progress is the **world we create for those who follow**.

IX. THE TECHNOLOGICAL EVOLUTION: A SYSTEM OF INNOVATION

A civilized nation harnesses technology to elevate society, balancing advancement with ethical considerations.

1. The Innovation Nexus: Driving Progress Through Research

Imagine a nation where technology is not merely a tool but a **catalyst for societal transformation**. Here, innovation acts as the beating heart of progress, fueling breakthroughs that elevate humanity and address its most pressing challenges. In this society, the **innovation nexus** becomes the hub of discovery, where science, technology, and creativity converge to shape a brighter future.

This nexus is not just a place—it is a **movement**, a collective effort to push the boundaries of possibility and turn ambition into reality.

Creating Hubs for Scientific Research and Technological Development

A truly advanced nation recognizes that **concentrated centers of innovation** are the engines of progress. These hubs serve as incubators where the brightest minds tackle complex problems and unlock new frontiers.

Key characteristics of these hubs include:

1. **Focus on Interdisciplinary Research**:

   o Scientists, technologists, and social scientists collaborate across disciplines, creating **holistic solutions** to global issues.

   o Projects bridge fields such as **biology, artificial intelligence, energy**, and **social sciences**, ensuring that breakthroughs address humanity's diverse needs.

2. **Leverage Advanced Technologies**:

   o Tools like **quantum computing**, **AI**, and **robotics** are harnessed to explore uncharted possibilities, from decoding genetic mysteries to designing autonomous transportation systems.

   o Laboratories are equipped with **state-of-the-art facilities**, fostering experimentation that challenges the limits of knowledge.

3. **Foster Global Cooperation**:

   o Partnerships with international research institutions create a **global network of knowledge**, enabling the exchange of ideas and resources.

   o Collaborative projects tackle universal challenges, from combating pandemics to exploring the cosmos.

Science underscores that concentrated efforts lead to exponential advancements.

Imagine:

- A global network of innovation hubs, where researchers in one country collaborate with engineers in another to solve pressing global problems.

- Urban centers transformed into **living laboratories**, testing sustainable technologies and futuristic designs.

By investing in these hubs, a nation positions itself as a **beacon of progress**, proving that **vision and collaboration can change the world**.

Incentivizing Innovation in Key Areas

Technology has the power to transform society, but only when directed toward **critical needs**. A truly civilized nation prioritizes innovation in areas that improve quality of life, safeguard the planet, and empower individuals.

1. **Healthcare**:

    o Early diagnosis tools leverage **AI and genomics**, preventing diseases before symptoms emerge.

    o Personalized medicine tailors treatments to individual genetic profiles, revolutionizing healthcare.

    o Pandemic response systems integrate **real-time data and predictive modeling** to prevent global crises.

2. **Education**:

    o Virtual reality classrooms immerse students in interactive learning experiences, breaking down barriers of geography and accessibility.

    o AI-driven platforms customize education to individual learning styles, ensuring that **every student thrives**.

3. **Sustainability**:

- o Renewable energy technologies, such as **solar, wind, and hydroelectric power**, reduce reliance on fossil fuels and combat climate change.

- o Smart agriculture systems optimize water and nutrient use, ensuring **food security for growing populations**.

- o Circular economy innovations create products designed for reuse and recycling, reducing waste and preserving resources.

Incentives for innovation include:

- **Grants and subsidies** for startups and research projects tackling societal challenges.

- **Tax benefits** to encourage businesses to invest in research and development.

- **Recognition programs** celebrating inventors and innovators who contribute to the greater good.

Science fiction often imagines societies transformed by bold technological leaps. A civilized nation turns this vision into reality, channeling imagination into actionable policies that ensure **technology serves humanity**.

Imagine:

- A national healthcare network powered by AI, where illnesses are predicted and prevented before they arise.

- Cities powered entirely by renewable energy, with carbon-neutral transportation and architecture.

These priorities ensure that **innovation becomes the engine of progress**, creating a society that thrives on ingenuity and compassion.

Encouraging Public-Private Collaboration in Technological Advancement

The most impactful innovations often emerge from the **synergy between public and private sectors**. By aligning the goals of governments, corporations, and communities, a nation maximizes its potential for progress.

1. **Co-Funding Research Initiatives**:

    o   Large-scale projects, such as **space exploration** or **green technology development**, are funded collaboratively, sharing financial responsibilities and risks.

    o   Grants and partnerships enable startups to **scale groundbreaking ideas**, accelerating their path to implementation.

2. **Building Innovation Ecosystems**:

    o   Networks of **universities, corporations, and government agencies** facilitate the exchange of ideas and resources, creating environments where innovation thrives.

    o   Startups and established companies collaborate in **incubators and accelerators**, driving rapid development and commercialization.

3. **Promoting Open Data Access**:

    o   Research findings are shared transparently, allowing scientists and innovators worldwide to **build on each other's discoveries**.

    o   Open-source platforms democratize technology, ensuring that its benefits are accessible to all.

History reminds us that collaboration multiplies potential while isolation stifles progress.

Imagine:

- Governments fund public infrastructure while private companies develop technologies to enhance it, from autonomous vehicles to smart grids.

- Open innovation networks where researchers from around the globe contribute to projects solving climate, health, or energy challenges.

By fostering **public-private collaboration**, a nation ensures that technological progress is **inclusive, efficient, and impactful**, driving innovation that benefits all.

Conclusion: Innovation as a Pathway to Progress

The **innovation nexus** is more than a hub—it is a **beacon of possibility** where science and technology converge to address humanity's greatest challenges. By:

- Creating **hubs for research and technological development**,

- Incentivizing **innovation in key areas like healthcare, education, and sustainability**, and

- Encouraging **public-private collaboration** to amplify impact,

The nation builds:

- A society at the **forefront of technological advancement**, tackling global challenges with creativity and determination.

- An economy driven by **knowledge, ingenuity, and progress**, empowering citizens to thrive in an era of rapid change.

- A legacy of innovation that demonstrates humanity's potential to **harness technology for the greater good**.

In this society, innovation is not just a goal—it is a **pathway to a brighter tomorrow**, where the fusion of research and creativity uplifts all. The innovation nexus becomes the **pulse of a civilization**, proving that progress is best achieved through vision, collaboration, and an unyielding commitment to excellence.

2. The Ethical Algorithm: Governing Technology with Responsibility

Imagine a society where **technological progress is guided by an ethical compass**, ensuring that innovation enhances humanity without compromising its most fundamental rights. In this **civilized nation**, the **ethical algorithm** governs the development, deployment, and use of technology, addressing challenges such as privacy, equity, and the societal impacts of rapid change. This ensures that progress is rooted in **responsibility, fairness, and inclusivity**.

In this vision, technology is not a force to be feared but a tool to **uplift humanity**, shaped by principles that prioritize the **greater good**.

Frameworks for Ethical AI and Automation to Prevent Misuse

Artificial intelligence and automation hold the potential to **revolutionize industries and improve lives**, but unchecked development risks misuse, exploitation, and harm. A truly civilized nation establishes **ethical frameworks** to ensure that these transformative technologies are deployed responsibly.

1. **Preventing Algorithmic Bias**:

   o AI systems are rigorously tested to identify and eliminate biases that could reinforce **social inequities**.

   o Standards for transparency ensure that citizens understand how decisions—such as those in hiring or criminal justice—are made, fostering **accountability and trust**.

2. **Regulating Autonomous Systems**:

   o Strict guidelines govern AI-driven decisions in **critical areas** like healthcare, law enforcement, and finance, ensuring they prioritize **human welfare** over efficiency.

   o Autonomous technologies are required to adhere to **ethical standards**, particularly in life-and-death scenarios like autonomous vehicles or medical diagnoses.

3. **Establishing Accountability**:

   o Developers and organizations are held responsible for the **ethical implications** of their technologies, with clear mechanisms for addressing harm caused by misuse or negligence.

   o Independent ethics councils oversee AI development, ensuring that innovation aligns with societal values.

Science underscores the dangers of unregulated AI, from privacy violations to the amplification of systemic bias.

Imagine:

- AI-driven hiring systems that prioritize **diverse talent** while removing unconscious biases from decision-making.

- Autonomous medical technologies that enhance diagnostics while **ensuring equitable access** to care.

By embedding ethics into every stage of technological development, the nation ensures that AI serves humanity, not exploits it. This creates a world where technology becomes a **trusted ally** in the pursuit of progress.

Addressing the Societal Impact of Rapid Technological Change

Technology often evolves faster than societal norms, policies, and infrastructure can adapt. This can lead to **inequality, disruption, and resistance to change**. A truly advanced nation anticipates and mitigates these challenges, creating pathways for a **smooth and equitable transition** into the future.

1. **Anticipating Economic Shifts**:

    o Automation and AI reshape industries, displacing traditional roles while creating new opportunities. The nation invests in **reskilling programs** and **social safety nets** to empower workers to thrive in emerging sectors.

    o Universal access to education and training ensures that no one is left behind in the **new economy**.

2. **Evaluating Societal Effects**:

    o Comprehensive **impact assessments** analyze how new technologies influence culture, behavior, and human relationships.

o   Insights from these assessments guide policies that minimize harm and maximize benefits, ensuring a **harmonious integration** of innovation into daily life.

3.   **Engaging in Public Discourse**:

o   Open forums, citizen panels, and educational campaigns encourage discussions about the implications of technological change, empowering people to **shape the trajectory** of innovation.

o   Governments and organizations actively seek public input on major initiatives, fostering **transparency and trust**.

Psychology reveals that people are more likely to embrace change when they understand its purpose and feel included in the process. **Imagine:**

•   Communities engaged in shaping the ethical guidelines for AI-driven urban planning.

•   Workers transitioning seamlessly into new roles through tailored reskilling programs, supported by the nation's commitment to **inclusive progress**.

By addressing the societal impacts of rapid technological change, the nation ensures that innovation becomes a **force for unity and empowerment**, not division or discord.

Protecting Privacy and Ensuring Equity in Access to Technology

In an era defined by data, privacy is a cornerstone of **individual autonomy**, and equitable access is essential for societal progress. A civilized nation safeguards its citizens and ensures that technology benefits **everyone, not just the privileged few**.

1.   **Strengthening Data Protection Laws**:

- o Regulations establish clear boundaries on how personal data is collected, stored, and used, ensuring that individuals retain control over their information.

- o Companies and governments are held accountable for breaches, creating a **culture of transparency and respect** for privacy.

2. **Promoting Cybersecurity**:

- o Investments in cybersecurity infrastructure protect citizens, businesses, and institutions from data breaches and cyberattacks.

- o Awareness campaigns educate the public on digital safety, empowering individuals to **protect themselves** in the digital age.

3. **Guaranteeing Equitable Access**:

- o Affordable internet, devices, and digital literacy programs bridge the **digital divide**, ensuring that all communities have the tools to thrive in a connected world.

- o Initiatives prioritize underserved and marginalized populations, creating opportunities for **inclusive innovation**.

History reminds us of the consequences of inequity and exploitation in technological advancement.

Imagine:

- Rural communities empowered by affordable internet access, connecting them to education, healthcare, and economic opportunities.

- A national data privacy framework that becomes a global standard, protecting citizens while fostering **innovation with integrity**.

By protecting privacy and ensuring equitable access, the nation creates a society where **technology empowers, uplifts, and connects**, leaving no one behind.

Conclusion: Technology Guided by Ethics

The **ethical algorithm** ensures that technological progress aligns with the principles of **justice, equity, and responsibility**. By:

- Establishing **ethical frameworks** for AI and automation,

- Addressing the **societal impacts** of rapid technological change, and

- Protecting **privacy and ensuring equitable access** to technology,

The nation builds:

- A society where technology enhances lives without compromising freedoms or values.

- A culture of trust, where citizens **embrace innovation** knowing it is developed and deployed responsibly.

- A legacy of progress that reflects humanity's ability to harness technology for the **greater good**.

In this vision, technology becomes a tool for **empowerment and progress**, guided by an ethical compass that ensures it serves humanity's highest aspirations. The nation proves that innovation need not come at the cost of morality but can be a **testament to humanity's capacity for wisdom and compassion**.

3. The Tech-Literate Citizen: Empowering Through Education

Imagine a civilization where **every individual is fluent in the language of technology**, confident in their ability to navigate the digital landscape, and empowered to shape their future. In this **civilized nation**, technology is not feared or misunderstood but embraced as a **universal tool for empowerment and innovation**. By prioritizing education, accessibility, and digital fluency, the nation cultivates a **tech-literate citizenry** that thrives in an interconnected, rapidly evolving world.

In this vision, technology becomes not just a tool but a **catalyst for personal and societal transformation**.

Integrating Technology Education at All Levels of Schooling

A truly advanced society recognizes that **technological literacy** is as fundamental as reading, writing, or mathematics. To prepare its citizens for a **future shaped by innovation**, it integrates technology education at every stage of learning, ensuring that no one is left behind.

1. **Early Education**:

   o Primary schools introduce foundational concepts such as **coding, digital ethics**, and **online safety**, fostering curiosity and responsible usage from a young age.

   o Interactive tools, like gamified coding apps and augmented reality (AR) lessons, make learning **engaging and intuitive**.

2. **Secondary Education**:

- o Specialized courses in **programming, data science**, and **robotics** cultivate technical skills, creativity, and problem-solving abilities.

- o Students participate in collaborative projects, such as **designing apps to address real-world problems** and blending innovation with societal impact.

3. **Higher Education and Vocational Training**:

- o Universities and vocational programs expand offerings in **emerging fields** like artificial intelligence (AI), cybersecurity, and green technology, ensuring a steady pipeline of skilled professionals.

- o Online learning platforms and certifications make advanced technical education accessible to **learners worldwide**.

Science reveals that early exposure to technology fosters critical thinking, creativity, and innovation.

Imagine:

- A curriculum where students learn **not just how technology works but how to shape it**, becoming the architects of a **digital future**.

- Classrooms equipped with cutting-edge tools like VR, allowing students to explore distant galaxies or conduct virtual dissections.

By integrating technology education at every level, the nation creates a **generation of digital pioneers** equipped to thrive in a world of constant innovation.

Programs to Reduce the Digital Divide and Increase Access to Digital Resources

Equity in access to technology is **essential for progress**. A truly civilized nation ensures that no one is excluded from the **opportunities of the digital age** by addressing the digital divide with comprehensive programs.

1. **Providing Affordable Internet Access**:

   o Broadband infrastructure is expanded to **rural and underserved communities**, connecting every corner of the nation.

   o Public-private partnerships subsidize internet costs for low-income households, making connectivity **universal**.

2. **Distributing Digital Devices**:

   o Subsidies and donation programs ensure that students and families in need receive **laptops, tablets, and smartphones**.

   o Schools and libraries are equipped with shared devices, creating **equal opportunities** for all learners.

3. **Establishing Digital Hubs**:

   o Community centers are transformed into **technology hubs**, equipped with cutting-edge devices and staffed with instructors who provide training and support.

   o Workshops on **basic tech skills, coding, and digital literacy** empower individuals to leverage technology in their personal and professional lives.

History reminds us of the devastating impact of exclusion. The scars of past inequities show that leaving communities behind in technological progress deepens societal divides.

Imagine:

- A remote village connected to the world through high-speed internet, its children excelling in **virtual classrooms** alongside peers from urban centers.

- Urban neighborhoods revitalized by **digital hubs**, where residents learn to code, create businesses, and connect with global opportunities.

By eliminating the digital divide, the nation ensures that **every citizen has a seat at the table of progress**.

Preparing Citizens to Navigate and Leverage an Increasingly Digital World

Technological fluency extends beyond technical skills, requiring the confidence and adaptability to use technology **responsibly and effectively**. A civilized nation prepares its citizens to **thrive in the digital era** by fostering critical thinking, innovation, and ethical engagement.

1. **Evaluating Digital Information Critically**:

   o Media literacy programs teach citizens to **recognize misinformation**, evaluate sources, and make informed decisions in a complex digital landscape.

   o Students learn to **decode algorithms** and understand how platforms shape their perspectives.

2. **Protecting Digital Privacy and Security**:

   o Education campaigns teach individuals to safeguard their personal data, navigate online threats, and use secure practices.

   o Citizens are empowered to take control of their digital identities, fostering **autonomy and safety**.

3. **Leveraging Digital Tools for Innovation**:

   o   Citizens learn to use technology to **solve problems, start businesses**, and connect with global communities.

   o   Programs emphasize entrepreneurial skills, enabling individuals to create **apps, platforms, and products** that address societal challenges.

Psychology shows that individuals who feel confident in their technological abilities are more likely to embrace digital opportunities and contribute meaningfully to progress.

Imagine:

• A society where seniors learn to use smartphones to **stay connected and access healthcare** while young innovators develop apps to tackle environmental challenges.

• Workshops that teach citizens to **transform their ideas into digital realities**, from e-commerce platforms to virtual art galleries.

By fostering technological fluency, the nation creates a **population of empowered innovators** ready to shape and benefit from the digital age.

Conclusion: A Society of Tech-Literate Innovators

Tech-literate citizens are the cornerstone of a nation that thrives in the digital era. By:

• **Integrating technology education** at every level of schooling,

• Implementing **programs to reduce the digital divide**, and

• **Preparing citizens to navigate and leverage** a digital world,

The nation ensures:

- A population that is not only adept at using technology but also **empowered to shape its trajectory**.

- Equitable access to **education, employment, and innovation**, breaking down barriers of geography and privilege.

- A society that adapts to and thrives in the face of technological change, proving that progress can be **inclusive and transformative**.

In this vision, technology becomes a **universal language of empowerment**, spoken fluently by every citizen. Together, their collective expertise and innovation propel the nation toward a brighter, more equitable future, proving that when knowledge is shared, and access is universal, the possibilities are **limitless**.

X. EMBODYING HOLISTIC WELL-BEING

A civilized nation prioritizes the physical, mental, and emotional well-being of its citizens, recognizing that flourishing individuals create a thriving society.

1. The Well-Being Ecosystem: Holistic Approaches to Health

Imagine a society where **health is not a privilege but a cornerstone of progress**, a foundation upon which individuals and communities thrive. In this **civilized nation**, well-being is approached **holistically**, addressing the physical, mental, and emotional needs of every citizen. The well-being ecosystem integrates policies, programs, and support systems to foster resilience, prevent illness, and nurture fulfillment, ensuring that flourishing individuals contribute to a **thriving society**.

In this vision, health is not just an individual pursuit but a **collective mission**, a reflection of the nation's commitment to its people.

Policies Ensuring Universal Access to Healthcare

A truly advanced nation ensures that healthcare is **accessible, equitable, and comprehensive**, providing every citizen with the care they need, regardless of income, geography, or background. Universal healthcare becomes the bedrock of societal progress, ensuring **no one is left behind**.

1. **Public Healthcare Systems**:

   o Investment in **state-of-the-art infrastructure, skilled staffing, and advanced technologies** ensures that medical care is high-quality and widely available.

   o Clinics, hospitals, and telemedicine networks reach urban centers and remote communities alike, creating a **seamless healthcare experience**.

2. **Affordable Medications and Treatments**:

   o Policies negotiate **fair pricing** for essential medications, ensuring affordability for all citizens.

   o Subsidies and programs provide free access to critical treatments for vulnerable populations.

3. **Telemedicine Initiatives**:

   o Remote care platforms bring **health consultations, diagnostics, and follow-ups** to citizens in rural and underserved areas.

o AI-powered health assistants guide patients, ensuring **timely intervention** and personalized care.

Science highlights that universal healthcare reduces poverty, boosts productivity, and fosters equality.

Imagine:

- A nation where **every citizen has access** to life-saving treatments without fear of financial ruin.

- Communities where healthcare professionals are empowered by cutting-edge technologies to deliver **compassionate, efficient care**.

Universal healthcare transforms society into a **network of care and support** where well-being becomes a shared priority.

Emphasizing Mental Health as a Critical Component of Societal Well-Being

Mental health is as vital as physical health, yet it remains **underrepresented in societal priorities**. A truly civilized nation elevates mental health, addressing it as a critical pillar of **holistic well-being**.

1. **Destigmatizing Mental Health**:

o Public awareness campaigns normalize conversations about **mental health**, breaking down barriers of shame and misunderstanding.

o Celebrities, leaders, and everyday citizens share their experiences, creating a **culture of openness and acceptance**.

2. **Expanding Mental Health Services**:

- o Schools, workplaces, and community centers integrate **counseling, therapy, and psychiatric care**, ensuring support is accessible where people live, learn, and work.

- o Digital platforms provide **confidential mental health resources**, offering 24/7 support for those in need.

3. **Integrating Mental Health into Primary Care**:

- o Routine medical visits include **mental health screenings**, encouraging early detection and intervention.

- o Healthcare providers receive **specialized training** to recognize and address mental health concerns, ensuring **comprehensive care**.

Psychology reveals that strong mental health fosters resilience, creativity, and social connection.

Imagine:

- A nation where children learn **emotional intelligence** alongside academics, equipping them to navigate life's challenges.

- Workplaces that prioritize employee well-being through **mental health days, support programs, and stress management workshops**.

By addressing mental health as an integral part of well-being, the nation cultivates a **population that is emotionally balanced, compassionate, and driven**.

Preventative Healthcare and Wellness Programs to Build Resilience

Prevention is the **cornerstone of resilience**, reducing the burden of disease and improving quality of life. A civilized nation prioritizes proactive health measures, empowering citizens to live healthier, more fulfilling lives.

1. **Preventative Screenings**:

   o Free or low-cost screenings for diseases like **diabetes, cancer, and heart conditions** ensure early detection and treatment.

   o Mobile health clinics bring preventative care to **underserved communities**, bridging gaps in access.

2. **Lifestyle Education**:

   o Community programs teach **nutrition, fitness, and stress management**, encouraging citizens to adopt healthier habits.

   o Schools integrate wellness education, ensuring children grow up with an understanding of how to care for their bodies and minds.

3. **Workplace Wellness Initiatives**:

   o Employers support employee health with **fitness programs, ergonomic environments**, and flexible schedules.

   o Policies encourage companies to implement **mental health support, smoking cessation programs**, and other proactive measures.

History reminds us that prevention saves lives and reduces costs. **Imagine:**

- Communities engaged in **neighborhood wellness initiatives**, from exercise classes to healthy cooking workshops.

- Workplaces transformed into **hubs of support**, where wellness is a priority for both employers and employees.

By building resilience through prevention, the nation creates a society capable of **withstanding and recovering from health challenges**, from pandemics to chronic diseases.

Conclusion: A Society Rooted in Holistic Health

The **well-being ecosystem** of a civilized nation is not an isolated effort—it is a comprehensive, collective mission to ensure that every citizen thrives. By:

- Ensuring **universal access to healthcare**,

- Elevating **mental health as a societal priority**, and

- Promoting **preventative healthcare and wellness programs**,

The nation achieves:

- A population that is **healthier, more productive, and more resilient**.

- Reduced disparities in health outcomes, fostering **equity and social cohesion**.

- A foundation for long-term prosperity, where well-being becomes the **bedrock of societal progress**.

In this vision, health is more than a personal journey—it is a **collective endeavor**, a testament to the nation's commitment to its people. By nurturing the physical, mental, and emotional well-being of its citizens, the nation paves the way for a future defined by **shared vitality, unity, and success**.

2. The Balance of Mind and Body: Promoting Healthy Lifestyles

Imagine a society where the **health of the mind and body** is seen as an interconnected symphony, and every citizen is empowered to live a life of vitality, resilience, and balance. In this **civilized nation**, public health is not limited to treating illness—it is about cultivating **holistic well-being**. By addressing physical, mental, and socio-economic factors, the nation creates a foundation for **flourishing individuals and thriving communities**.

In this vision, health becomes a **dynamic balance**, nurtured by choices, opportunities, and supportive systems, ensuring **harmony between mind, body, and society**.

Programs Encouraging Physical Activity and Nutritious Eating

A truly advanced nation recognizes that **physical activity and nutrition** are cornerstones of a thriving society. By integrating these habits into daily life, it ensures that health is not a luxury but a **shared reality for all**.

1. **Community Fitness Initiatives**:

   o Public gyms, sports facilities, and parks offer **free or subsidized access** to encourage widespread participation.

   o Organized activities such as **yoga classes, walking groups,** and community sports leagues create opportunities for fitness and social bonding.

2. **Healthy Food Accessibility**:

- ○ Local farmers' markets are promoted, connecting communities with fresh, affordable produce while supporting sustainable agriculture.

- ○ Subsidies for nutritious food ensure that even underserved areas have access to **affordable, healthy options**, reducing reliance on processed and unhealthy alternatives.

3. **Educational Campaigns**:

- ○ Public service announcements and interactive programs teach citizens about the **benefits of balanced diets and regular exercise**.

- ○ Schools incorporate nutrition and fitness education, encouraging children to adopt **healthy habits for life**.

Science highlights that regular exercise and nutritious eating significantly reduce the risk of chronic diseases, from heart disease to diabetes.

Imagine:

- A nation where parks are alive with citizens engaging in fitness activities, supported by **free access to outdoor gyms and walking trails**.

- Urban areas transformed into **food oases**, where fresh produce is as accessible as convenience stores.

By making fitness and nutrition a part of daily life, the nation fosters a culture of **vitality and resilience**, ensuring that every citizen has the tools to thrive.

Incorporating Mindfulness and Stress Management Into Public Health Initiatives

Mental health is inseparable from physical well-being, and a **civilized society** prioritizes both with equal vigor. By embracing **mindfulness and stress management**, the nation creates a foundation for **emotional balance and resilience**.

1. **Mindfulness Training in Schools**:

   o   From an early age, students learn techniques such as **meditation, deep breathing**, and emotional regulation, fostering a generation equipped to handle life's challenges.

   o   Mindfulness-based practices are integrated into school routines, enhancing **focus, creativity**, and emotional intelligence.

2. **Corporate Wellness Programs**:

   o   Workplaces promote mental well-being by offering **flexible schedules, mindfulness sessions, and mental health days**.

   o   Stress-reducing initiatives, such as onsite yoga classes and digital detox programs, enhance **employee satisfaction and productivity**.

3. **Community Mental Health Hubs**:

   o   Local centers provide **therapy, support groups, and workshops** on stress management, making mental health resources accessible to all.

   o   Programs tailored to specific community needs address issues like trauma recovery, addiction, and anxiety, fostering **collective healing**.

Psychology confirms that mindfulness reduces stress, enhances focus, and improves emotional well-being.

Imagine:

- Communities where citizens gather for **group meditation sessions**, creating moments of calm and connection in urban hubs.

- Workplaces transformed into **supportive environments** where mental health is prioritized alongside professional development.

By integrating mindfulness and stress management into public health, the nation nurtures a population that is **emotionally balanced, adaptable**, and capable of thriving in the face of challenges.

Addressing the Socio-Economic Factors That Influence Health Disparities

Health is deeply intertwined with **socioeconomic structures**, and a truly civilized nation recognizes that equitable access to resources is essential for eliminating disparities. By addressing these root causes, the nation ensures that **everyone has the opportunity to lead a healthy life**.

1. **Reducing Barriers to Healthcare**:

   o Affordable medical services, fitness facilities, and nutritious food options are made accessible to **marginalized and underserved communities**.

   o Telemedicine and mobile clinics bring care to rural and remote areas, bridging gaps in **geographic access**.

2. **Affordable Housing and Safe Environments**:

- o Policies prioritize the creation of **safe, clean, and affordable housing**, recognizing that living conditions are directly linked to health outcomes.

- o Urban planning integrates green spaces, pedestrian-friendly areas, and pollution control measures, creating **healthier environments**.

3. **Job Security and Fair Wages**:

- o Fair compensation enables individuals to prioritize health, ensuring they can afford medical care, nutritious food, and recreation.

- o Workplace policies support **work-life balance**, reducing stress and promoting **overall well-being**.

History reminds us that health disparities weaken societies, creating cycles of poverty and illness.

Imagine:

- Neighborhoods where **affordable housing is designed with wellness in mind**, complete with parks, fitness centers, and community gardens.

- A workforce where individuals are empowered by **fair wages** to invest in their health and the well-being of their families.

By addressing socio-economic factors, the nation ensures that **health is not a privilege but a shared right**, creating a foundation for **collective progress and equity**.

Conclusion: Harmony in Health

The **balance of mind and body** is more than an ideal—it is the lifeblood of a thriving society. By:

- Promoting **physical activity and nutritious eating**,

- Incorporating **mindfulness and stress management** into public health initiatives and

- Addressing **socio-economic health disparities**,

The nation achieves:

- Citizens empowered to lead **vibrant, balanced lives** with the tools to maintain physical and mental well-being.

- Communities strengthened by a culture of **health and vitality**, where well-being permeates every level of society.

- A foundation for **equity and opportunity**, fostering resilience and progress for future generations.

In this vision, health becomes a **shared responsibility** nurtured by individuals, communities, and institutions working in harmony. Together, they create a society where the **balance of mind and body fosters lasting vitality, unity, and success**. This equilibrium not only enriches lives but also propels the nation toward its **greatest potential**, embodying the essence of what it means to flourish as a people.

3. The Happiness Index: Measuring Societal Progress

Imagine a nation where progress is not confined to economic growth but **defined by the well-being of its citizens**. In this visionary society, success is measured not by numbers but by **joy, purpose, and fulfillment**. The **Happiness Index** becomes the guiding star, offering a comprehensive metric to evaluate societal progress, where human flourishing is at the heart of every policy and decision.

This framework redefines the essence of a thriving civilization: one where people lead **balanced, meaningful lives** and communities flourish in unity.

Beyond GDP: Metrics That Assess Quality of Life

A truly advanced nation understands that **GDP alone is an incomplete measure** of progress. While economic growth is important, it must align with improvements in quality of life. The **Happiness Index** incorporates multidimensional metrics that provide a fuller picture of societal well-being:

1. **Health and Longevity**:

   o Metrics evaluate access to **comprehensive healthcare**, life expectancy, and mental well-being.

   o National initiatives track reductions in **chronic illness, mental health disparities**, and preventable diseases.

2. **Education and Opportunity**:

   o Indicators measure **access to quality education**, vocational training, and upward mobility.

   o Programs assess lifelong learning opportunities, ensuring citizens can adapt to a rapidly evolving world.

3. **Environmental Health**:

   o Metrics track **air and water quality**, access to green spaces, and the success of **sustainability initiatives**.

   o Surveys assess citizen satisfaction with urban planning and environmental stewardship.

4. **Personal Happiness and Fulfillment**:

   o National surveys measure individuals' satisfaction with their **lives, relationships, and sense of purpose**.

- o Tools evaluate stress levels, emotional resilience, and the quality of social connections.

Science confirms that nations prioritizing happiness experience **greater social cohesion, innovation**, and productivity.

Imagine:

- Citizens living in **clean, green cities** designed for harmony between humanity and nature.

- Governments use happiness metrics to create policies that foster **holistic progress**.

By going beyond GDP, the nation reimagines **progress as human flourishing**, creating a society rooted in well-being and equity.

Encouraging Community and Connection as Vital Contributors to Well-Being

Human beings are inherently social, and **strong communities and connections** are essential for well-being. A truly civilized nation nurtures these bonds, recognizing that a sense of **belonging** strengthens resilience and enhances the quality of life.

1. **Community-Building Initiatives**:

   - o Local governments support **events, volunteer programs**, and shared spaces that encourage interaction and collaboration.

   - o Projects revitalize neighborhoods with **public parks, libraries**, and cultural centers, fostering **unity and creativity**.

2. **Policies for Inclusivity**:

   - o Environments are designed to **celebrate diversity**, ensuring every citizen feels valued and accepted.

    ○ Programs address barriers to inclusion, from language support to accessibility improvements.

3. **Support for Family and Relationships**:

    ○ Resources for parenting, eldercare, and relationship counseling strengthen **interpersonal bonds**.

    ○ Flexible leave policies enable families to **spend quality time together**, enriching their connections.

Psychology reveals that individuals with strong social ties are healthier, happier, and more engaged.

Imagine:

- Communities thriving through **cultural festivals, dialogue forums**, and neighborhood projects that unite citizens from all walks of life.

- Families strengthened by **policies that prioritize time together**, creating lasting connections across generations.

By fostering community and connection, the nation cultivates a society where empathy, trust, and collaboration become the **fabric of progress**.

Fostering Environments That Support Work-Life Balance and Personal Growth

A thriving society values **work-life balance**, recognizing that meaningful careers should not come at the expense of health or personal fulfillment. A civilized nation creates systems that **empower citizens to pursue professional and personal aspirations** in harmony.

1. **Flexible Work Policies**:

- o Remote work options, **flexible schedules**, and part-time opportunities accommodate diverse lifestyles and family needs.

- o Initiatives encourage **healthy work environments** where employees feel valued and supported.

2. **Universal Leave Policies**:

- o Generous parental leave, paid time off, and vacation days allow citizens to rest, recover, and reconnect.

- o Policies normalize **mental health days**, reducing burnout and promoting overall well-being.

3. **Opportunities for Personal Growth**:

- o Lifelong learning programs provide access to **education, creative outlets, and skill development**.

- o Recreational activities, from hiking trails to art classes, enrich lives and foster **self-discovery**.

The scars of burnout and overwork remind us that the relentless pursuit of economic gain erodes happiness and productivity.

Imagine:

- Workplaces designed with **break areas, wellness programs**, and creative spaces that inspire employees to thrive.

- Cities filled with **community theaters, art studios, and innovation hubs** where citizens pursue their passions.

By fostering work-life balance and personal growth, the nation creates a society where individuals can **flourish in every aspect of life**, contributing to a collective sense of fulfillment.

Conclusion: Redefining Progress Through Well-Being

The **Happiness Index** redefines societal success by placing **well-being at the heart of progress**. By:

- Adopting metrics that go **beyond GDP**, prioritizing quality of life,

- Encouraging **community and connection** as vital contributors to well-being and

- Fostering environments that support **work-life balance and personal growth**,

The nation achieves:

- Citizens who lead lives that are not only prosperous but also **meaningful and joyful**.

- Communities that flourish as **empathy, trust, and collaboration** become the norm.

- Progress aligned with values of **equity, sustainability, and shared purpose**.

In this vision, the **true wealth of a nation** is not measured in numbers but in the smiles of its people, the strength of its communities, and the vitality of its culture. By prioritizing happiness and well-being, the nation paves the way for a future where **every citizen thrives**, proving that the greatest achievements are those that enrich the **human spirit**.

Conclusion

A truly civilized nation is not defined by its wealth or power but by its commitment to the **flourishing of its people and the planet**. This chapter has unveiled the key attributes of such a nation, where governance is transparent, opportunity is abundant, and innovation is guided by ethics.

It is a society where individuals unlock their potential, communities unite in shared purpose, and progress is measured by well-being rather than wealth. It is a world where cultural richness is celebrated, environmental resilience is prioritized, and technology becomes a tool for collective elevation.

As you reflect on these principles, let them serve as a **rallying cry for action**. Whether you are a leader, a visionary, or a builder of dreams, you have a role in shaping a future where humanity's boundless potential can flourish.

The path forward is not without challenges, but the rewards are immeasurable. Together, we can create a legacy of hope, innovation, and shared success—a civilization that stands as a testament to the power of unity, creativity, and resilience. Let us rise as architects of a future where progress and humanity walk hand in hand.

THE SIREN'S CALL: NAVIGATING MISGUIDED IDEAS

ᨀᨀᨀ

The Siren's Call is not just a whisper—it is a symphony that weaves itself into the fabric of society, its haunting melody drawing civilizations into the abyss. Misinterpreting this warning, dismissing it as alarmist or irrelevant, is to ignore the discordant notes already resonating in our world. It is to mistake comfort for safety, stagnation for stability, and division for identity. The darkness that follows is not sudden—it creeps in, thread by thread, unraveling the tapestry of progress until only shadows remain.

The dangers are insidious. The allure of simplicity blinds societies to the complexity of their challenges. The seeds of stagnation choke the growth of innovation and ambition. The loss of individuality extinguishes the sparks of freedom and creativity. Walls of division fracture unity, and unchecked control suffocates progress. Technology, wielded without foresight, becomes a tool of unintended devastation. All the while, blind optimism hums a reassuring tune, drowning out the warnings and leaving humanity vulnerable to collapse.

To misinterpret this warning is to embrace the Siren's Call, to march willingly into the dissonance of a fractured and unrecognizable future. It is to lose sight of the delicate harmony that sustains civilization, replacing it with the cacophony of despair.[3]

I. The Allure of Simplicity: The Deceptive Promise of Easy Solutions

In the labyrinth of progress, complexity is an unavoidable reality. Yet, as challenges grow more intricate, the Siren Song of Simplicity emerges—a melody that promises relief from uncertainty and order amidst chaos. It entices societies with the illusion of easy solutions, whispering that a single answer can resolve even the most multifaceted problems. But beneath this comforting refrain lies a harrowing truth: simplicity, when taken to extremes, erodes critical thinking, undermines innovation, and fosters misguided ideas that accelerate societal collapse.

Philosophy and cognitive neuroscience expose the peril of this illusion. Nobel laureate Daniel Kahneman's research on cognitive biases highlights humanity's preference for simplicity, even when it obscures the truth. The desire for clear and concise answers, while comforting, often leads to oversimplified solutions that fail to address the nuances of real-world problems. The allure of simplicity may offer temporary solace, but it threatens to blind societies to the complexity that progress demands.

---

[3] This structure creates a logical progression from the foundational errors (simplicity, stagnation) to the systemic consequences (division, tribalism) and culminating in existential threats (unchecked technology, collapse). It maintains narrative cohesion while emphasizing the escalating stakes, compelling readers to confront each danger with increasing urgency.

1. The Mirage of Silver Bullets

The Mirage of Silver Bullets is among the most dangerous manifestations of simplicity. It is the belief that a single, transformative solution can resolve a crisis, neglecting the interconnectedness of modern challenges. This dangerous mindset prioritizes immediate relief over comprehensive strategies, leaving societies vulnerable to unforeseen consequences.

The Peril of Oversimplification

Imagine a world grappling with a global energy crisis, its ecosystems collapsing under the weight of unsustainable consumption. A promising breakthrough in nuclear fusion captures the world's imagination, hailed as the ultimate solution. Governments and corporations divert all resources toward this technology, abandoning other renewable energy research and conservation efforts.

However, nuclear fusion, though revolutionary, cannot solve the broader systemic issues—economic inequality, geopolitical tensions, and infrastructure disparities—that contribute to the crisis. As the world's resources are funneled into a single endeavor, the neglected elements of the problem fester, and the fragile solution begins to crack under pressure. The promise of the silver bullet becomes a shattering illusion, leaving humanity adrift in a worsening crisis.

Science Fiction Parallel

Science fiction echoes this warning. Picture a futuristic society that discovers an inexhaustible energy source capable of powering entire planets. The discovery is heralded as humanity's salvation. Yet, in their zeal, society fails to consider how the distribution of this energy would deepen existing inequalities. The wealthiest nations hoard the technology, leaving poorer regions to languish in darkness.

As unrest spreads, protests erupt, and the once-brilliant promise of the new energy source gives way to conflict and collapse. The energy breakthrough, instead of becoming a beacon of hope, becomes a catalyst for division and destruction. This cautionary tale reminds us that no solution exists in a vacuum; every breakthrough must be woven into the broader fabric of society.

A Warning Etched in Shadows

The Mirage of Silver Bullets tempts with its simplicity, but its cost is profound. By focusing solely on singular solutions, societies neglect the interconnected nature of their challenges, leaving vital efforts underfunded and critical vulnerabilities unaddressed. The promise of simplicity blinds leaders to the complex interplay of factors required for sustainable progress.

The Call to Action: Embrace the Complexity of Progress

To resist the Siren Song of Simplicity, we must recognize that progress demands multifaceted approaches. A thriving civilization is not built on singular solutions but on the harmonious interplay of diverse strategies. This requires investment in innovation, a commitment to collaboration, and the courage to confront complexity rather than flee from it.

Let us reject the illusion of the silver bullet and instead weave a tapestry of solutions that address the full spectrum of humanity's challenges. Together, we can compose a future that thrives not on the simplicity of a single answer but on the resilience and ingenuity of a civilization unafraid to embrace the complexity of progress.

2. The Tyranny of Binary Thinking

In the pursuit of progress, the human mind often seeks clarity, preferring simplicity over ambiguity. Yet, as the Siren Song of Binary Thinking rises, it offers not clarity but constraint, framing complex challenges as false dichotomies. It whispers that the world exists only in black and white, forcing societies into divisive camps and stifling the creativity needed to navigate the gray areas where true solutions lie. Beneath this deceptive tune lies a chilling truth: the tyranny of binary thinking is not a path to progress but a barricade, one that polarizes debates, erodes collaboration and accelerates societal fracture.

Philosophy and cognitive psychology illuminate the dangers of such oversimplification. Nobel Prize-winning psychologist Daniel Kahneman's exploration of cognitive biases reveals humanity's tendency to oversimplify complex problems into either/or choices. This false dichotomy limits innovative thinking and fuels divisiveness, leaving societies paralyzed in the face of nuanced challenges. The allure of binary thinking promises decisiveness but delivers discord.

False Dichotomies: The Illusion of Choice

Societal challenges are rarely black-and-white, yet binary thinking insists otherwise. Consider the false choice between environmental conservation and economic growth—a narrative that pits sustainability against prosperity, ignoring the vast potential for synergy between the two.

Imagine a nation torn between preserving its natural resources and expanding its industrial base. Politicians and citizens align themselves with one of two factions, each accusing the other of undermining the nation's future. Conservationists demand an immediate halt to industrial projects, while industrialists decry environmental regulations as shackles on economic freedom. Meanwhile, opportunities for innovative solutions—sustainable industries, green technologies, and balanced policies—are left unexplored. The inability to navigate the gray area leads to stagnation, missed opportunities, and a fractured society.

Epic Fantasy Allegory: A Kingdom Divided

In the realm of epic fantasy, the dangers of binary thinking take on allegorical form. Imagine a kingdom bound by an ancient prophecy, one that forces its citizens to choose between two opposing paths. One faction believes the prophecy demands strict adherence to tradition, while the other insists on total transformation. The kingdom splits along these lines, each side clinging to its interpretation and refusing compromise.

As tensions escalate, the kingdom's once-unified purpose dissolves. Farmers refuse to trade with craftsmen aligned with the opposing faction. Warriors, divided in their loyalties, weaken the kingdom's defenses. The inability to find a middle ground or consider alternative paths leads to internal collapse. The kingdom's grand legacy is reduced to ruins, a haunting testament to the dangers of binary thinking.

A Warning Etched in Shadows

The Tyranny of Binary Thinking offers the illusion of decisiveness but at a grave cost. By reducing complex problems to false dichotomies, societies become trapped in cycles of polarization and inaction. Innovation and collaboration wither, leaving challenges unresolved and opportunities squandered. The promise of simplicity blinds leaders to the intricate interplay of factors needed for sustainable progress.

The Call to Action: Break Free from Binary Chains

To resist the Siren Song of Binary Thinking, we must embrace the complexity of societal challenges. True progress arises not from choosing between extremes but from forging innovative paths that integrate diverse perspectives. This requires courage—the courage to reject oversimplification and the willingness to explore the gray areas where true solutions reside.

Let us discard the false choices that divide us and instead compose a symphony of nuanced solutions that harmonize progress with sustainability, tradition with innovation, and individual ambition with a collective purpose. By breaking free from binary chains, we can ensure a future where humanity thrives not on division but on the strength of its unity and creativity. Together, we can rewrite the melody of progress, transforming discord into harmony and simplicity into a future as rich and complex as the tapestry of human potential.

II. The Seeds of Stagnation: Early Threats to Progress

Beneath the glittering façade of civilization lies a hidden peril—an insidious force sowing the seeds of stagnation and decay. Like a shadow creeping across the horizon, these early threats masquerade as comfort and convenience, their true danger hidden in plain sight. These seeds, seemingly harmless at first, germinate into forces that stifle innovation, corrode ambition, and hollow out the foundations of progress.

Imagine a world where the siren songs of stagnation and instant gratification weave a seductive melody. They lull societies into a false sense of security, promising endless prosperity without effort and blinding them to the compounding dangers of their choices. The allure of stability and quick rewards becomes a trap—a gilded cage that shackles the human spirit and condemns future generations to struggle in the ruins of what could have been.

This chapter is a warning, a thriller set in a dystopian future that grows not from sudden catastrophe but from the quiet neglect of long-term vision. It explores the perilous allure of unchanging perfection and fleeting satisfaction, unraveling how these forces undermine the very pillars of civilization. From the forgotten kingdoms of epic fantasy to the shattered empires of science fiction, the narrative unfolds as a cautionary tale etched into the histories of both reality and imagination.

The seeds of stagnation may seem small, but their roots run deep. They undermine creativity, erode resilience, and rob humanity of the tools needed to confront the challenges ahead. These early threats demand our attention, for their danger lies not in their immediate impact but in the slow, suffocating grip they exert on the future.

Let us not ignore the warning signs. The seeds of stagnation are being sown even now. Will we let them take root, or will we act with the foresight and courage needed to preserve the symphony of progress? This is not a tale of despair but a call to action. The choices we make today determine whether humanity thrives in brilliance or fades into the quiet decay of complacency.

1. The Siren Song of Stagnation: A Symphony of Lost Potential

In the labyrinth of human progress, there lies a treacherous snare: the Siren Song of Stagnation. It whispers of a perfect world—unchanging, safe, and comfortable. But beneath its alluring melody lies the specter of decay, a subtle paralysis that smothers ambition, innovation, and evolution. Stagnation is not the utopia it pretends to be; it is the graveyard of civilizations, the quiet killer of progress.

From the echoes of cognitive neuroscience, we know that the human brain thrives on novelty and challenge. Dr. Mihaly Csikszentmihalyi, the pioneer of flow theory, revealed that engagement and fulfillment stem from striving for new heights, not from dwelling in idle comfort. When societies embrace stagnation, they deny this fundamental need, creating a mental and cultural atrophy that paves the way to decline.

Lurking Threats: The Allure of the Golden Cage

The Empire in Twilight

Imagine a glittering galactic empire, its technology unrivaled, and its citizens basking in the glow of prosperity. Yet, within this golden cage lies its doom. Complacency has replaced ambition; adaptation is deemed unnecessary. As external threats emerge—be they cosmic phenomena, ecological collapse, or adversarial forces—the empire's brilliance becomes its blindness. It is the chilling paradox of stagnation: the greater the comfort, the deeper the vulnerability.

The Kingdom Frozen in Time

History echoes similar warnings in the myths and fables of epic fantasy. Consider a kingdom fortified by unyielding traditions. Its defenders cling to ancient strategies, its leaders to rituals that once symbolized strength but now signify inertia. Meanwhile, adversaries innovate. A once-unassailable bastion falls, its rigid walls crumbling under the weight of obsolescence. This is the fate of those who resist the currents of change.

The Shadows of the Past: Clinging to Dead Echoes

Even in the aftermath of catastrophe, the Siren Song persists. Picture a post-apocalyptic world where remnants of humanity cling to relics of a bygone era, unwilling to adapt to their new reality. Their traditions, once their salvation, now bind them to irrelevance. Social structures that once flourished become anchors in a changing tide. The knowledge they need to thrive slips away lost in the dust of nostalgia.

The Neuroscience of Stagnation: A Silent Decline

Psychology uncovers the silent peril of stagnation. Human cognition is wired for growth, for the pursuit of goals that stretch and challenge us. When societies prioritize stability over evolution, they erode the mechanisms of creativity and problem-solving. Dr.

Carol Dweck's research on mindset warns of the dangers of a fixed mentality—where fear of failure stifles the pursuit of progress. A stagnant society becomes a monotone hum, drowning out the vibrant melody of potential.

A Warning Etched in Stars

To heed the Siren Song of Stagnation is to choose decay disguised as serenity. It is a call to reject the uncomfortable, to avoid the unfamiliar. Yet history, science, and the echoes of philosophy reveal its hollowness. Progress demands discomfort; innovation requires disruption. The future is forged not in the safety of unchanging perfection but in the crucible of adaptation and growth.

The Call to Action: Reclaim the Dawn

We must silence the Siren Song of Stagnation before it envelops us. The architects of tomorrow cannot cling to the foundations of yesterday. A truly enlightened civilization harmonizes the wisdom of the past with the evolution demanded by the future. This is not a rejection of tradition but a transformation—a reinvention of values, practices, and ambitions.

The danger is clear, and the stakes are immense. Will we allow ourselves to be lulled into complacency, or will we rise as architects of a future dawn? Let the warning be heard: the cost of stagnation is a silent decline, but the reward of adaptation is boundless progress. Let us choose the path of vibrancy and potential before the Siren's call drowns the symphony of humanity.

2. The Siren Song of Instant Gratification: A Symphony of Future Sorrow

In the shadows of progress lies a dangerous melody, the Siren Song of Instant Gratification. It entices with promises of immediate rewards, urging societies to seize fleeting gains at the cost of a sustainable future. Like a drug that offers temporary euphoria, it blinds civilizations to the compounding dangers of short-term thinking. But this seductive tune carries a dire warning: a society that sacrifices tomorrow for today risks an irreversible collapse.

From the lens of psychology, the allure of instant gratification stems from humanity's evolutionary wiring. The "pleasure principle," as Sigmund Freud described it, drives us to seek immediate satisfaction. However, cognitive neuroscience reveals the paradox: the prefrontal cortex, responsible for long-term planning and self-control, is underutilized in the face of such temptations. This clash between impulsive desires and disciplined foresight mirrors the broader struggles of civilizations at critical crossroads.

Lurking Perils: The Mirage of Immediate Gains

The Myopic Gamble

Imagine a bustling metropolis that sacrifices its forests to fuel its economic machine. For a time, wealth abounds. Towering skyscrapers rise as testaments to prosperity. Yet, beneath the surface, ecosystems collapse, water supplies dwindle, and the air thickens with toxins. The temporary surge in wealth gives way to environmental ruin, leaving future generations to pay the price. This is the myopic gamble of prioritizing immediate gains over the long-term balance of nature and society.

The Future We Forget

Science fiction warns of civilizations undone by their short-sightedness. Picture a world clinging to obsolete technologies, unwilling to invest in the research and development needed to face new challenges. As novel threats arise—be they pandemics, environmental shifts, or technological adversaries—this society finds itself defenseless, its vulnerabilities laid bare. The future they ignored becomes a harbinger of their downfall, a cautionary tale etched into the annals of time.

A Kingdom Built on Sand

Epic fantasy offers another allegory. Consider a prosperous kingdom whose rulers focus on hoarding wealth and consuming resources. Forests fall, rivers run dry, and the land itself rebels against its exploitation. Though the coffers of the elite brim with gold, their foundations crumble beneath them. This is the fate of those who mistake transient prosperity for enduring strength—a kingdom built on the shifting sands of greed.

The Shadows of Survival: A Perpetual Cycle of Need

Even in the ashes of collapse, the siren's song persists. Picture a post-apocalyptic wasteland where leaders prioritize survival over rebuilding. Infrastructure is neglected, education forgotten, and innovation sacrificed. Society, desperate to meet its immediate needs, remains trapped in a cycle of short-term fixes and is unable to rise from its despair. The lingering legacy of instant gratification condemns it to perpetual stagnation.

The Psychology of Sacrifice: A Beacon of Hope

Hope, however, is not lost. Research in psychology reveals a path forward. Dr. Angela Duckworth's concept of "grit" emphasizes the power of perseverance and long-term vision. Societies that cultivate hope and optimism are more likely to embrace delayed gratification and sustainable practices. Leaders who inspire with visions of a better future can rally their people to make sacrifices today for the promise of a thriving tomorrow.

A Warning Etched in Civilization's Bones

The Siren Song of Instant Gratification is a trap—a melody that seems sweet but conceals bitter consequences. It lures nations into sacrificing their foundations for fleeting pleasures, trading resilience for fragility. But civilizations that resist this temptation, that invest in sustainability, education, and innovation, can break free from the siren's grasp.

The Call to Action: A New Symphony of Sustainability

To secure a prosperous and equitable future, humanity must compose a new melody—one that harmonizes progress with foresight. This requires more than rejection of the siren's tune; it demands a commitment to a long-term vision. By investing in sustainable infrastructure, protecting the environment, and fostering innovation, we can create a world where progress is not a fleeting crescendo but a symphony that echoes for generations.

Let this be a call to action: resist the allure of immediate gratification. The decisions we make today will resonate for centuries. Will we succumb to the hollow promises of the siren, or will we rise as architects of a future dawn, weaving a society where progress and sustainability form a harmonious duet? The choice is ours, and the future hangs in the balance.

III. The Subtle Loss of Individuality: Threats to Innovation and Freedom

Beneath the surface of progress, a silent peril looms—a force that whispers promises of unity, harmony, and shared purpose. Yet, this is no noble call to collaboration. It is the Siren Song of Conformity, luring societies into the shadowed depths where individuality is sacrificed, ambition is dulled, and freedom is a fading echo. This is the subtle erosion of self-determination, a creeping threat that suffocates the sparks of innovation and leaves civilization vulnerable to stagnation and collapse.

The loss of individuality begins not with a roar but with a whisper—an allure of sameness, a promise that uniformity will bring peace and prosperity. But beneath this alluring veneer lies the terrifying truth: without the vibrant melody of personal ambition, the symphony of progress becomes a monotonous drone. The engines of creativity falter, and societies that once thrived on the brilliance of their diverse minds descend into a chilling sameness, their potential lost to the abyss of collective mediocrity.

From the sterile silence of scientific laboratories devoid of dissent to the rigid hierarchies of kingdoms that suppress creative thought, history, and imagination echo the same warning: individuality is the foundation of resilience, creativity, and freedom. Without it, societies become brittle, unable to adapt to unforeseen challenges, and doomed to crumble under their own weight.

This chapter delves into the haunting cost of conformity—a world where the pursuit of harmony eclipses the power of ambition, where diverse talents are silenced in favor of sameness, and where the spark of innovation flickers and dies. It is a warning against the creeping dangers of the hive mind, the crushing monotony of uniformity, and the stifling embrace of collective stagnation.

Will humanity resist this siren's call, or will we let the subtle loss of individuality extinguish the vibrant fire of progress? The choice is ours. The stakes are nothing less than the future of freedom, innovation, and the boundless potential of human achievement. Let us navigate this perilous path with vigilance, for the cost of inaction is the quiet descent into a world where humanity's most powerful force—its individuality—is forever lost.

1. The Chilling Symphony of Sameness: A Requiem for Progress

In the quest for fairness, a shadowy melody emerges—the Tyranny of Equality. It whispers promises of harmony, a utopia where burdens and rewards are evenly shared and where every individual is treated identically. But beneath this seemingly benevolent tune lies a dystopian truth: in the pursuit of absolute equality, we risk erasing the very essence of humanity—our individuality. Without the spark of diversity, the engines of innovation stall, and the symphony of progress is reduced to a monotonous hum.

From the perspective of psychology, individuality is essential for human motivation and well-being. Abraham Maslow's hierarchy of needs underscores the human desire for self-actualization—the drive to realize one's unique potential. A society that silences this individuality risks stagnation, eroding not only progress but the very spirit that makes us human.

Lurking Perils: The Danger of Uniformity

The Meritocratic Engine Stalls

Meritocracy is the engine that drives progress, rewarding effort, skill, and ingenuity. But imagine a world where all outcomes are equal, regardless of contribution. The scientist receives the same recognition as the idle dreamer; the innovator is indistinguishable from the conformist. The desire to excel vanishes, and with it, the breakthroughs that push civilization forward. Scientific advancements falter, creativity withers and the great machinery of human potential grinds to a halt.

The Symphony of Silence

Science fiction offers grim visions of societies stripped of individuality. Picture a civilization where roles are arbitrarily assigned—engineers till the fields, poets are conscripted into the military. Without diverse talents aligned with innate abilities, the society falters. Challenges demanding creativity and adaptability become insurmountable, leaving the once-thriving civilization defenseless against inevitable crises.

The Crumbling Kingdom: Uniformity in Ruin

Epic fantasy provides a timeless allegory. Imagine a once-mighty kingdom where rigid laws enforce absolute equality. Warriors are forced to become farmers and artists to labor as blacksmiths. This forced conformity erases the kingdom's strength—its specialized skills. Inefficiency grows, vulnerability increases and the kingdom collapses under its own weight. The lesson is clear: strength lies not in sameness but in the dynamic interplay of diverse talents.

The Tower of Babel Crumbles Again

Even in a post-apocalyptic wasteland, the Tyranny of Equality looms. Picture a community struggling to rebuild, its leaders insisting that every individual perform identical tasks. The doctor builds while the engineer farms, vital expertise wasted in the name of uniformity. Progress halts, and the chance for renewal is lost. The lesson resonates: when individuality is silenced, survival itself is threatened.

The Psychology of Ambition: A Society Without Dreams

Psychology reveals that human beings are driven by achievement, growth, and self-expression. Dr. Carol Dweck's research on growth mindset highlights the importance of striving for improvement. But in a society where ambition is stifled, where personal growth is irrelevant, apathy replaces aspiration. Without dreams to pursue, the human spirit withers. A monotony of sameness engulfs the culture, robbing it of its dynamism and its capacity to envision a better future.

A Warning Etched in History

The Tyranny of Equality promises harmony but delivers a chilling dystopia—a society devoid of individuality, creativity, and progress. The vibrant tapestry of human potential is replaced by a sterile canvas of uniformity. History, philosophy, and science converge to warn us that strength lies not in making everyone the same but in celebrating the diversity that fuels innovation.

The Call to Action: Embrace the Power of Individuality

To resist the Siren Song of Sameness, we must reclaim the power of individuality. A thriving civilization is not a monotonous hum but a symphony where each unique voice contributes to greater harmony. This requires a commitment to meritocracy, a celebration of diverse talents, and a rejection of policies that stifle ambition.

Let us heed this warning. The future is not built on sameness but on the vibrant interplay of individual contributions. We must nurture a society where innovation and creativity thrive, where the unique skills of every citizen are celebrated, and where the symphony of progress resounds with the power of individuality. Only then can we ensure that the promise of humanity is not lost to the chilling silence of uniformity.

2. The Crushing Symphony of Monotony: A Warning Against the Hive Mind

Amid the vast expanse of human potential lies a shadowy seduction—the Tyranny of Uniformity. It promises efficiency, a society where every individual sings the same note in perfect harmony. But beneath this veneer of order lies a chilling truth: such uniformity is not the strength of a cohesive civilization but the suffocation of its very soul. Without the dynamic interplay of diverse ideas and perspectives, the engines of progress stall, leaving a society defenseless against the tides of change.

From cognitive neuroscience, we understand that the brain thrives on complexity and novelty. Neuroplasticity—the brain's ability to adapt and evolve—relies on exposure to diverse inputs and perspectives. A society stripped of diversity risks cognitive stagnation as the monotony of thought erodes its capacity for innovation and adaptation.

Lurking Perils: The Illusion of Efficiency

The Sterile Science Lab

Innovation is born in the clash of ideas, the vibrant debate of minds unafraid to dissent. Yet, imagine a world where scientific communities enforce conformity. Dissenting voices are silenced, creativity stifled by rigid protocols. Complex challenges—climate change, global pandemics, interstellar exploration—go unanswered because no one dares to question the norm. The once-thriving engine of discovery sputters, its potential extinguished by the chilling embrace of uniformity.

The Doomed Starship

Science fiction warns of civilizations undone by their lack of diversity. Picture a sprawling interstellar empire where a single ideology dominates. Independent thought is eradicated in the name of unity. When an unexpected threat emerges—a rogue artificial intelligence, a cosmic anomaly—the society is paralyzed. Bereft of the diverse perspectives needed to confront the challenge, its rigidity becomes its downfall. The lesson is stark: without adaptability, even the stars cannot save us.

The Stagnant Kingdom: Creativity Crushed by Conformity

Epic fantasy offers its own cautionary tale. Picture a kingdom where all artists are forced to paint the same scenes, warriors are trained in identical tactics, and scholars recite only approved texts. When a cunning adversary arrives with new strategies, the kingdom's inability to innovate ensures its defeat. Its rigid adherence to conformity becomes its fatal flaw, a chilling reminder that progress demands more than sameness—it demands the courage to think differently.

The Tower of Babel Resurrected

Even in the ashes of collapse, uniformity can rise again like a specter. Imagine a post-apocalyptic community clinging to a single method of rebuilding. Engineers, doctors, and artists are stripped of their individual expertise and forced to follow a rigid, one-size-fits-all plan. The result? Inefficiencies mount, setbacks multiply, and progress slows to a crawl. The tools of survival lie unused, victims of a narrow, oppressive vision.

The Silenced Symphony: A Monotony of Minds

Psychology reveals the cost of stifled individuality. Human motivation flourishes when people feel they contribute something unique to society. Dr. Edward Deci's work on self-determination theory emphasizes that autonomy, competence, and relatedness are critical drivers of human fulfillment. A society that demands conformity extinguishes these motivators, replacing them with apathy and disengagement. The vibrant symphony of individual voices becomes a monotonous drone, and the wellspring of innovation runs dry.

A Warning Written in Shadows

The Tyranny of Uniformity promises streamlined efficiency but delivers a barren landscape of stagnation. It silences the cacophony of human ingenuity, replacing it with the dull hum of monotony. History, science, and imagination converge to warn us: true progress demands diversity—not just of background, but of thought, skill, and perspective.

The Call to Action: Celebrate the Beautiful Cacophony

To resist the Hive Mind, we must champion individuality as the cornerstone of progress. A thriving civilization is not a monotonous tune but a rich tapestry of voices, each contributing to a greater harmony. This requires more than tolerance—it demands an active celebration of difference.

Let us build a society that honors diverse perspectives and fosters spaces where ideas clash and innovation flourishes. The stakes are high, and the costs of inaction are immense. The survival of civilization depends not on forcing conformity but on embracing the beautiful cacophony of human thought.

The Hive Mind may promise order, but it delivers a chilling monotony—a requiem for creativity, adaptability, and progress. Let us not succumb to its seductive whispers. Instead, let us compose a symphony that resonates with individuality, a thriving testament to the power of diversity and the boundless potential of humanity.

3. The Siren Song of Conformity: A Symphony Stifled by Stagnation

In the quest for harmony, a shadow looms—the Siren Song of Conformity. It whispers of order, promising a world where everyone moves in lockstep toward shared goals, where discord is silenced, and individuality is sacrificed for the collective. But beneath this alluring melody lies a chilling truth: a society that crushes individuality in the name of conformity extinguishes the very essence of progress. Without the spark of personal ambition and the freedom to dream, innovation falters, and the vibrant tapestry of human potential unravels.

From the perspective of psychology, this peril becomes even clearer. The work of Dr. Edward Deci and Dr. Richard Ryan on self-determination theory reveals that autonomy, mastery, and purpose are critical for human motivation. A society that denies these drivers of personal growth risks stagnation, creating an environment where creativity and ambition are stifled under the weight of sameness.

Lurking Perils: The Hollow Promise of Harmony

A Symphony of Stars, Not Clones

True progress lies not in unison but in harmony, where individual ambition complements collective goals. Imagine a society where personal achievement is celebrated, inspiring others to reach new heights. Scientists innovate, artists create, and visionaries lead—not in isolation but in collaboration. The melody of individual effort enhances the symphony of collective action, driving progress forward. Yet, when conformity silences these voices, the orchestra becomes a dull, repetitive tune incapable of inspiring greatness.

A Galactic Tapestry of Talents

Science fiction warns of civilizations that crumble when diversity of thought and skill is lost. Picture a galactic federation facing existential threats. In such a future, survival depends on a tapestry of talents: engineers, diplomats, strategists, and visionaries, each contributing their unique strengths. But when conformity takes hold, this rich diversity is replaced by a monotonous uniformity. Challenges arise that no single mindset can solve, and the once-thriving civilization collapses under the weight of its homogeneity.

The Nation's Chorus of Achievement: Strength in Diversity

Epic fantasy reminds us that strength lies in the contributions of individuals from all walks of life. Imagine a kingdom where artisans, warriors, and scholars each play a vital role in its prosperity. The blacksmith forges weapons for defense, the farmer provides sustenance, and the philosopher guides with wisdom. Together, they create a resilient and thriving society. Yet, if forced into conformity, this vibrant chorus is silenced, leaving the kingdom vulnerable to both internal decay and external threats.

From Ashes, We Rise with Ambition

Even in the aftermath of catastrophe, ambition endures as a beacon of hope. Picture a post-apocalyptic community struggling to rebuild. The innovative engineer designs water purification systems, the resourceful farmer cultivates resilient crops, and the determined leader inspires collective effort. Their unique contributions fuel the community's recovery, proving that individuality is the foundation of resilience.

Without this ambition, the ashes remain, and the promise of renewal fades.

The Psychology of Aspiration: A Society Driven to Achieve

Psychology underscores the importance of personal ambition in driving societal progress. When individuals are motivated by a sense of accomplishment, they strive to improve their lives and contribute to their communities. Dr. Angela Duckworth's research on grit demonstrates that perseverance and passion for long-term goals are critical for success. A society that nurtures these traits fosters innovation, resilience, and progress. Without them, the human spirit languishes in mediocrity, and the engines of advancement grind to a halt.

A Warning Written in Shadows

The Siren Song of Conformity may promise a world of harmony and order, but its true cost is the stagnation of society. It stifles the dreams of individuals, crushes the diversity of thought, and extinguishes the flames of progress. History, science, and imagination converge to warn us that true strength lies in the interplay of individual ambition and collective effort, not in the sterile monotony of enforced uniformity.

The Call to Action: Celebrate the Individual within the Collective

To resist the Siren Song of Conformity, we must embrace a new vision of unity—one that celebrates individuality as the driving force of collective achievement. A truly thriving civilization is not a monotonous tune but a symphony where each unique melody enriches the whole. This requires a commitment to fostering ambition, celebrating achievement, and creating space for diverse perspectives to flourish.

Let us build a society that harmonizes the power of collective action with the vibrant energy of individual ambition. The stakes are immense, but the rewards are greater. The future of innovation, progress, and resilience depends on our ability to embrace the richness of human diversity.

The Siren Song of Conformity is a whisper of stagnation, but the symphony of individuality is a roar of progress. Let us choose the path of vibrancy, where every voice contributes to the grand tapestry of human potential, ensuring a future that is as dynamic as it is harmonious.

IV. The Idolization of Stability: A Symphony Frozen in Time

Stability is often hailed as the foundation of progress—a secure platform from which societies can flourish. Yet, when stability becomes an obsession, it transforms into a trap, prioritizing the status quo over evolution. This is the Idolization of Stability, a Siren Song that promises peace but delivers stagnation. It whispers that change is dangerous and that clinging to tradition ensures survival. But beneath its soothing melody lies a stark truth: a society frozen in time becomes brittle, unable to adapt to the shifting tides of progress, and vulnerable to collapse.

From a philosophical perspective, Heraclitus reminds us, "The only constant is change." Evolution is not the enemy of stability but its greatest ally. Cognitive neuroscience further underscores this truth, as human adaptability is hardwired into our biology. Societies that resist change favoring rigid norms over innovation, lose their resilience and risk obsolescence. The Idolization of Stability is not the foundation of progress—it is the barrier that holds it hostage.

1 The Danger of Cultural Rigidity

Cultural rigidity is the cornerstone of the Idolization of Stability. It is the refusal to evolve, to adapt to new realities and opportunities.

While tradition provides a foundation, rigidity turns it into a shackle, preventing societies from responding to the demands of a rapidly changing world.

Erosion of Adaptability

Imagine a society that prides itself on its unchanging traditions, refusing to adapt to technological advancements. As the world progresses around them, they remain steadfast in their ways, dismissing automation, renewable energy, and digital infrastructure as fleeting fads. At first, their traditions seem noble, a testament to their cultural identity. But as industries innovate, global economies evolve, and environmental challenges escalate, their refusal to adapt isolates them.

Their once-thriving economy falters, their infrastructure decays, and their youth, seeking opportunity, abandon their homeland. The society becomes a relic—a museum of what once was, rather than a beacon of what could be. Their idolization of stability renders them obsolete, and their cultural rigidity becomes their undoing.

Post-Apocalyptic Parallel

Even in the face of survival, rigidity can doom a community. Picture a post-apocalyptic world where climate crises have devastated traditional farming methods. A community, bound by their ancestral ways, resists adopting new agricultural techniques like hydroponics or vertical farming. They view these innovations as betrayals of their heritage, clinging to outdated methods even as their crops fail and famine spreads.

As resources dwindle, desperation grows. The community fragments, blaming each other for their suffering, while neighboring groups that embraced change thrive and rebuild. Their unwillingness to adapt turns their traditions into a tombstone, marking the collapse of a culture that could not evolve.

A Warning Etched in Shadows

The Danger of Cultural Rigidity is a silent threat, its grip tightening as societies cling to the illusion of security in an ever-changing world. This rigidity erodes adaptability, isolates communities, and leaves nations ill-prepared to face the challenges of the future. The Siren Song of Stability may promise comfort, but its cost is immense: a society frozen in time, left behind by progress, and vulnerable to collapse.

The Call to Action: Embrace the Symphony of Adaptation

To resist the Idolization of Stability, we must embrace adaptability as the cornerstone of progress. Stability is not found in resisting change but in navigating it, weaving tradition and innovation into a harmonious symphony. This requires courage—the courage to challenge rigid norms and the wisdom to evolve without losing our identity.

Let us discard the chains of cultural rigidity and instead compose a future where progress thrives alongside heritage. By fostering adaptability, we can ensure that humanity remains resilient, vibrant, and ready to face the uncertainties of tomorrow. Together, we can rewrite the melody of stability, transforming it from a frozen refrain into a dynamic overture that resonates with the boundless potential of a world unafraid to evolve.

2 The Fear of Disruption

Change is the catalyst of progress, but with it comes disruption—a force that unsettles the familiar and challenges the status quo. The Fear of Disruption emerges as a Siren Song, luring societies and institutions into a state of paralysis. It whispers that stability must be preserved at all costs and that innovation is a threat to tradition and order. Yet beneath this cautious refrain lies a chilling truth: the refusal to embrace disruption stifles innovation, leaving societies vulnerable to stagnation and decline.

Philosophers like Friedrich Nietzsche remind us that creation often emerges from destruction, and psychology underscores this with research on adaptability and resilience. Disruption, though uncomfortable, is the crucible of growth. Societies that reject it in favor of stability become brittle, their resistance to change transforming potential opportunities into existential threats. The Fear of Disruption is not a shield—it is a cage.

Stifling Innovation: The Cost of Resistance

Fear of disruption often manifests in the rejection of groundbreaking ideas, as leaders cling to familiar structures rather than risk the upheaval of change. Consider a corporation entrenched in its traditional hierarchies, wary of adopting artificial intelligence (AI) for fear of destabilizing its workforce and power dynamics.

The Corporate Cautionary Tale

Imagine a corporation that dominates its industry, thriving on legacy systems and established practices. The advent of AI presents an opportunity to revolutionize operations, improve efficiency, and unlock untapped potential. Yet, the board resists, fearing that automation will upend their workforce and threaten the roles of middle management.

While they debate, smaller, more agile competitors embrace AI, streamlining their processes, cutting costs, and offering innovative products. Within a decade, the once-dominant corporation finds itself overtaken, its refusal to disrupt its hierarchy leading to its obsolescence. What began as a fear of change ends as a cautionary tale, a stark reminder that clinging to the familiar can be as dangerous as embracing the unknown.

The Broader Implications

The Fear of Disruption is not confined to corporations. Governments, educational institutions, and entire nations often resist transformative ideas, preferring stability over progress. Whether it is rejecting renewable energy technologies due to existing fossil fuel investments or resisting healthcare reform to maintain outdated systems, the refusal to adapt leaves societies vulnerable to being outpaced by the future.

A Warning Etched in Shadows

The Fear of Disruption offers comfort, but its cost is immense. By stifling innovation, societies, and institutions become relics of the past, their relevance eroded by the relentless march of progress. The Siren Song of Stability may promise security, but it is an illusion— a lullaby that silences the dynamism and creativity essential for survival in an ever-changing world.

The Call to Action: Harness the Symphony of Disruption

To resist the Fear of Disruption, we must reframe our understanding of change. Disruption is not the enemy—it is the conductor of progress, orchestrating the evolution of systems and ideas. Embracing disruption requires courage: the courage to challenge established hierarchies, take risks, and prioritize innovation over comfort.

Let us reject the stagnation of stability and instead compose a future where disruption becomes a symphony of growth. By fostering an environment where groundbreaking ideas are welcomed, and transformative technologies are embraced, we can ensure that humanity remains at the forefront of progress. Together, we can rewrite the melody of disruption, transforming it from a discordant threat into a harmonious prelude to a brighter, more dynamic future.

V. Walls of Division: The Isolation of Communities and Nations

A shadow stretches across the horizon—a silent threat that whispers promises of safety, autonomy, and self-sufficiency. These are the Walls of Division, an invisible force that rises to separate communities, nations, and individuals. They appear as barriers against chaos, as shields protecting identity and independence. But beneath their deceptive strength lies a harrowing truth: these walls do not fortify—they isolate. They do not protect—they imprison. And they do not unify—they divide, severing the connections that humanity needs to thrive.

As the Siren Songs of solitude and isolation echo through the corridors of progress, they erode the very foundations of collaboration and innovation. The world becomes fragmented, its potential trapped behind borders of fear and mistrust. The vibrant symphony of cooperation fades into a muted refrain, and the engines of progress grind to a halt. What emerges is a fractured future—communities locked in silos, nations blind to their shared challenges, and individuals estranged from their collective power.

History and psychology warn us of the perils of division. Humanity's greatest triumphs have always come through unity—through the weaving of diverse voices into a harmonious whole. Science, too, reminds us that challenges like climate change, pandemics, and technological advancement demand global collaboration. Without it, the world risks being consumed by its own disconnection.

This chapter delves into the sinister allure of isolation and the devastating cost of division. It is a warning against the seductive whispers of solitude, self-sufficiency, and dissonance—a call to tear down the walls that divide us and embrace the limitless potential of unity. For within these walls lies not safety but the seeds of stagnation, not strength but the threat of collapse.

The choice is clear: we can retreat behind these barriers, allowing them to imprison our ambitions, or we can break free and build a future united in purpose and progress. The fate of humanity depends not on the walls we erect but on the bridges we build. Let us not succumb to the Siren Songs of division but instead compose a symphony of connection, where every voice is part of a greater harmony, and every nation stands as a vital note in the grand melody of our shared future.

1. The Siren Song of Solitude: A World Doomed by Walls

In a world fraught with uncertainty, the Siren Song of Solitude rises—a seductive melody promising safety behind walls, a haven where nations thrive alone, free from the chaos beyond. It whispers of self-sufficiency, of independence unmarred by external complications. But beneath this seemingly tranquil tune lies a harrowing truth: isolationism is a mirage, a false refuge that conceals the seeds of stagnation, vulnerability, and collapse.

From the perspective of science, the dangers of isolationism are stark. Global challenges—climate change, pandemics, economic instability—ignore the barriers humanity erects. They flow across borders with the inevitability of tides, their destructive force amplified when nations retreat into silos. History and psychology echo the same lesson: no fortress is strong enough to withstand the storms of a connected world. Only through cooperation and trust can humanity face its shared challenges.

Lurking Perils: The Illusion of Safety Behind Walls

A Divided Planet, a Shared Threat

Imagine a world where nations turn inward, retreating behind fortified borders in a desperate bid for security. A deadly pandemic sweeps the globe, but without international collaboration, there is no unified response. Scientific advancements languish in isolated laboratories, and resources are hoarded rather than shared. Meanwhile, rising sea levels creep inexorably inland, destroying coastal cities with no coordinated mitigation efforts. The walls, once seen as protection, become the silent witnesses to humanity's greatest failures.

A Galaxy Divided Falls

Science fiction offers a chilling glimpse of the cost of division. Picture a sprawling interstellar civilization, with each planet guarding its knowledge and resources in isolation. When a hostile alien force emerges, the fractured species are unable to unite. Their lack of collaboration becomes their undoing. The galaxy's brilliance is extinguished, not by the enemy, but by the refusal to recognize that survival demands unity.

A Kingdom Under Siege

Epic fantasy paints an equally grim portrait. Imagine a kingdom that prides itself on its self-sufficiency, rejecting alliances and fortifying its borders against perceived threats. When a powerful enemy arises, the isolated kingdom finds itself outmatched. Its walls, though high and strong, cannot compensate for the absence of allies or shared knowledge. The kingdom falls, a stark reminder that no fortress can stand alone against the tide of an interconnected world.

The Wasteland of Missed Opportunities

Even in the ruins of civilization, the Myth of Isolationism persists. Picture a post-apocalyptic wasteland where communities barricade themselves, hoarding resources and distrusting outsiders. Innovation slows, progress halts, and rebuilding becomes a distant dream. The remnants of humanity, locked within their isolated enclaves, doom themselves to a bleak and stagnant future, their potential squandered by fear and suspicion.

The Walls Around Our Hearts

Psychology reveals the human cost of isolation. Trust and cooperation are fundamental to feelings of safety and progress. A world dominated by fear and suspicion builds not only physical barriers but also emotional ones. Societies that isolate themselves suffer from stagnation, their innovation stifled by a lack of shared perspectives. The walls are meant to protect instead of imprison, leaving humanity's spirit to wither within the confines of solitude.

A Warning Etched in Shadows

The Siren Song of Solitude promises peace but delivers a chilling reality: a world divided, paralyzed by fear, and doomed to face its challenges alone. It replaces the dynamic strength of collaboration with the frailty of isolation, leaving humanity vulnerable to the very threats it seeks to escape. The lesson is clear—walls do not make us stronger; they make us weaker, fragmenting the unity essential for survival and progress.

The Call to Action: Tear Down the Walls

In the face of mounting global challenges, the answer is not to retreat but to unite. A truly civilized society thrives on the interconnectedness of its people, fostering trust, collaboration, and shared knowledge. This requires more than dismantling physical barriers; it demands tearing down the walls of mistrust and fear that divide nations and communities.

Let us reject the Myth of Isolationism and embrace the power of unity. Only by working together can we confront the crises of today and build a future resilient enough to withstand the storms of tomorrow. The Siren Song of Solitude may promise safety, but true security lies in the strength of collective effort. Let us choose unity over division and collaboration over isolation, ensuring that humanity rises together, stronger and more connected than ever before.

2. The Siren Song of Isolation: A Symphony Muted by Discord

In the intricate dance of human progress, the Siren Song of Isolation emerges—a haunting melody that promises independence, autonomy, and self-reliance. It whispers of a world where walls shield individuals and nations from the complexities of cooperation, where self-sufficiency reigns supreme. Yet, beneath this alluring tune lies a stark truth: isolation, far from empowering, silences the symphony of collaboration and stifles the creativity and progress that arise when diverse minds unite.

Psychology underscores humanity's deep-seated need for connection. Dr. Abraham Maslow's hierarchy of needs places belonging at its foundation, highlighting that individuals flourish when they are part of a supportive collective. Beyond personal well-being, cooperation ignites innovation, driving solutions that are greater than the sum of their parts. When isolation takes hold, this synergy collapses, leaving society fractured and vulnerable.

2.1. The Amplification of Individuality: A Symphony Strengthened by Collaboration

Contrary to the whispers of isolationism, collaboration is not the enemy of individuality; it is its amplifier. True cooperation does not erase personal achievement but elevates it, creating a grand symphony where each unique voice contributes to a powerful and harmonious whole. The interplay of talents, perspectives, and ambitions is the bedrock of progress.

Science of Shared Brilliance

Scientific discovery thrives on the cross-pollination of ideas. Imagine a team of researchers from diverse disciplines—chemists, biologists, and engineers—collaborating on a groundbreaking medical treatment. Each brings their unique expertise to the table, their perspectives weaving together to unravel a complex challenge. Alone, their efforts might falter, but together, they spark innovation and unlock breakthroughs that transform lives.

A Galactic Concord of Expertise

Science fiction expands this vision to a cosmic scale. Picture a galaxy threatened by a monumental crisis—a supernova threatening to engulf entire systems. Individual civilizations lack the resources to confront the threat alone. Yet, through collaboration, pooling their knowledge, and uniting their efforts, they craft a solution. Each civilization's unique strength becomes part of a collective force, forging a brighter future for all. Isolation, in contrast, would doom them to extinction, their strengths squandered in solitude.

The Nation's Chorus of Achievement

Epic fantasy paints a parallel allegory. Imagine a thriving kingdom where warriors defend, farmers sustain, and artisans enrich. Together, they create a society where every role is essential and celebrated. This synergy does not diminish individual contributions; it magnifies them. Each person's efforts inspire and bolster the others, forging a community that thrives on cooperation.

From Ashes, We Rise Together

Even in the desolate aftermath of catastrophe, the value of collaboration shines. Imagine a post-apocalyptic world where isolated communities struggle to survive. But when they come together—sharing resources, knowledge, and manpower—they rebuild stronger than ever. The farmer grows food to nourish the engineer, who restores the water supply, while the teacher educates the next generation. Through shared effort, they transform despair into hope and isolation into resilience.

Psychology of Shared Purpose

Human motivation is deeply intertwined with a sense of purpose and belonging. Studies show that people perform better and feel more fulfilled when they see their contributions making a tangible difference. Collaboration fosters this shared purpose, creating an environment where individuals not only thrive but inspire others to excel.

A Warning Etched in Shadows

The Siren Song of Isolation may promise freedom and self-sufficiency, but its cost is profound: a society divided, its potential muted by the silence of disconnected voices. Without collaboration, innovation falters, progress stalls and the human spirit languishes. The lesson is clear: no individual, community, or nation can thrive in isolation. Strength lies in unity, and the power of the collective surpasses the limits of the singular.

The Call to Action: Embrace the Power of Collaboration

To resist the Siren Song of Isolation, we must champion the symphony of cooperation. A thriving civilization does not suppress individuality but amplifies it, weaving unique contributions into a harmonious whole. By fostering collaboration, we create a world where innovation flourishes, challenges are overcome, and every voice plays a vital role in the grand symphony of human progress.

Let us reject the isolationist myth and embrace the transformative power of unity. The challenges of tomorrow demand more than individual effort; they require the collective strength of humanity working together. Only by uniting our voices can we compose a future that resonates with hope, resilience, and boundless potential.

2.2. The Siren Song of Stagnation: A Symphony Silenced by Self-Sufficiency

In the quiet chambers of progress, a sinister melody rises—the Siren Song of Stagnation. It promises self-sufficiency, a world where innovation is no longer necessary, and tradition reigns supreme. This song whispers of a society that stands still, content in its supposed perfection. But beneath this deceptive refrain lies a chilling truth: a civilization that rejects collaboration for isolation extinguishes the spark of progress. Without the vibrant exchange of ideas, the engines of innovation sputter, and the symphony of advancement fades into silence.

Psychology and history offer profound insights into this peril. Human ingenuity thrives not in isolation but in connection, where ideas meet, clash, and evolve into groundbreaking solutions. Studies on group creativity reveal that diverse perspectives and collaboration ignite innovation. When societies turn inward, they trade the dynamism of shared knowledge for the monotony of self-reliance, and their potential is quietly suffocated.

Lurking Perils: The Illusion of Self-Sufficiency

The Symphony of Ideas: Collaboration Unleashes Potential

Far from stifling creativity, cooperation amplifies it. Imagine a group of engineers tackling a technological challenge. Each brings a unique perspective—one sees the structural limitations, another the mechanical intricacies, and a third the user experience. Together, their ideas converge, transforming obstacles into breakthroughs. Without this collaboration, the spark of innovation would wither, leaving only unrealized potential.

A Galactic Concord of Discovery

Science fiction warns of the dangers of stagnation in a rapidly advancing universe. Picture a coalition of interstellar civilizations facing a challenge like faster-than-light travel. Alone, each species struggles to overcome the barriers of their own understanding. But by combining their knowledge—melding the precision of one species with the creativity of another—they achieve the impossible. Isolation would have condemned them to remain stranded, their ambitions confined by their own limitations.

The Nation's Innovation Engine

Epic fantasy echoes these themes. Imagine a team of artisans and architects working together to create a grand cathedral. Each brings a unique skill: the mason carves intricate stone, the glassworker crafts stunning stained glass, and the mathematician designs flawless structural integrity. Their collective effort produces a masterpiece that none could achieve alone. Collaboration transforms their individual talents into an enduring legacy.

From Ashes, We Rise with Invention

Even in the bleakest of settings, collaboration is a lifeline. In a post-apocalyptic wasteland, communities unite to rebuild. A scientist develops new irrigation techniques, a farmer adapts them to the barren land, and a craftsman constructs the tools needed for the process. Their pooled knowledge and shared purpose allow them to thrive where isolated efforts would have failed. Cooperation turns desperation into resilience.

Psychology of the Brainstorm

Human creativity is most potent when ideas intersect and evolve. Group brainstorming sessions demonstrate this principle, where even the most unconventional suggestions inspire innovative solutions. The interplay of minds builds momentum, refining raw ideas into groundbreaking innovations. Without collaboration, the creative process stalls, leaving societies trapped in the inertia of stagnation.

A Warning Etched in Shadows

The Siren Song of Stagnation offers the illusion of stability, but its cost is devastating: a society frozen in time, its potential wasted, its innovation extinguished. History, imagination, and science remind us that progress is a symphony, not a solo performance. Only through the vibrant interplay of ideas can humanity overcome its greatest challenges and reach new heights.

The Call to Action: Ignite the Symphony of Ideas

To resist the Siren Song of Stagnation, we must embrace the transformative power of collaboration. A thriving society values the contributions of every individual, weaving their talents into a collective force that propels humanity forward. By fostering environments where ideas collide and evolve, we can reignite the flame of progress and ensure a brighter future.

Let us reject the isolationist mirage and champion a culture of shared innovation. In the symphony of human achievement, every mind and voice has a role to play. Together, we can compose a masterpiece that transcends the limitations of isolation and resonates with the boundless potential of unity.

2.3. The Siren Song of Compulsion: A Symphony Strained by Coercion

---

In the orchestration of progress, a discordant note emerges—the Siren Song of Compulsion. It hums with the allure of order and stability, promising unity through enforced cooperation. Yet beneath this seemingly harmonious refrain lies a dangerous truth: compulsion suffocates innovation, silences creativity, and extinguishes the intrinsic motivation that fuels true progress. A society driven by coercion may achieve compliance, but it will never unlock the boundless potential of self-driven purpose.

Psychology underscores the transformative power of intrinsic motivation. Decades of research demonstrate that people achieve their greatest heights when driven by a sense of purpose, passion, and internal reward. Coercion, by contrast, breeds resentment, resistance, and disengagement. When societies lean too heavily on external control, they rob individuals of their autonomy and dim the creative spark that drives innovation and resilience.

Lurking Perils: The Fragility of Enforced Obedience

The Symphony of Self-Driven Spirit

True progress thrives on the fire of intrinsic motivation. Picture a scientist who works tirelessly to cure a disease—not for external accolades but for the profound satisfaction of saving lives. Their late nights, failed experiments, and relentless determination are driven by an inner purpose. In contrast, a researcher forced to meet quotas under rigid control lacks the passion to persevere. The result is mediocrity, not innovation.

A Galactic Concord of Free Spirits

Science fiction warns of civilizations trapped by their own systems of control. Imagine a team of explorers facing the uncharted reaches of space. Those driven by a thirst for discovery push boundaries, take creative risks and adapt to unforeseen challenges. But if bound by orders from a rigid authority, their courage falters, and their creativity stagnates. The lesson is clear: intrinsic motivation fuels not only progress but survival in the face of the unknown.

The Nation's Champions of Choice

Epic fantasy echoes the power of purpose-driven action. Picture a knight who fights not for gold or fame but to uphold justice and protect the innocent. This unwavering belief in a greater good sustains them through grueling battles and impossible odds. In contrast, a mercenary motivated solely by external rewards may falter when the cost becomes too great. True heroes rise from intrinsic motivation, their deeds shaping legacies that inspire generations.

From Ashes, We Rise with Willpower

Even in the aftermath of a catastrophe, intrinsic motivation lights the path to recovery. Imagine a post-apocalyptic community where individuals are driven by a shared vision of a brighter future. Their determination to rebuild, innovate, and persevere stems not from orders but from a collective desire to thrive. This internal fire transforms survival into progress, creating a society stronger and more united than before.

Psychology of the Self-Directed

The human spirit thrives on autonomy and purpose. Dr. Edward Deci's self-determination theory reveals that people are most engaged and creative when driven by intrinsic motivation rather than external rewards or coercion. When societies foster environments where individuals feel valued, empowered, and free to pursue their passions, they unleash a force of creativity and productivity that compulsion can never achieve.

A Warning Etched in Shadows

The Siren Song of Compulsion may promise stability, but its cost is the erosion of individuality, creativity, and engagement. Societies that prioritize enforced obedience over intrinsic motivation risk stagnation, their progress hollow and their potential unrealized. History, psychology, and imagination converge to warn us: lasting power lies in empowering individuals, not controlling them.

The Call to Action: Empower the Symphony of Self-Driven Spirits

To resist the Siren Song of Compulsion, we must champion the power of intrinsic motivation. A thriving society does not demand obedience; it nurtures autonomy and purpose. By fostering environments where individuals are free to innovate, explore, and contribute their unique talents, we ignite a collective spirit that propels humanity forward.

Let us reject the limitations of coercion and embrace the boundless potential of empowerment. In the grand symphony of human progress, every individual is both a soloist and a contributor to the greater harmony. Together, we can compose a future where creativity flourishes, resilience thrives, and the spark of self-driven purpose illuminates the path to a brighter tomorrow.

2.4. The Siren Song of Scattered Focus: A Symphony Strained by Dissonance

In the intricate dance of human progress, a chaotic melody arises—the Siren Song of Scattered Focus. It entices with the promise of unfettered freedom, a world where every pursuit is valid and all voices equally amplified. Yet beneath this beguiling harmony lies a perilous truth: distraction is not liberation. A society consumed by divided loyalties and unbridled chaos loses the power of directed resolve—the singular focus that transforms potential into achievement and ambition into an enduring legacy.

From the lens of psychology, focus is the foundation of creativity and mastery. Dr. Mihaly Csikszentmihalyi's concept of "flow" highlights that true innovation arises when individuals can immerse themselves fully in their tasks. A society that fosters endless distractions or encourages shallow engagement risks losing this essential focus, trading profound progress for fleeting stimulation.

Lurking Perils: The Cost of Divided Loyalties

The Symphony of Focused Resolve

Progress demands the power of unwavering attention. Imagine a scientist working tirelessly to decode the secrets of a deadly disease. Every late night in the lab, every failed experiment, and every small breakthrough builds toward a monumental discovery. Yet, if this scientist is pulled away by administrative distractions or forced to juggle competing priorities, their focus falters, and progress stagnates. Directed resolve is the crucible where breakthroughs are forged.

A Galactic Concord of Unwavering Attention

Science fiction amplifies this concept to a cosmic scale. Picture a team of engineers racing against time to prevent a cosmic disaster—a black hole on the verge of engulfing a star system. Their success depends entirely on their ability to concentrate on identifying the anomaly and developing a solution. If their attention fractures—due to bureaucratic interference, political squabbles, or personal rivalries—their civilization faces annihilation. Focus, not chaos, is the key to survival.

The Nation's Masters of Craft

Epic fantasy offers a parallel tale. Imagine a master craftsman shaping a monument to their kingdom's glory. Each strike of the chisel, each brush of paint, is deliberate, guided by an unwavering vision. Yet, if the artisan is plagued by interruptions—petty disputes, excessive demands from patrons, or diversions—they cannot achieve their masterpiece. Only through concentrated effort can talent be transformed into enduring greatness.

From Ashes, We Rise with Purpose

Even in a post-apocalyptic wasteland, the value of focus is paramount. Picture a fractured community, its survival contingent on rebuilding infrastructure, securing food supplies, and innovating new technologies. When individuals dedicate themselves fully to their roles—whether cultivating crops, constructing shelters or designing water filtration systems—the community thrives. But if distractions abound, progress halts, and survival becomes an ever-receding goal.

Psychology of the Absorbed Mind

The human mind excels in environments that allow for deep thinking and concentration. A system plagued by constant distractions dilutes creativity and problem-solving. In contrast, a society that fosters immersion enables its citizens to develop mastery and achieve breakthroughs. The absorbed mind becomes a wellspring of innovation, propelling collective progress forward.

A Warning Etched in Shadows

The Siren Song of Scattered Focus may promise unbridled freedom, but its cost is devastating: a society fragmented, its energy dissipated, and its potential unrealized. Without directed attention, even the most gifted individuals and ambitious projects falter, leaving behind a cacophony of missed opportunities. History, imagination, and science unite to warn us: progress requires focus, and focus requires structure and purpose.

The Call to Action: Embrace the Symphony of Focused Minds

To resist the Siren Song of Scattered Focus, we must champion a culture of directed attentiveness. A thriving society empowers its citizens to immerse themselves fully in their pursuits, fostering environments where distractions are minimized and concentration can flourish. This focus transforms potential into progress and chaos into creation.

Let us reject the seductive distractions of dissonance and instead compose a symphony of focused resolve. In this harmony, every individual contributes their unique melody to a collective vision of achievement. Together, we can channel the boundless energy of humanity into a legacy of innovation, resilience, and enduring progress, ensuring that the symphony of civilization crescendos toward a brighter future.

VI. The Siren Song of Tribalism: A Symphony of Fragmentation

In the symphony of human progress, tribalism is the discordant note that threatens to dismantle the harmony of unity. Rooted in humanity's ancient instincts to form in-groups and out-groups, tribalism whispers promises of belonging, identity, and loyalty. Yet beneath its comforting refrain lies a harrowing truth: the Siren Song of Tribalism fosters division, deepens mistrust, and fragments the collective spirit necessary for innovation and survival. Left unchecked, it can transform societies into fractured, stagnant echoes of their former potential.

Psychology highlights the dangers of tribalism through the lens of social identity theory. Humans are hardwired to form bonds with those who share their beliefs, values, or characteristics. While this fosters community, it also amplifies division, creating barriers between groups and hindering collaboration. Tribalism, when unchecked, becomes a force that erodes empathy, limits perspective, and stifles progress.

1. The Fragmentation of Identity

The Fragmentation of Identity is among the most insidious consequences of tribalism. As individuals retreat into echo chambers, their identities become narrowly defined by the groups they align with, leaving society fractured and incapable of addressing shared challenges.

Echo Chambers: The Amplification of Division

Social media has become the catalyst for modern tribalism, amplifying divisions and creating echo chambers where individuals only encounter ideas and perspectives that reinforce their existing beliefs. Imagine a society where algorithms curate every interaction, ensuring that citizens only engage with those who share their worldview. Over time, opposing perspectives become incomprehensible, and ideological divides widen into chasms.

Without exposure to diverse ideas, creativity stagnates, and the ability to solve complex societal challenges is lost. Debates devolve into vitriolic conflicts, and progress grinds to a halt. The once-vibrant exchange of ideas that fueled innovation becomes a cacophony of isolated voices, each speaking only on its own.

Science Fiction Warning: A Fractured Galaxy

Science fiction offers a chilling glimpse of tribalism on a cosmic scale. Imagine a future where humanity colonizes the stars, spreading across countless planets. Instead of uniting under a shared identity, these colonies fragment into factions, each prioritizing its own interests and cultures.

As resources become scarce and communication falters, mistrust festers, and conflicts ignite. What could have been a golden age of interstellar collaboration devolves into factional warfare. Technologies meant to unite and uplift humanity are turned toward destruction, and the dream of a thriving galactic civilization crumbles into ruin. This cautionary tale underscores the destructive power of tribalism when unity is forsaken.

A Warning Etched in Shadows

The Fragmentation of Identity offers the illusion of security and belonging, but its cost is catastrophic. As societies retreat into isolated factions, empathy erodes, collaboration diminishes, and progress stalls. The Siren Song of Tribalism may promise solidarity within groups, but it fractures the broader collective spirit essential for addressing shared challenges.

The Call to Action: Weave the Tapestry of Unity

To resist the Siren Song of Tribalism, we must embrace the richness of diverse identities without allowing them to divide us. True progress arises when societies foster environments where different perspectives can coexist, collaborate, and enrich the collective vision. This requires a commitment to breaking down echo chambers, encouraging open dialogue, and promoting shared goals.

Let us reject the fragmentation of identity and instead compose a symphony of unity, where every voice contributes to a greater harmony. Together, we can build a future where humanity's strength lies not in isolated factions but in the interconnected tapestry of our shared existence. By fostering collaboration across divides, we can ensure that the melody of progress continues to resonate through the ages, unbroken by the dissonance of tribalism.

2. The Erosion of Shared Purpose

In the symphony of human progress, shared purpose is the rhythm that binds diverse voices into a harmonious whole. It is the unifying force that elevates societies beyond their divisions, allowing them to collaborate on shared goals and overcome common challenges. Yet, the Siren Song of Tribalism leads to the Erosion of Shared Purpose, whispering that individual or regional interests should take precedence over collective ambition. Beneath this tempting refrain lies a devastating truth: the loss of shared purpose fractures societies, paralyzes progress, and leaves humanity adrift in disunity.

Philosophy and psychology warn of the dangers of such fragmentation. John Locke's social contract theory highlights the necessity of shared goals for a functional society, while modern psychology reveals how a sense of purpose fosters resilience, cooperation, and innovation. Without shared purpose, nations become fragmented, global efforts falter, and the interconnected fabric of humanity unravels.

Loss of National and Global Identity

The Erosion of Shared Purpose manifests most starkly in the collapse of national and global identities. As societies fragment, their ability to address pressing challenges disintegrates, leaving them vulnerable to internal and external crises.

Fragmentation at the National Level

Imagine a nation divided by regional disputes, where factions prioritize their local interests over the collective good. Political infighting escalates as each region seeks to assert dominance, refusing to collaborate on issues that require national unity. Infrastructure deteriorates, education systems falter, and healthcare collapses as resources are squandered on internal rivalries instead of addressing the needs of the populace.

Natural disasters strike, but the government's fractured leadership is incapable of mounting an effective response. The nation, once a beacon of strength and innovation, becomes a patchwork of weakened regions, its shared identity and purpose lost. The promise of progress is replaced by stagnation, and the cracks of division widen into an irreparable chasm.

Global Fragmentation and the Collapse of Unity

On a global scale, the consequences are even more catastrophic. Imagine a world facing a climate crisis, where rising sea levels threaten entire nations and extreme weather events become the norm. Yet, instead of uniting to combat this shared threat, countries turn inward, prioritizing short-term gains over global cooperation.

Technological advancements that could mitigate the crisis are hoarded by wealthy nations, while poorer countries bear the brunt of the devastation. The lack of a shared purpose not only exacerbates the crisis but also sows resentment and distrust among nations. The world, fractured by tribalistic priorities, is unable to mount a unified response, and humanity's collective future becomes increasingly bleak.

A Warning Etched in Shadows

The Erosion of Shared Purpose offers the illusion of autonomy and localized strength, but its cost is immense. Without a unifying vision, societies become fragmented, and their ability to confront challenges crumbles. The Siren Song of Tribalism may promise freedom from collective constraints, but it isolates individuals and regions, leaving them vulnerable and adrift.

The Call to Action: Rekindle the Flame of Shared Purpose

To resist the Erosion of Shared Purpose, we must reignite the collective ambition that unites humanity. Shared purpose does not erase individuality or local identity; it elevates them, weaving them into a greater tapestry of progress. This requires fostering national and global unity, prioritizing collaboration over division, and committing to goals that benefit all of humanity.

Let us reject the dissonance of fragmentation and instead compose a future where shared purpose resonates as the guiding melody of our progress. Together, we can rebuild the connections that bind us, ensuring that humanity moves forward as one. By mending the fractures of tribalism, we can create a symphony of unity where the power of our collective spirit drives us toward a brighter and more harmonious future.

VII. The Strangling Progress: The Illusion of Control

In the intricate symphony of human progress, a haunting melody lingers—the Siren Song of Control. It promises order, efficiency, and security under an all-encompassing grasp, luring societies with the illusion that centralized authority and rigid systems can solve every problem. Yet beneath its seductive tune lies a chilling truth: the quest for absolute control does not foster progress—it strangles it. Like a conductor silencing the orchestra's individual instruments, the illusion of control extinguishes the vibrant interplay of freedom, innovation, and collaboration that drives civilization forward.

History and imagination warn us of this perilous trap. From oppressive empires to dystopian futures ruled by iron fists, the lesson is clear: unchecked authority, selfish isolation, and hoarded power are not the hallmarks of a thriving society but the harbingers of its stagnation. The more tightly control is gripped, the more the creativity and individuality needed for growth slip away, leaving behind a discordant and disjointed world.

This chapter explores the many faces of the Illusion of Control—from the seductive promises of central authority to the fractures caused by unchecked selfishness, isolation, and disunity. It is a journey through a perilous landscape where progress is stifled, freedoms are suffocated, and societies crumble under the weight of their own rigidity.

The question is not whether the Siren Song of Control will sing—it already does. The question is whether we will heed its warnings or allow ourselves to be lulled into complacency. Will we succumb to the myth that power, hoarded and wielded unilaterally, is the answer? Or will we rise as architects of a freer, more dynamic future where the melody of human ingenuity plays unbound by the chains of control?

The stakes are immense. The cost of failure is the slow, suffocating descent of civilization into monotony and decay. The choice before us is not merely one of governance or systems—it is a choice between thriving and fading, between a future illuminated by possibility or shadowed by oppression. Let us turn away from the Illusion of Control and embrace the harmonious potential of a world where liberty, collaboration, and diversity compose the true symphony of progress.

1. The Siren Song of Central Control: A Symphony Stifled

In the grand orchestra of human progress, a haunting melody emerges—the Siren Song of Central Control. It promises order, efficiency, and unity under a single, guiding hand. It whispers of a utopia where chaos is vanquished by the steady rhythm of an all-encompassing authority. Yet beneath this seemingly harmonious tune lies a sobering truth: absolute control strangles creativity, stifles innovation, and dulls the vibrancy of human ambition. A society that surrenders entirely to centralized power risks silencing the very voices that propel it forward.

History and philosophy reveal the dangers of such overreach. While centralized systems can achieve great feats, their rigid structures often suffocate the adaptability and diversity essential for lasting progress. The lesson is clear: balance is the cornerstone of a thriving society, where centralized power supports rather than suppresses local initiative and individual freedom.

1.1. Decentralization: A Call to Progress, Not Regression

Against the seductive pull of central control stands the liberating force of decentralization. Often dismissed as chaotic or regressive, decentralized systems are, in truth, dynamic engines of innovation and resilience. By distributing power and decision-making, they create an agile and empowered society, one capable of adapting to challenges and seizing opportunities with unparalleled speed.

Science Unbound – The Agile Symphony

Imagine a decentralized network of research institutions, each free to pursue its own avenues of inquiry. Without the sluggish oversight of a central bureaucracy, breakthroughs emerge at an accelerated pace. New technologies, medicines, and ideas flourish as researchers follow their instincts and expertise. This agility transforms stagnation into momentum, ensuring that progress is unburdened by the weight of excessive control.

Science Unbound – The Symphony of Empowerment

Even within organizations, decentralization fosters creativity and innovation. Picture a company where employees are empowered to make decisions at every level. This sense of ownership fuels motivation, sparks ideas, and drives rapid adaptation to change. The result is not chaos but a symphony of empowered minds, each contributing to the collective success.

The Symphony of a Thousand Stars

Science fiction amplifies this truth on a galactic scale. Imagine a sprawling interstellar federation, its worlds as diverse as the stars themselves. A centralized government struggles to understand and address the unique needs of each planet. However, when governance is decentralized, each star system thrives, and its autonomy allows it to innovate and respond to local challenges. United by a common purpose, this federation becomes a testament to the strength of decentralized power.

The Symphony of a Thousand Cities

Epic fantasy offers a similar vision. Consider a vast empire weighed down by bureaucratic inefficiency, its central authority unable to meet the needs of its distant provinces. Now, picture a tapestry of self-governing city-states, each vibrant with its own culture and innovations. Their collective diversity creates a resilient and thriving civilization, one enriched by the unique contributions of each community.

The Symphony of Rebirth

Even in the ashes of societal collapse, decentralization proves its worth. Imagine a post-apocalyptic world where a central authority cannot be established. Communities must rely on their own resources, forging networks of cooperation and resource-sharing. This decentralized structure not only ensures survival but paves the way for a resilient and adaptable future.

The Symphony of Ownership

Psychology reinforces the value of decentralization. People are more engaged and motivated when they feel ownership over the decisions that shape their lives. Decentralized systems empower individuals and communities, fostering active participation and a deeper sense of responsibility. This collective ownership becomes the foundation of a vibrant and innovative society.

A Warning Etched in Shadows

The Siren Song of Central Control promises unity and efficiency, but its cost is immense: the loss of individual initiative, the suppression of diversity, and the erosion of innovation. A society that surrenders to absolute control trades its future for a fleeting sense of order, its potential forever muted by the weight of overreach.

The Call to Action: Orchestrate a Harmonious Balance

To resist the Siren Song of Central Control, we must embrace the dynamic power of decentralization. A truly civilized nation balances the strength of centralized authority with the freedom of local innovation, creating a symphony where every voice contributes to greater harmony. This balance fosters resilience, adaptability, and progress, ensuring that no single note dominates the melody of civilization.

Let us reject the false allure of absolute control and instead compose a future where liberty and collaboration thrive together. In this symphony of governance, centralized power supports rather than stifles, and the collective spirit of humanity propels us toward a brighter, more harmonious dawn.

1.2. Socialization: A Symphony of Strength, Not Silence

Amid the complex chords of progress, the Siren Song of Misconception rises—a melody warning that socialization silences individuality and that a society fostering collective responsibility sacrifices personal ambition. Yet this notion is a dangerous fallacy. A truly civilized nation understands that socialization is not an inhibitor of progress but its amplifier. It is the harmony between individual initiative and a strong social fabric that weaves the most vibrant tapestry of human achievement.

History, science, and psychology illuminate the power of shared purpose. Socialization does not suppress individuality; it nurtures it. When people are unburdened by the weight of poverty, inequality, or lack of opportunity, they are free to explore, innovate, and excel. A robust social fabric does not homogenize—it fortifies, creating a chorus of empowered voices, each contributing to a symphony of strength and resilience.

Lurking Perils and Unseen Potential: The Power of Socialization

Science Unchained

Imagine a society where every person has access to quality healthcare and education. In this society, no one is held back by illness or lack of opportunity. The scientist who might cure a deadly disease, the artist who inspires generations, and the entrepreneur who creates transformative technologies are all unshackled, free to pursue their full potential. This is not a loss of individuality but its flourishing—a society enriched by the unleashed talents of its people.

The Symphony of Skills

Education and infrastructure are the cornerstones of collective success. Picture a nation where every individual has the tools to succeed—a chorus of skilled minds contributing to the collective good. This is a society where innovation thrives, productivity soars, and prosperity is shared. Far from silencing voices, it amplifies them, creating a symphony of progress that echoes across generations.

A Galactic Concord

Science fiction envisions a future where humanity must unite against existential threats like resource scarcity or climate change. Imagine a world where nations collaborate to develop sustainable energy sources or mitigate rising sea levels. This is not a loss of sovereignty or individuality but a harmonious global effort for survival—a testament to the strength of coordinated action.

The Automated Age

As automation reshapes the workforce, the need for a social safety net becomes more pressing. Imagine a future where technological advances displace traditional jobs. A robust social structure ensures stability, providing people the freedom to adapt, retrain, and innovate. This is not suppression but empowerment—a society where people are free to evolve alongside technology.

The Nation's Chorus

Epic fantasy offers a timeless allegory of socialization's power. Imagine a thriving kingdom supported by a network of guilds and institutions—artisans crafting, scholars teaching, warriors protecting. Each group contributes its unique skills to the nation's success, creating a vibrant symphony of cooperation. This harmony does not erase individuality but magnifies its impact.

From Ashes, We Rise Together

Even in the wake of catastrophe, the value of socialization remains undeniable. Picture a post-apocalyptic world where communities pool their resources and expertise to rebuild. Engineers repair infrastructure, farmers cultivate crops, and teachers educate the next generation. This is not conformity but survival born of collaboration—a testament to the strength of shared purpose.

The Symphony of Belonging

Psychology underscores the importance of belonging and cooperation. Humans are social creatures who thrive in environments that foster connection and shared responsibility. A society that nurtures these bonds strengthens its collective spirit, fueling progress and resilience. Socialization is not a threat to individuality but its greatest ally, providing the foundation upon which innovation and ambition can thrive.

A Warning Etched in Shadows

The misconception that socialization silences individuality leads to a fragmented society where opportunity is hoarded; progress stagnates, and resilience withers. A truly enlightened nation recognizes that individual liberty and social responsibility are not opposing forces—they are complementary. Together, they create a framework for justice, prosperity, and enduring progress.

The Call to Action: Weave the Symphony of Socialization

To resist the Siren Song of Misconception, we must embrace a nuanced understanding of socialization as a force that strengthens rather than silences. A thriving society fosters individual achievement while providing the support systems needed to ensure that everyone can contribute their unique melody to greater harmony.

Let us move beyond simplistic fallacies and orchestrate a future where collective achievements and individual prosperity coexist. In this symphony of progress, every voice is valued, every talent amplified, and every person empowered to play their part in a melody that resonates through history and into the future. Together, we can compose a world where socialization is not a threat but a triumph—a beautiful harmony woven from the threads of empowered individuals working as one.

2. The Siren Song of Selfishness: A Symphony Disjointed

The human spirit is a marvel of ambition and ingenuity, capable of reaching incredible heights when fueled by individual initiative. Yet, lurking in the shadows of progress is the Siren Song of Selfishness—a deceptive melody that champions unfettered individualism at the expense of collective purpose. It promises empowerment and freedom but delivers fragmentation, disunity, and stagnation. Left unchecked, selfishness transforms the harmony of society into a discordant cacophony, where the pursuit of personal gain erodes the very foundations of progress.

History and philosophy teach us that no individual, enterprise, or community exists in isolation. The achievements of humanity—its technologies, societies, and civilizations—are built on the interplay of individual brilliance and collective effort. A thriving civilization is a symphony where every voice contributes to a greater melody, blending private success with the shared goals of society.

2.1. The False Dichotomy: A Symphony in Need of All Instruments

At the heart of the Siren Song of Selfishness lies a dangerous myth: the belief that individual success and collective well-being are irreconcilable opposites. This false dichotomy suggests that social cohesion can only be achieved by dismantling private wealth or suppressing ambition. Yet, a truly enlightened society recognizes the power of balance—a harmony where individual and collective efforts amplify one another, creating a dynamic and thriving system.

Science of Harmony

Imagine a society where private enterprise drives relentless innovation—pioneering new technologies, medicines, and ideas. Yet, without collective investment in infrastructure—roads to transport goods, power grids to sustain industries, and schools to educate workers—this innovation is stifled. It's like a virtuoso musician without an instrument; the melody is lost. Only when individual and collective strengths converge does the symphony of progress truly play.

A Galactic Collaboration

Science fiction explores this balance on an interstellar scale. Picture a future where humanity embarks on an audacious journey to the stars. Private corporations, driven by ambition and profit, develop advanced technologies. Yet, the sheer scale of interstellar exploration demands global collaboration—a unified space agency pooling resources, knowledge, and expertise. This is not suppression of individual achievement but a crescendo of collective action, where the dreams of individuals fuel humanity's greatest endeavors.

The Nation's Song

Epic fantasy offers an age-old allegory of synergy. Consider a prosperous kingdom where artisans craft exquisite goods, their creativity driving economic growth. But without public investment in roads, bridges, and marketplaces, their goods remain confined. Prosperity emerges only when individual enterprise harmonizes with collective infrastructure—an elegant dance of independence and interdependence, creating a nation where every voice contributes to the grand melody.

From Ashes, We Rise Together

Even in the chaos of a post-apocalyptic world, balance proves essential. Picture communities rebuilding amidst the ruin. Barter and trade drive the recovery, with individuals contributing their ingenuity and skills. Yet, without collective efforts to restore critical infrastructure—clean water systems, food distribution networks, and security—their progress falters. It is the interplay of individual drive and collective action that lifts society from the ashes and into renewal.

The Symphony of Shared Purpose

Psychology reinforces the need for harmony between individual and collective goals. Research shows that people are more motivated when they see their contributions benefiting both themselves and their communities. A society that invests in its citizens—through education, healthcare, and infrastructure—fosters a sense of shared purpose. This shared purpose becomes a powerful motivator, driving progress that benefits all.

A Warning Etched in Shadows

The Siren Song of Selfishness entices with its promises of unfettered freedom, yet its cost is immense: fractured communities, unrealized potential, and a society unable to face collective challenges. A truly civilized nation rejects the false dichotomy of individual versus collective, recognizing instead that progress lies in their interplay—a symphony where every note matters.

The Call to Action: Embrace the Symphony of Balance

To resist the Siren Song of Selfishness, we must champion a future where individual ambition and collective effort harmonize. A thriving society nurtures private initiative while investing in shared resources, creating a dynamic balance that amplifies progress. By fostering this synergy, we weave a melody that ensures prosperity, resilience, and innovation.

Let us reject the dissonance of unchecked self-interest and embrace the power of working together. In this grand symphony, every voice contributes to a brighter, more unified future, where the achievements of individuals are amplified by the strength of the collective. Together, we can compose a world where progress is not a solitary endeavor but a shared masterpiece.

2.2. The Siren Song of Isolation: A Nation Vulnerable in the Face of the Storm

In the symphony of civilization, no note rings more vital than unity in the face of danger. Yet, the Siren Song of Isolation hums a seductive tune, promising strength through self-reliance and the illusion that a fragmented defense is as mighty as a unified force. It whispers that a nation need not rely on collective might and that individuals and communities standing alone can face any storm. Beneath this alluring melody, however, lies a chilling truth: unchecked isolation weakens the shield of a nation, leaving it defenseless when the tempests of crisis strike.

History and psychology illuminate the flaws in this dangerous fantasy. True strength lies in synergy—a coordinated force that harnesses the brilliance of individuals within the framework of a collective purpose. Without this unity, a nation becomes a patchwork of vulnerabilities, its defenses scattered and its resolve fractured.

Lurking Perils: The Fragility of Fragmented Defense

Strength in Unity: A Symphony of Shields

A formidable defense is not the result of isolated excellence but of orchestrated synergy. Imagine a military where every soldier is a master of their craft, yet their brilliance is amplified by coordinated maneuvers and shared purpose. Like instruments in a symphony, their individual skills blend into a powerful crescendo, creating a defense that is both agile and unbreakable. Without this harmony, even the most skilled warriors become isolated notes lost in chaos.

Science of Steel

The strength of a military lies in its commitment to its people. Picture an army that invests in the training, well-being, and morale of its soldiers, fostering a powerful esprit de corps—a spirit of camaraderie that binds them together. Each soldier is not only an individual master of their craft but also a vital part of a cohesive whole. This unity transforms them into an unstoppable force capable of withstanding any assault.

A Galactic Bulwark

Science fiction envisions a future where humanity faces cosmic threats. Imagine a united galactic navy pooling the resources, knowledge, and expertise of countless star systems. This collective action forms an impenetrable bulwark against extraterrestrial dangers, a symphony of firepower and strategy that ensures survival. Without this unity, isolated planets stand no chance, their defenses overwhelmed by the vastness of the threat.

The Nation's Steel Legion

Epic fantasy echoes the importance of cohesion. Picture a kingdom that understands the power of discipline and strategy. Its army is not merely a collection of skilled warriors but a synchronized force, trained in coordinated maneuvers and united by a common purpose. This synergy allows them to face any foe, creating a storm of steel that sweeps away the encroaching darkness.

From Ashes, We Rise Together

Even in a post-apocalyptic wasteland, the need for collective defense persists. Picture a community where individuals are trained in self-defense and prepared to protect their loved ones. Yet, without a coordinated strategy, they remain vulnerable to larger, more organized threats. It is the combination of individual preparedness and a unified defense plan that enables a society to withstand violence and rebuild from the ashes.

The Psychology of the Pack

Psychology reinforces the power of unity. Soldiers who feel part of a team, driven by a shared mission, perform better and persevere through challenges. A strong sense of belonging and shared responsibility creates a fighting spirit that surpasses individual courage, transforming a group of individuals into a cohesive and unstoppable force.

A Warning Etched in Shadows

The Siren Song of Isolation may promise freedom and self-reliance, but its cost is devastating: a nation left vulnerable, its strength fractured, and its people unprotected. True security lies not in fragmentation but in the collective strength of a united society. Without this synergy, a nation becomes a house of cards, unable to withstand the storms of crisis.

The Call to Action: Forge the Symphony of Strength

To resist the Siren Song of Isolation, we must embrace the transformative power of unity. A thriving nation is not a collection of isolated parts but a symphony of interconnected efforts where individual initiative harmonizes with collective action. By fostering this unity, we build a defense that is as resilient as it is powerful.

Let us reject the illusion of fragmented self-reliance and instead compose a future where every citizen contributes to the collective shield. Together, we can ensure that our nation stands strong in the face of any storm, a symphony of courage and strength that protects and uplifts all its people.

2.3. The Siren Song of the Iron Fist: A Discordant Symphony of Control

In the grand orchestra of governance, the Siren Song of the Iron Fist hums a dangerous melody. It tempts society with promises of efficiency, swift decision-making, and a singular, unyielding vision. It suggests that the chaos of democratic deliberation can be silenced under the rule of an all-powerful leader—a conductor who wields absolute control over the symphony. Yet, beneath this seemingly orderly tune lies a discordant truth: unchecked authoritarianism stifles the voices of the many, extinguishes innovation, and ultimately chokes the progress it claims to protect.

History, science, and imagination warn us of the perils of authoritarian control. While the allure of swift and decisive leadership is strong, true progress arises from collective participation—a harmonious balance where every voice contributes to the melody. Without this synergy, the symphony falters, and the spirit of a nation withers under the weight of suppression.

Lurking Perils: The Fragility of Absolute Control

The Power of Consent: A Symphony Played by All

Democracy is not chaos; it is the foundation of legitimacy. Imagine a society where leaders derive their power not from force but from the consent of the governed. This creates a system where citizens are actively engaged, their voices shaping the decisions that guide their future. Democratic participation transforms governance from a solo performance into a symphony played by all, amplifying trust and shared purpose.

Science of Stability

Studies show that democracies are more stable and peaceful than authoritarian regimes. Picture a nation where citizens actively participate in governance, their involvement fostering a sense of shared responsibility. This engagement propels progress, ensuring that the collective will drives innovation and resilience. In contrast, authoritarian control breeds resentment and stagnation, silencing the creative energy of the populace.

A Galactic Concord

Science fiction envisions a united galactic society built on democratic principles. Picture a federation of planets where each member world has a voice in shaping interstellar policy. This collaboration ensures decisions are made for the collective good, creating a harmonious alliance capable of withstanding the challenges of the cosmos. In contrast, a galaxy ruled by an iron-fisted dictator risks fracturing under the weight of discontent and rebellion.

The Nation's Just Chorus

Epic fantasy offers timeless lessons in leadership. Imagine a kingdom led by a wise monarch who governs with the consent of their people, actively listening to their concerns. This ruler fosters unity and prosperity, ensuring that every voice contributes to the kingdom's progress. In contrast, a tyrant, driven by their own desires, alienate their subjects and erode the very foundation of their rule.

From Ashes, We Rise Together

Even in the aftermath of catastrophe, democratic leadership shines as a beacon of hope. Picture a post-apocalyptic community electing leaders to guide their recovery. This process ensures accountability, trust, and shared purpose, creating a foundation for rebuilding that is stronger and more resilient. The collective voice shapes the future, transforming adversity into a shared triumph.

The Instruments of Harmony: Qualifications and Accountability

Leadership is not merely about holding power; it is about wielding it wisely. Democratic systems ensure that leaders are chosen for their qualifications and held accountable for their decisions. Imagine a society where leaders possess the knowledge and vision to tackle complex challenges, supported by advisors who enrich their understanding. This is governance as a symphony, where expertise and collaboration produce a melody of progress.

Science of Solutions

Effective leadership requires adaptability and insight. Imagine leaders who navigate the complexities of technological advancements, climate change, or economic transformation with wisdom and foresight. This adaptability ensures that the symphony of progress evolves, remaining vibrant and innovative.

The Wise Ruler's Counsel

Epic fantasy underscores the value of wise leadership. Picture a king who surrounds himself with capable advisors, seeking their counsel before making decisions. This collaboration ensures that governance benefits from diverse perspectives, creating a kingdom where every voice contributes to harmony.

A Warning Etched in Shadows

The Siren Song of the Iron Fist may promise swift and decisive action, but its cost is immense: the silencing of voices, the suppression of creativity, and the erosion of trust. Authoritarian control transforms the symphony of governance into a discordant solo, one that stifles the progress it seeks to command. True strength lies in collective participation, where every voice matters, and every note contributes to the greater melody.

The Call to Action: Embrace the Symphony of Participation

To resist the Siren Song of the Iron Fist, we must champion the transformative power of democracy. A thriving society values consent, qualifications, and accountability, creating a system where leadership is guided by the will and wisdom of the people. This harmony empowers individuals to shape their future, fostering innovation, resilience, and trust.

Let us reject the allure of absolute control and instead compose a future where governance is a symphony played by all. Together, we can build a world where every voice contributes to the grand melody of progress, ensuring a legacy of freedom, innovation, and unity for generations to come.

2.4. The Siren Song of Self-Interest: A Symphony Without Passion

In the grand orchestra of human progress, a single, discordant note threatens to drown out the melody—the Siren Song of Self-Interest. It promises prosperity through individual gain alone, a world where the pursuit of personal profit becomes the sole motivator for achievement. Yet beneath this seemingly logical refrain lies a chilling truth: a society that values financial reward above all else risks extinguishing the intrinsic motivations that fuel creativity, purpose, and progress. This is a symphony without passion, one that leaves humanity adrift in apathy.

History, psychology, and imagination reveal a richer tapestry of human motivation. While the promise of reward is an effective motivator, it is not the only one. People are driven by purpose, mastery, and the desire to leave a positive mark on the world. A society that recognizes and nurtures this diversity of motivation creates a harmonious balance, propelling progress not through greed but through inspiration and shared purpose.

Lurking Perils: The Limitations of Self-Interest

Beyond the Coin: A Symphony of Motivation

The absence of a profit motive does not signal the end of innovation but the beginning of a more profound drive. Imagine a research scientist who spends countless hours in a lab, fueled not just by the promise of accolades but by the intrinsic passion to uncover life-saving treatments. Their motivation is a symphony, where external rewards blend seamlessly with internal purpose to create a force that transcends monetary value.

A Galactic Calling

Science fiction amplifies this idea. Picture a future where humanity faces a galaxy-wide energy crisis. A team of engineers dedicates their expertise not to wealth but to the opportunity to solve a problem that could improve billions of lives. Their motivation stems from a mix of personal purpose and collective responsibility, creating a powerful catalyst for innovation. This blend of intrinsic and extrinsic motivation ensures that even the most daunting challenges are met with resilience and ingenuity.

The Hero's Heart

Epic fantasy reminds us that the greatest heroes often act not for wealth but for something far more profound. Imagine a knight who stands against an evil sorcerer, not for treasure but for duty, justice, and the love of their people. This intrinsic drive—the desire to protect, serve, and strive for the greater good—fuels acts of courage and determination that echo through the ages.

From Ashes, We Rise with Purpose

Even in a post-apocalyptic wasteland, the human spirit finds purpose. Picture a community coming together to rebuild their world, driven not by promises of riches but by the shared goal of creating a better future. They repair homes, cultivate crops, and innovate solutions, not for personal gain but for the survival and prosperity of their children and their neighbors. This intrinsic motivation transforms despair into hope and adversity into opportunity.

Psychology of the Human Drive

Psychology teaches us that people are motivated by much more than financial reward. Dr. Edward Deci and Dr. Richard Ryan's self-determination theory highlights the importance of autonomy, mastery, and purpose in fostering creativity and satisfaction. Imagine an artist who paints for the joy of expression, a scientist driven by curiosity, or a teacher who thrives on nurturing young minds. These intrinsic motivators are the foundation of a society where progress and fulfillment coexist.

A Warning Etched in Shadows

The Siren Song of Self-Interest may be tempting, but its limitations are profound. A society driven solely by financial gain becomes shallow, its creativity stifled, its progress hollow. True innovation and achievement arise not from greed but from a richer symphony of motivations—a balance of purpose, passion, and shared responsibility that transcends mere profit.

The Call to Action: Embrace the Symphony of Motivations

To resist the Siren Song of Self-Interest, we must cultivate a society that values the diverse range of human drives. A thriving civilization empowers individuals to pursue knowledge, creativity, and the greater good, blending personal ambition with collective progress. This harmony transforms self-interest into a vibrant tapestry of motivations, ensuring a future fueled by inspiration, resilience, and unity.

Let us reject the limitations of a single note and instead compose a symphony where every chord matters. Together, we can build a world where the pursuit of personal gain is not the only melody but one among many, creating a dynamic and flourishing society. This is the true song of progress—a melody that resonates with the passion, purpose, and potential of all humanity.

2.5. The Siren Song of Scarcity: A Symphony Strained by Disunity

In the grand symphony of human progress, a discordant melody whispers its chilling refrain—the Siren Song of Scarcity. It seduces societies with the illusion of limitation, insisting that resources, wealth, and potential are finite and that competition is the only path to survival. It paints a grim picture of division and distrust, where hoarding replaces collaboration, and disunity extinguishes the synergy that fuels innovation and growth. Beneath this seemingly pragmatic tune lies a devastating truth: the Myth of Scarcity is not a path to progress but a barrier, one that fractures the collective spirit and stalls the engines of civilization.

History, science, and psychology teach us otherwise. The most profound achievements of humanity—the eradication of diseases, the conquest of space, the rebuilding of shattered societies—have all been born from unity, from the harmonization of wealth and effort into a shared purpose. A society that recognizes the power of abundance, the potential of collaboration, and the strength of shared goals creates a symphony where every note contributes to a crescendo of progress.

Lurking Perils: The False Promise of Scarcity

The Engine of Abundance: A Symphony Fueled by Unity

Progress is not achieved through competition alone but through the synergy of collective resources and human effort. Imagine a global initiative to combat climate change. Nations pool their wealth, scientists share their expertise, and engineers innovate solutions. This combined effort transforms what seems insurmountable into a shared triumph. Division and scarcity cannot fuel this engine; only unity can.

A Galactic Collaboration

Science fiction envisions a future where vast resources and collaboration are essential for humanity's greatest endeavors. Picture a coalition of civilizations working together to construct a starship capable of interstellar travel. This monumental task demands not only the wealth of entire star systems but also the ingenuity and dedication of countless individuals. The fusion of resources and effort ensures the success of such an ambitious project, while disunity would doom it to failure.

The Nation's United Effort

Epic fantasy offers its own allegories of abundance through unity. Imagine a kingdom building a massive dam to control floods or a towering wall to defend against an invading army. These monumental feats require more than centralized authority; they demand the collective effort of citizens, laboring side by side, driven by a shared purpose. The union of wealth and humans will transform vulnerability into strength.

From Ashes, We Rise Together

Even in the desolation of a post-apocalyptic world, the power of collective action prevails. Imagine a community pooling resources to rebuild its infrastructure. Engineers repair power grids, farmers cultivate crops, and educators restore knowledge. Each person's contribution, no matter how small, becomes part of a greater whole. This unity turns despair into hope and scarcity into abundance.

Psychology of the Collective Spirit

Psychology underscores the profound impact of working together toward a shared goal. People feel a deeper sense of accomplishment and purpose when they contribute to collective achievements. Imagine the pride and unity of a community that rebuilds its homes and infrastructure together, transforming challenges into a testament to their resilience and collaboration.

A Warning Etched in Shadows

The Siren Song of Scarcity may tempt with its promises of security through hoarding and competition, but its cost is immense. It fractures societies, fosters distrust, and undermines the synergy essential for progress. The truth is clear: abundance is not a myth but a reality born of unity, collaboration, and the harmonization of resources and human effort.

The Call to Action: Compose the Symphony of Abundance

To resist the Siren Song of Scarcity, we must embrace a vision of unity and shared purpose. A thriving society recognizes that wealth and effort when combined, become a powerful force for progress. By fostering collaboration, investing in collective goals, and rejecting the illusion of limitation, we unlock the potential to achieve the extraordinary.

Let us not be seduced by the discord of scarcity but instead orchestrate a future where every resource, talent, and voice contributes to a grand symphony of progress. Together, we can ensure a world where abundance is not a distant dream but a shared reality, resonating with the harmony of human ambition and unity.

VIII. The Perils of Unchecked Technology: A Symphony of Unintended Consequences

Technology has always been humanity's double-edged sword—a tool for progress and innovation that also harbors the seeds of disruption and chaos. In the relentless march of technological advancement, the Siren Song of Unchecked Technology whispers promises of prosperity and ease, luring societies into a state of complacency. Yet beneath its alluring tune lies a chilling truth: when technology evolves without foresight or regulation, it becomes a force of unintended consequences, destabilizing the very foundations it was meant to strengthen.

From the perspective of cognitive neuroscience, the allure of technological progress is deeply rooted in humanity's drive for efficiency and control. But as philosopher Hannah Arendt warned, unchecked innovation risks reducing human dignity to a mere byproduct of mechanization. Societies that fail to consider the ethical, economic, and social ramifications of technological advances risk unraveling into inequality, unrest, and fragmentation.

1 The Dark Side of Automation

Automation, heralded as a revolution in efficiency, is one of the clearest examples of the double-edged nature of technology. While it promises to alleviate human labor, its unchecked implementation often displaces workers, deepens economic disparities, and sows the seeds of societal unrest.

Economic Displacement: The Human Cost of Automation

Imagine a society where automation sweeps through industries, from manufacturing to service, replacing human labor with machines. Factories once bustling with activity now stand silent, their workforce displaced by precision robotics. Supermarkets eliminate cashiers in favor of automated checkouts while self-driving vehicles render professional drivers obsolete.

At first, the efficiency gains seem promising. Profits soar, production accelerates, and goods become cheaper. But the cost is borne by the workers left behind. With no safety nets or retraining programs in place, millions find themselves unemployed, their skills rendered obsolete. Economic inequality widens, resentment grows, and protests erupt, creating a fractured society where innovation has outpaced compassion.

Epic Fantasy Allegory: The Rebellion of the Displaced

In an epic fantasy realm, imagine a kingdom where alchemical automatons replace laborers in the fields and workshops. At first, the kingdom's leaders celebrate the newfound productivity, using the automatons to amass wealth and expand their influence. But the laborers, cast aside and left to fend for themselves, grow resentful.

The economic disparity festers, turning once-loyal subjects into disillusioned rebels. A rebellion erupts, not out of greed or ambition, but out of desperation. The kingdom, blinded by its pursuit of progress, collapses under the weight of its displaced populace. The automaton revolution, meant to secure prosperity, instead becomes a harbinger of chaos and collapse.

A Warning Etched in Shadows

The Dark Side of Automation is a cautionary tale of progress without preparation. The Siren Song of Efficiency promises wealth and innovation, but its unchecked implementation exacerbates inequality, displaces workers, and destabilizes societies. Technology, when wielded without foresight, becomes a force of division rather than unity.

The Call to Action: Orchestrate a Balanced Symphony of Progress

To resist the Dark Side of Automation, we must harmonize technological advancement with ethical foresight and social responsibility. Innovation must be paired with systems that support displaced workers, such as retraining programs, universal basic income, and policies that prioritize human dignity alongside progress.

Let us reject the complacency of unchecked innovation and instead compose a future where technology serves humanity rather than subjugates it. By weaving ethical considerations into the fabric of technological advancement, we can ensure that progress uplifts all, creating a symphony of innovation that resonates with equity, resilience, and compassion. Together, we can write a new chapter where technology enhances, rather than disrupts, the human experience.

2 The Loss of Humanity

As humanity steps into the age of artificial intelligence, a new Siren Song emerges—a melody promising unparalleled efficiency, precision, and problem-solving capabilities. Yet beneath this futuristic tune lies a haunting truth: as AI evolves, it brings with it profound ethical dilemmas that, if ignored, could erode the very essence of human agency. The Loss of Humanity is not a distant threat but a looming reality, one that challenges the values, autonomy, and identity that define civilization.

Philosophers and ethicists, from Aristotle to modern thinkers like Nick Bostrom, have long warned of the risks of delegating moral and critical decisions to entities devoid of human conscience. Cognitive neuroscience reveals that humans derive meaning and fulfillment from agency—the ability to make choices and shape their destinies. When artificial intelligence encroaches upon this domain, humanity risks becoming passive observers in a world shaped by algorithms.

Ethical Dilemmas in AI

The integration of AI into governance, warfare, and personal autonomy raises questions that societies are ill-prepared to answer. Without careful oversight and ethical foresight, these technologies could strip humanity of its moral compass, leaving critical decisions to systems incapable of empathy or accountability.

Governance: The Algorithmic State

Imagine a future where governments rely on AI to make policy decisions, allocate resources, and enforce laws. While these systems are designed for efficiency, they lack the nuance to consider the human consequences of their actions. Citizens become statistics, and their needs and struggles are reduced to data points in a cold calculation.

In such a society, fairness becomes a casualty of optimization. Biases embedded in the algorithms, often unintentional, perpetuate systemic inequalities. Dissent is suppressed as algorithms flag and neutralize perceived threats without human judgment. The government, once a servant of the people, transforms into a faceless entity ruled by artificial logic, eroding trust and agency.

Warfare: The Autonomous Battlefield

The use of AI in warfare introduces ethical questions with no easy answers. Imagine a battlefield dominated by autonomous drones capable of identifying and eliminating targets without human intervention. These machines operate with precision but lack the moral discernment to differentiate between combatants and civilians.

In their relentless pursuit of efficiency, such systems escalate conflicts, making war more detached and devastating. Accountability becomes a murky concept as nations deflect responsibility for atrocities, blaming "malfunctions" in their AI systems. Humanity's capacity for empathy, negotiation, and restraint is replaced by cold, unfeeling automation.

Personal Autonomy: The Erosion of Choice

As AI systems become more integrated into daily life, from healthcare to personal assistants, the line between assistance and control blurs. Imagine a world where algorithms predict and influence every decision, from career paths to romantic relationships. While this may seem convenient, it erodes the sense of autonomy that defines human existence.

Over time, individuals become reliant on AI, losing the ability to make independent choices. The rich complexity of human experience—marked by mistakes, growth, and discovery—gives way to a sterile existence dictated by optimized outcomes. Humanity becomes an audience to its own lives, watching as algorithms take the stage.

A Warning Etched in Shadows

The loss of humanity is a silent threat, and its danger is growing as societies embrace AI without addressing its ethical implications. The Siren Song of Progress promises solutions to humanity's greatest challenges but risks reducing people to passive participants in a world increasingly governed by machines. Without foresight, the very technologies meant to empower us could rob us of our humanity.

The Call to Action: Safeguard the Symphony of Human Agency

To resist the Loss of Humanity, we must place ethical considerations at the forefront of technological development. AI must be a tool that enhances human agency, not a replacement for it. This requires global cooperation to establish guidelines that prioritize accountability, transparency, and empathy in AI systems.

Let us reject the complacency of unchecked advancement and instead compose a future where technology serves humanity's highest ideals. By fostering innovation that respects autonomy, preserves morality, and uplifts human dignity, we can ensure that progress remains a shared journey. Together, we can create a world where the harmony of human agency and artificial intelligence leads to a brighter, more compassionate dawn.

IX. The Tyranny of Optimism: Ignoring the Warnings

Optimism is the engine of progress, the belief that humanity can overcome challenges and build a brighter future. Yet, when taken to extremes, optimism becomes a tyrant, blinding societies to legitimate dangers. The Tyranny of Optimism emerges as a Siren Song, promising that progress alone will solve all problems. It whispers that the future is secure, that crises will pass, and that warnings are needless distractions. Beneath this alluring melody lies a sobering truth: unbridled optimism fosters complacency, leaving societies unprepared for crises that could have been mitigated.

Philosophy and psychology warn against this perilous mindset. Soren Kierkegaard's concept of "infinite resignation" highlights the dangers of ignoring reality in favor of wishful thinking. Cognitive biases like optimism bias further reveal humanity's tendency to underestimate risks. When warnings are dismissed, societies gamble with their future, trading preparation for peril.

1 The Peril of Complacency

The Peril of Complacency is one of the most insidious consequences of unchecked optimism. It leads to the dismissal of early warnings, the prioritization of immediate gains over long-term safety, and the illusion that progress alone can shield humanity from disaster.

Ignoring Early Warnings: A Precipice of Neglect

Imagine a society where scientists issue dire warnings about an impending natural disaster—a massive earthquake, a superstorm, or a volcanic eruption. The evidence is clear, but leaders, driven by economic optimism, prioritize growth over preparation. They dismiss the scientists as alarmists, redirecting funds to infrastructure projects that promise short-term gains.

When a disaster strikes, the unprepared society faces catastrophic losses. Cities crumble, lives are lost, and the economy collapses under the weight of devastation. What could have been a manageable crisis becomes an existential catastrophe, a grim reminder that optimism without caution is a dangerous delusion.

Science Fiction Mirror: A Star's Final Warning

Science fiction offers a chilling parallel. Imagine a planet orbiting a dying star, its sun on the verge of a supernova. Scientists detect early signs of instability and propose urgent action: planetary evacuation or the construction of a protective shield. But the planet's leaders, confident in their technological prowess, dismiss these warnings as exaggerated.

As time runs out, the star's explosion obliterates the planet. The once-thriving civilization, blinded by its faith in unproven solutions, becomes a cautionary tale etched into the cosmos. The planet's hubris—its tyranny of optimism—leads to its annihilation.

A Warning Etched in Shadows

The Peril of Complacency tempts with its promises of safety and progress but exacts a heavy toll. By ignoring warnings and underestimating risks, societies leave themselves vulnerable to crises that could have been mitigated or averted. The Siren Song of Optimism may promise security, but it lulls leaders and citizens into a false sense of safety, blind to the dangers that lie ahead.

The Call to Action: Balance Hope with Vigilance

To resist the Tyranny of Optimism, we must balance hope with caution and ambition with preparation. Optimism should inspire action, not blind complacency. Societies must value the voices of scientists, thinkers, and visionaries who sound the alarm, weaving their warnings into proactive strategies for resilience.

Let us reject the illusion of infallibility and instead compose a future where progress is fortified by preparedness. By listening to the warnings of those who see beyond the immediate horizon, we can safeguard humanity against crises and ensure that optimism remains a force for growth, not a harbinger of downfall. Together, we can create a symphony of progress where hope and vigilance harmonize to illuminate a secure and vibrant future.

2 The Blind Faith in Progress

Progress is humanity's most potent tool—a testament to our ingenuity, ambition, and resilience. Yet, when faith in progress becomes blind, it morphs into a dangerous illusion. The Siren Song of Blind Faith in Progress whispers that advancement is inherently good and that every step forward is a step toward utopia. It lures societies into ignoring the ethical, social, and environmental consequences of their pursuits. Beneath this hopeful melody lies a chilling truth: unchecked progress risks creating a world where humanity becomes the victim of its own innovation.

From a philosophical standpoint, thinkers like Aldous Huxley and Hans Jonas have cautioned against unexamined progress. Cognitive neuroscience reveals that humans, driven by a desire for control and accomplishment, often overlook the long-term ramifications of their actions. The Blind Faith in Progress is not a path to a brighter future—it is a perilous road where ethical boundaries are blurred, and unintended consequences loom large.

Ignoring Ethical Boundaries: A Pandora's Box

The pursuit of progress without ethical oversight opens a Pandora's box of unintended consequences. Biotechnology, for example, holds the promise of miraculous cures and human enhancement but also raises profound ethical dilemmas that, if ignored, could destabilize societies.

The Perils of Genetic Inequality

Imagine a world where biotechnology advances to the point where parents can choose their children's genetic traits—intelligence, physical appearance, even personality. At first, these innovations seem revolutionary, offering the potential to eradicate genetic diseases and improve quality of life.

However, as access to these technologies becomes a luxury afforded only by the wealthy, a new class divide emerges—those genetically enhanced and those left behind. The promise of equality through innovation is shattered, replaced by a world where privilege is hardwired at birth. This genetic inequality breeds resentment, division, and unrest, unraveling the social fabric that once held humanity together.

Unforeseen Ecological Impacts

Biotechnology's reach extends beyond humanity. Imagine scientists genetically modifying crops to withstand extreme weather and pests, heralding an agricultural revolution. Yet, these modifications inadvertently disrupt ecosystems, wiping out pollinators like bees or allowing invasive species to thrive unchecked.

The ecological balance, meticulously maintained over millennia, collapses under the weight of unintended consequences. Entire ecosystems vanish, taking with them critical resources on which humanity depends. The pursuit of progress, blind to its environmental impact, becomes a harbinger of ecological disaster.

A Warning Etched in Shadows

The Blind Faith in Progress tempts societies with its promise of miracles, yet its cost is immense. By ignoring ethical boundaries and long-term consequences, humanity risks creating a world defined by inequality, environmental collapse, and moral ambiguity. The Siren Song of Progress without foresight is not a call to advancement but a warning of potential ruin.

The Call to Action: Forge an Ethical Compass for Innovation

To resist the Blind Faith in Progress, we must anchor advancement in ethical principles. Innovation must not outpace humanity's capacity for responsibility. This requires global collaboration to establish ethical guidelines for biotechnology, artificial intelligence, and other transformative fields, ensuring that progress uplifts rather than divides.

Let us reject the illusion of infallible progress and instead compose a future where innovation serves humanity's highest ideals. By weaving ethics into the fabric of technological development, we can ensure that the miracles of tomorrow are not shadows of regret. Together, we can create a symphony of progress where humanity's drive for advancement harmonizes with its duty to safeguard equality, dignity, and the planet. This is not a limitation of progress—it is its highest potential realized.

X. The Crescendo of Collapse: The Most Dangerous Threats

A shadow looms over the horizon of human progress, its presence a harbinger of discord and collapse. The grand symphony of civilization—crafted through centuries of shared effort and bound by the threads of trust, cooperation, and empathy—teeters on the edge of dissonance. Fraying at its edges, the tapestry of humanity faces its greatest threat: the unraveling of the very ideals that have sustained it. Without swift action, the harmony that underpins progress may disintegrate into chaos, leaving behind a fractured and unrecognizable world.

From the lens of psychology and philosophy, the roots of this peril become evident. Dr. Carol Gilligan's ethics of care and Immanuel Kant's moral imperatives remind us that fairness, mutual respect, and shared purpose are essential for societal cohesion. As these pillars erode, distrust festers, relationships fracture, and communities spiral into isolation. The most dangerous threats to civilization are not external forces but internal rifts—the unraveling threads of justice, cooperation, and empathy.

This chapter confronts these existential dangers, exploring the critical need to reweave the fabric of humanity. It is a call to action to restore the ideals that unite us and repair the fractures that threaten our collective future. Through justice, cooperation, and empathy; we can confront the Crescendo of Collapse and ensure that the symphony of civilization continues to rise toward a brighter dawn.

1. The Unraveling Tapestry: A Symphony Strained by Discord

A haunting dissonance pervades the air—a discordant echo of a once-grand symphony. The tapestry of humanity, woven with the threads of shared experience and purpose, is unraveling. Distrust between nations has fractured the foundation of cooperation, ideological divides have splintered communities, and individuals are left alienated in a sea of disconnection. Each tear in this intricate fabric threatens to destroy the harmony of progress, leaving only a frayed remnant of what could have been.

The solution lies in reclaiming the golden thread of shared humanity. Like a skilled artisan restoring a masterpiece, we must mend the tears in our social fabric with the foundational ideals of justice, cooperation, and empathy. These principles are not merely abstract concepts; they are the lifeblood of progress, the melody that guides humanity toward a brighter future. Unless we act decisively to reharmonize our collective efforts, the potential for unity and innovation will slip through our grasp, leaving us adrift in a sea of discord.

1.1. Justice: The Cornerstone of Trust

Justice is the thread that holds the social fabric together. Without it, the bonds of trust and cooperation unravel, leaving societies vulnerable to collapse. Justice ensures fairness, equity, and opportunity, fostering a sense of belonging and shared purpose. It is the foundation upon which civilizations are built and the guiding principle that ensures their stability.

Justice: A Galactic Imperative

Imagine a future where humanity has colonized the stars, creating diverse and complex galactic societies. Justice becomes the cornerstone of these communities, ensuring that the rights and opportunities of every individual are protected. Societies built on fairness and equity thrive, fostering trust and cooperation among diverse populations. Without justice, these interstellar colonies would descend into chaos, torn apart by mistrust and inequality.

Justice: A Nation's Unifying Force

Epic fantasy provides a timeless lesson in the power of justice. Picture a kingdom where farmers, warriors, and scholars alike are treated with respect and fairness. This shared sense of justice fosters loyalty and unity, strengthening the kingdom's social fabric and fueling its prosperity. A just society is not merely a moral ideal; it is a practical necessity for enduring strength and harmony.

Justice: Rebuilding with Equity

Even in the desolation of a post-apocalyptic wasteland, the value of justice remains paramount. Imagine a community rising from the ashes, striving to rebuild its shattered world. Without fairness and shared purpose, divisions would quickly emerge, threatening their fragile recovery. Justice becomes the foundation of stability, ensuring that every individual has an equal stake in the future.

Psychology of Trust and Respect

Psychology underscores the transformative power of justice. Studies reveal that individuals are more likely to cooperate and build strong relationships when they feel treated with dignity and respect. A society that prioritizes fairness fosters trust, creating an environment where progress and innovation flourish. Justice is not merely a moral virtue; it is the key to unlocking the full potential of human collaboration.

A Warning Etched in Shadows

The unraveling of justice is not a distant threat but an immediate danger. Without it, societies fracture, trust disintegrates, and progress grinds to a halt. The Siren Song of Division and Discord tempts us with its promises of power and individual gain, but its cost is the disintegration of the very foundation of humanity's greatest achievements.

The Call to Action: Weave the Threads of Justice

To resist the Crescendo of Collapse, we must prioritize justice as the cornerstone of a thriving civilization. A truly enlightened society ensures fairness, equity, and opportunity for all, fostering a sense of shared purpose that binds communities together. By restoring trust and strengthening the social fabric, we can ensure that the melody of progress continues to rise, carrying humanity toward a brighter future.

Let us not allow the tapestry of civilization to fray into chaos. Instead, let us weave the golden thread of justice into every facet of our shared existence, creating a harmonious world where every voice is valued and every effort contributes to the symphony of human achievement.

Together, we can turn discord into harmony and ensure that the Crescendo of Collapse becomes the overture to a future dawn.

1.2. Cooperation: The Strength in Unity

In the symphony of human progress, cooperation is the melody that unites us, weaving a powerful harmony that amplifies our strengths and transcends our limitations. Humanity's greatest achievements—the exploration of space, the eradication of diseases, the rebuilding of shattered worlds—have been born from collaboration. Yet, as the Siren Song of Division grows louder, the threads of unity begin to fray. It whispers of self-sufficiency and competition, luring societies into isolation and disunity. Beneath this deceptive tune lies a harrowing truth: without cooperation, humanity's potential is squandered, and our collective future darkens.

From the perspective of psychology and history, the importance of cooperation is clear. Humans are inherently social creatures, thriving on connection and shared purpose. Research by Dr. Abraham Maslow and Dr. Edward Deci highlights how collaboration fosters belonging and intrinsic motivation, enabling individuals to achieve more together than they ever could alone. A fractured society, by contrast, breeds isolation, despair, and inevitable decline.

Lurking Perils and Transformative Potential

Cooperation: A Galactic Concord

Science fiction offers a powerful vision of collaboration's potential. Imagine a colossal asteroid hurtling toward Earth, its impact threatening extinction. No single nation possesses the resources or technology to avert disaster. Yet, through a united global effort—nations sharing expertise, pooling technology, and working in unison—humanity deflects the asteroid, saving billions. This is the strength of unity: a force capable of overcoming even existential threats.

Cooperation: A Nation's Fortified Walls

Epic fantasy echoes this message in tales of united societies. Picture a kingdom where warriors defend, farmers sustain, and artisans innovate. Together, they form a robust system where every role is vital, and each contribution strengthens the whole. The kingdom's defenses are unyielding, and its prosperity is flourishing because cooperation replaces division. In unity, the nation finds its greatest strength.

Cooperation: Rebuilding from the Ashes

Even in the bleak aftermath of catastrophe, cooperation remains the key to survival. Imagine a post-apocalyptic wasteland where fractured communities hoard resources, competing for survival. This fractured society is doomed to fail. Only through collaboration—pooling resources, sharing knowledge, and working together—can they rebuild infrastructure, ensure well-being, and rise from the ashes. Cooperation transforms scarcity into abundance, and chaos into order.

Psychology of Belonging and Purpose

Psychology reveals that humans derive a profound sense of fulfillment from collaboration. Working together toward a shared goal fosters connection and purpose, creating a sense of belonging that strengthens the social fabric. In contrast, societies fractured by competition and mistrust descend into isolation and despair. Rebuilding unity is not only a moral imperative but a psychological necessity for collective progress.

A Warning Etched in Shadows

The absence of cooperation is not merely a failure of organization—it is a harbinger of collapse. Societies that prioritize division over unity find themselves adrift, unable to address their most pressing challenges. The Siren Song of Division may promise independence, but its cost is the erosion of progress, resilience, and hope.

The Call to Action: Harmonize the Symphony of Unity

To resist the dissonance of division, we must reclaim the melody of cooperation. A thriving society does not rise from isolated efforts but from the harmonious interplay of diverse talents, perspectives, and ambitions. By fostering collaboration across divides—between nations, communities, and individuals—we create a force capable of overcoming humanity's greatest challenges.

Let us mend the tears in our social fabric and rediscover the strength in unity. Together, we can compose a future where cooperation propels us forward, ensuring that every voice contributes to the grand symphony of progress. This is our shared mission, our collective purpose—to weave a tapestry of hope, resilience, and achievement that resonates through the ages.

1.3. Empathy: The Bridge Across Divides

In the symphony of civilization, empathy is the bridge that spans divides, transforming discord into harmony and isolation into understanding. It is the ability to see the world through another's eyes, the cornerstone of strong relationships, and the foundation of a compassionate society. Yet, as the Siren Song of Indifference grows louder, empathy begins to wane. Its absence leaves societies fractured, their social fabric torn by misunderstanding, mistrust, and conflict. Without empathy, humanity risks unraveling into a cacophony of isolation and division.

Psychology highlights the transformative power of empathy. Dr. Brené Brown's research on vulnerability and connection reveals that empathy fosters trust, cooperation, and resilience. It is through empathy that communities heal, nations unite, and civilizations thrive. Without it, the fractures between individuals, cultures, and ideologies widen, threatening the stability of the entire tapestry of human progress.

Lurking Perils and Aspirational Visions

Empathy: Understanding Alien Cultures

Science fiction envisions a future where humanity encounters alien life forms. In this new frontier, empathy will be humanity's greatest asset. Imagine an alien race with values, behaviors, and perspectives vastly different from our own. Without empathy, misunderstandings could escalate into catastrophic conflict— potentially interstellar war. However, with empathy, humanity can bridge these cultural divides, fostering peaceful relations and shared progress that transcends planetary boundaries.

Empathy: A Nation's Wise Ruler

Epic fantasy echoes the critical role of empathy in leadership. Picture a kingdom ruled by a tyrant blind to the suffering of their people. Excessive taxes crush the poor, while the ruler squanders resources on personal luxuries. Resentment festers, and the once-loyal citizens rise in rebellion. The kingdom collapses into chaos, its grand tapestry unraveled by a lack of compassion. Now, contrast this with a wise ruler who listens to their people, understands their struggles, and governs with empathy. Such leadership fosters loyalty, unity, and social cohesion, ensuring the nation's resilience and prosperity.

Empathy: Rebuilding with Understanding

Even in the desolation of a post-apocalyptic world, empathy is essential for survival. Imagine a fractured community where factions cling to past grievances, refusing to cooperate. Their lack of understanding prolongs suffering, hindering efforts to rebuild. Yet, when empathy takes root, they begin to see each other's humanity to understand the pain and fears that drive their divisions. This shared understanding becomes the foundation for cooperation, enabling them to build a more inclusive and sustainable future.

Psychology of Connection and Trust

Empathy is the golden thread that mends the social fabric. It allows us to connect on a deeper level, fostering trust, cooperation, and resilience. Societies that prioritize empathy thrive, and their citizens are united by a sense of shared purpose and mutual respect. Conversely, a society devoid of empathy teeters perpetually on the brink of collapse, its people isolated by indifference and alienated by mistrust.

A Warning Etched in Shadows

The absence of empathy is not a mere weakness; it is a fatal flaw. A society that turns its back on empathy creates a world of isolation and conflict, where misunderstandings escalate into crises and unity becomes an unattainable dream. The Siren Song of Indifference may promise simplicity and self-preservation, but its cost is immense: the loss of connection, trust, and progress.

The Call to Action: Build the Bridge of Empathy

To resist the Siren Song of Indifference, we must embrace empathy as the cornerstone of civilization. By fostering understanding, compassion, and connection, we can bridge divides and mend the fractures that threaten our shared future. Empathy is not just an ideal—it is the bridge that transforms isolation into collaboration and conflict into harmony.

Let us weave empathy into the fabric of our societies, creating a world where every voice is heard and every life valued. Together, we can compose a symphony of shared humanity, ensuring that the melody of progress resonates across divides and through generations to come. Empathy is the key to building a future that is not just brighter but truly united.

Conclusion: A Spark of Vigilance: A Call to Resist the Siren's Call

The Siren's Call is not a distant myth but an ever-present danger, a haunting melody that entwines itself into the fabric of our choices. It tempts us with illusions of safety, simplicity, and control, and it whispers promising utopia while leading us toward dystopia. Beneath its alluring harmonies lie the seeds of stagnation, the erosion of individuality, the walls of division, the tightening grip of control, and the devastating crescendo of collapse.

Each misguided idea threatens to unravel the symphony of human progress, replacing unity with discord and hope with despair. The seductive appeal of stagnation promises comfort but delivers decay. The loss of individuality assures harmony but stifles the innovation and freedom that fuel progress. Isolation lures us with the illusion of strength yet fractures the bonds that sustain us. The illusion of control promises order but chokes the vibrant interplay of liberty and creativity. And the crescendo of collapse warns us of the ultimate price of division: the irreversible fracturing of our shared humanity.

We stand at a precipice. The echoes of these siren songs are already reverberating through our world, weaving themselves into policies, ideologies, and behaviors. Each note draws us closer to the abyss, where the tapestry of our civilization may unravel into chaos. To ignore these dangers is to doom ourselves to repeat the failures of the past, to march willingly into a future where the promise of progress is silenced by our own complacency.

Yet, within this darkness lies a spark—a choice. The Siren's Call may be seductive, but it is not inevitable. The power to resist lies within us in the ideals that have always propelled humanity forward: justice, cooperation, empathy, freedom, and unity. These are the true notes of our symphony, the harmonious counterpoint to the discord of misguided ideas.

This is a call to vigilance. It is a plea to awaken to the dangers that lurk within these false promises and to rise as architects of a future dawn. Let us rewrite the melody of progress, replacing dissonance with harmony, division with collaboration, and stagnation with boundless potential. The Siren's Call does not have to be our downfall—it can be the spark that ignites our resolve to build a brighter, more resilient civilization.

The time to act is now. The stakes are nothing less than the survival of the symphony of humanity. Will we succumb to the seductive whispers of ruin, or will we rise, united, to compose a masterpiece worthy of future generations? The choice is ours, and the world waits for the melody we will create.

WHISPERS FROM THE FUTURE: A GUIDE TO AN ENLIGHTENED TOMORROW

᭙᭙᭙

A New Dawn Beckons: A Symphony of Humanity Awaits. The future whispers to us across the vast expanse of time, a message carried on the golden light of a new epoch. We, the inheritors of this potential, stand before you – the architects of today. This is not a mere call for progress but a summons to usher in a dawn of unparalleled human achievement.

Arise, Fellow Architects!

Challenges are not harbingers of defeat but the crucible from which this new epoch will be forged. Harriet Beecher Stowe's words echo through time: *"When you get into a tight place...never give up then, for that is just the place and time that the tide will turn."* Cling to your vision with unwavering determination. Let your will be the unyielding force that propels you forward and your imagination the compass that guides you toward a symphony of human potential.

The Architect's Canvas: A Masterpiece of Harmony Awaits

The future unfolds before you not as a rigid blueprint but as a vibrant artist's canvas. This canvas represents a harmonious society where individual aspirations flourish alongside collective endeavors. We, the inheritors of this potential, call upon you to become the artists who paint this masterpiece.

John Foster reminds us: *"When a firm, decisive spirit is recognized...it is curious to see how the space clears around a man and leaves him room and freedom."* Just as a resolute individual carves their path, a society with a clear vision cultivates an environment where individuality and collectivity can coexist in perfect harmony.

Willpower is the brushstroke that brings this vision to life. Embrace the freedom to explore your individuality while recognizing the power of collective action. Together, we can transform this canvas into a masterpiece of harmony and shared prosperity.

Together We Ascend: A Call to Action!

By nurturing these principles, you cultivate the seeds that will blossom into a magnificent new era. Embrace the potential that lies dormant within you, and answer the call to usher in this new epoch. The choice is yours: will you be a passive observer or a torchbearer leading humanity towards a brighter dawn?

Embrace persistence, cultivate these core principles, and together, we can ascend to a new epoch of human potential – a symphony where individual brilliance harmonizes with collective action.

I. FOUNDATIONAL PRINCIPLES: THE BLUEPRINT FOR TOMORROW

As the dawn of a brighter future stretches before us, humanity must turn its gaze inward and upward—to the values, principles, and aspirations that define our collective potential. To build the bridge to an enlightened tomorrow, we need more than fleeting ideals; we need a blueprint that serves as a guide for every note, every step, and every contribution to the grand symphony of progress.

This blueprint is not a static design; it is a living framework—a tapestry woven with purpose, enriched by diverse threads, and strengthened by the resilience of humanity. It is a vision that calls upon each of us to be architects, not mere bystanders, of a harmonious future.

Within this framework, we find the foundational principles that ensure the melody of tomorrow is both aspirational and enduring:

- **The Architect's Canvas: A Blueprint for Harmony** reminds us that the balance between individual brilliance and collective good is the cornerstone of a transcendent civilization. By harmonizing these dualities, we create a society where every voice contributes to a greater whole.

- **The Synergy of Knowledge: A Tapestry Woven from Diverse Threads** emphasizes the power of interdisciplinary collaboration. When diverse perspectives converge, innovation flourishes, crafting solutions that address humanity's most complex challenges.

- **The Power of Empathy: A Bridge Across Divides** teaches us that compassion is the unifying thread that binds cultures, ideologies, and generations. Empathy transforms understanding into action and fosters a world where diversity becomes a source of strength.

- **The Call for Sustainability: A Covenant with the Planet** urges us to honor our shared home, Earth. By harmonizing environmental, social, and economic systems, we ensure a legacy of balance and prosperity for future generations.

- **The Heritage of Flexibility: A Symphony of Adaptation** highlights the importance of resilience in the face of change.

Flexibility enables us to rise above uncertainty, to innovate, and to continually refine the melody of progress.

These principles form the foundation of humanity's greatest endeavor: to build a future where harmony, creativity, and purpose converge. This is more than a vision—it is a call to action, an invitation to each of us to pick up our instruments and join the symphony.

Will you embrace this blueprint? Will you lend your voice to the melody of progress? Together, we can compose a masterpiece that echoes through time, a testament to what humanity can achieve when united by a shared purpose and guided by enduring principles.

The journey begins here. The symphony awaits. Let us create.

A. The Architect's Canvas: A Blueprint for Harmony

Balancing Individual Excellence with Collective Good to Create a Transcendent Civilization

Henry Wadsworth Longfellow once wrote, *"An enlightened mind is not hoodwinked; it is not shut up in a gloomy prison till it thinks the walls of its own dungeon are the limits of the universe, and the reach of its own chain the outer verge of intelligence."* These words echo through time as a rallying cry to dreamers, visionaries, and architects of a brighter tomorrow. They invite us to see beyond the confines of our current limitations and recognize the boundless potential that lies within us, both as individuals and as a collective.

Embrace the Duality: Collective Good and Individual Excellence

The foundation of an enlightened society lies in the delicate balance of individual brilliance and collective harmony. Just as a symphony relies on the unique voice of each instrument to create a masterpiece, so too does a transcendent civilization flourish when every individual contributes their distinct melody.

Imagine a future where governance and societal structures act not as restrictive walls but as scaffolding, elevating all to reach their highest potential. Envision a world where talent, ingenuity, and passion are not only nurtured but celebrated, where the success of one becomes the shared prosperity of many. In this grand design, humanity thrives not by suppressing individuality but by harmonizing it within the collective symphony.

The Focused Pursuit: From Dreamers to Doers

As Francis Parkman observed, *"Achieving greatness requires concentrated work."* This truth reveals a vital distinction between those who dream and those who transform dreams into reality. Vision without action is a song left unsung. To bring forth a harmonious future, we must pair lofty aspirations with determined effort, crafting our ambitions into tangible achievements.

Let us honor the dreamers who dare to envision what others deem impossible, and let us celebrate the doers who, through grit and resolve, bring those visions to life. Every note of this symphony requires focus, discipline, and the courage to forge ahead—even when the path is uncertain.

Transform the Blueprint: A Symphony of Action

A blueprint alone is inert, a silent possibility waiting for the spark of action to ignite its potential. As architects of the future, we are called not just to imagine but to build. Dedicate yourselves to transforming these principles into living, breathing realities. Whether through innovation, collaboration, or simple daily acts of kindness, every contribution plays a role in constructing a civilization that shines as a beacon of unity, creativity, and progress.

Picture a society where education equips every child with the tools to explore their passions, where communities are strengthened by empathy and shared purpose, and where innovation addresses humanity's greatest challenges with bold and ethical solutions. This is the world we can create—a testament to what is possible when individuals unite in service of the greater good.

The Final Question: Will You Answer the Call?

The blueprint is drawn. The melody is composed. The baton awaits in your hand. The future calls for each of us to step forward, embrace the duality of individual and collective potential, and contribute our unique notes to humanity's grand symphony.

Will you answer this call? Will you join in the chorus of progress and possibility? Together, we can craft a legacy that will inspire generations to come—a civilization built not just for survival but for flourishing. The melody of a brighter tomorrow is waiting. Now is the time to conduct.

B. The Synergy of Knowledge: A Tapestry Woven from Diverse Threads

Emphasizing Interdisciplinary Collaboration as the Catalyst for Groundbreaking Solutions

As we embark on this transformative journey toward a harmonious future, a profound tool stands before us: **The Synergy of Knowledge**. Albert Einstein's timeless wisdom reminds us, *"The important thing is not to stop questioning. Curiosity has its own reason for existing."* In an era defined by complexity, curiosity is more than a virtue—it is a necessity. It is the driving force that compels humanity to transcend traditional boundaries and discover innovative solutions in the uncharted intersections of knowledge.

Embrace Interdisciplinary Learning: A Symphony of Innovation

Imagine a world where the boundaries of disciplines dissolve into a seamless exchange of ideas. Picture biologists collaborating with artists to design ecosystems that inspire and sustain life or engineers partnering with philosophers to ensure technology serves ethical and humane purposes. These partnerships create a dynamic fusion of insights, sparking innovations that bridge the gap between progress and human well-being.

- **Historical Context Meets Modern Solutions:** Let history guide science to illuminate the social impacts of technological advancements, providing lessons from the past to inform ethical progress.

- **Functionality Merges with Aesthetic Brilliance:** Imagine art and engineering collaborating to create not just functional but profoundly beautiful structures that elevate the human experience.

- **A Canvas of Possibility:** Within these intersections lies the seedbed of solutions that are as innovative as they are holistic.

Interdisciplinary learning invites us to expand our vision, fostering creativity, inclusivity, and empathy. It transforms knowledge into a living tapestry woven from the vibrant threads of diverse perspectives.

The Instruments of Progress: Building Blocks for a Brighter Dawn

This synergy of knowledge forms the foundation upon which the symphony of humanity will be built. The following principles serve as the keystones of this grand composition:

- **The Power of Empathy:** Empathy bridges divides, enabling humanity to collaborate across cultures and perspectives. In its resonance lies a unified chorus of voices driven by a shared purpose.

- **The Call for Sustainability:** Sustainability must become a guiding covenant with our planet. By weaving ecological balance into societal structures, we ensure a future where humanity and nature thrive in harmony.

- **The Spark of Innovation:** Curiosity is the fuel that propels the symphony of progress. Let this spark ignite within you, catalyzing ideas that address the world's most pressing challenges.

- **The Strength of Unity:** A symphony requires not discord, but harmony. Let humanity stand shoulder-to-shoulder, transforming isolated efforts into a collective masterpiece.

A Call to Action: Weaving the Future Together

The synergy of knowledge is not merely an ideal; it is a call to action. It asks each of us to rise beyond the silos of singular thought and embrace the rich possibilities that arise when we learn, collaborate, and innovate together.

- **Become Master Weavers:** Seek opportunities to engage across disciplines, blending your unique expertise with the insights of others to create transformative solutions.

- **Foster Interconnection:** Build bridges where barriers exist. Let your curiosity guide you toward partnerships that push the boundaries of possibility.

- **Join the Symphony:** The melody of the future awaits your contribution. With every action, every collaboration, and every innovative idea, you add your note to the harmonious composition of humanity's destiny.

Are you ready to raise your instrument and join the symphony? The tapestry is waiting, and its intricate melody will only come alive when we work together to weave its vibrant threads. The future is calling—will you answer?

C. The Power of Empathy: A Bridge Across Divides

Fostering Compassion and Understanding to Strengthen Unity Across Cultures and Ideologies

As we strive to build a harmonious future, we must recognize empathy as the transformative thread that weaves together the tapestry of society. Carroll Duvall Lewis's timeless words resonate deeply: *"The only true wealth is that you give away, and the only opportunity to secure happiness for yourself is to try to make someone else happy."* These sentiments illuminate empathy not as a fleeting emotion but as the cornerstone of an evolving and thriving civilization.

In an increasingly interconnected world, empathy transcends its role as a virtue and becomes a necessity—a bridge that connects humanity across cultural divides, ideological differences, and generational gaps.

Imagine a World Built on Empathy

Picture a future where the melody of human experience forms a rich and vibrant symphony. Each note, representing a unique perspective, contributes to the harmony of a shared purpose. Empathy enables us to step beyond the confines of our own experiences and see the world through the eyes of others. It challenges us to walk a mile in another's shoes, to feel their joys and sorrows, and to recognize the interconnectedness of all humanity.

This capacity for empathy fosters collaboration, understanding, and unity in ways that no other force can. When compassion guides our actions, the world becomes a place where diversity is celebrated, conflicts are resolved through dialogue, and progress is driven by collective goodwill.

Cultivating Empathy: A Practice for Transformation

Empathy is not an inherent gift but a skill that can be nurtured and developed. By incorporating empathy into our daily lives, we become catalysts for meaningful change. Consider these actionable steps to cultivate empathy:

- **Practice Active Listening:** Truly hear and understand others without judgment or interruption. Engage with their perspectives as if they were your own.

- **Demonstrate Compassion in Action:** Show kindness and understanding even in moments of disagreement. Let your actions reflect your care for others.

- **Seek Out Diverse Experiences:** Expand your horizons by interacting with people from different cultures, backgrounds, and beliefs.

- **Engage in Perspective-Taking:** Imagine yourself in someone else's situation to deepen your understanding of their challenges and triumphs.

- **Volunteer Your Time:** Dedicate your energy to helping others. Experience the profound fulfillment of making a positive impact on someone's life.

- **Practice Mindfulness:** Cultivate awareness of your own thoughts and emotions, enabling you to connect more deeply with those of others.

- **Empathize Through Storytelling:** Explore the lives of fictional characters in books, movies, or theater to gain insights into different perspectives and emotions.

Empathy: The Foundation for a Harmonious Future

Empathy transforms the threads of knowledge and understanding into bridges that connect us all. It fosters resilience, solidarity, and hope in the face of challenges. By embracing empathy, we create a society where collaboration flourishes, and every individual is valued.

Imagine governments designing policies with compassion at their core, corporations building inclusive cultures, and communities coming together to uplift their most vulnerable members. These are not abstract ideals but tangible realities made possible through the power of empathy.

A Call to Action: Building Bridges Through Empathy

The melody of progress awaits your contribution. Will you embrace the transformative power of empathy to bridge divides and unify humanity? The challenge before us is profound, but the reward is extraordinary: a world where compassion reigns, and harmony thrives.

The baton is in your hands. Let empathy guide your actions, inspire your words, and shape the future you wish to see. Together, we can compose a symphony of understanding, a legacy of love, and a bridge to an enlightened tomorrow.

Are you ready to join the symphony? The melody of empathy is waiting—let it flow through you and connect us all.[4]

---

[4] **The Instruments of Progress: Building Blocks for a Brighter Dawn**

D. The Call for Sustainability: A Covenant with the Planet

Harmonizing Environmental, Social, and Economic Systems for Long-Term Prosperity

As we weave the intricate tapestry of a harmonious future, we must never lose sight of the foundation upon which all life is built: our shared home, Earth. Mahatma Gandhi's wisdom resonates with timeless clarity: *"The Earth has enough for everyone's needs, but not for everyone's greed."* This statement reminds us that the choices we make today will determine the legacy we leave behind.

Sustainability is not merely an ideal—it is the covenant we must uphold to ensure that the symphony of humanity flourishes in harmony with the planet. It calls upon us to embrace balance in all its forms—environmental, social, and economic—and to act as stewards of a thriving world.

Environmental Sustainability: A Song of Balance

Imagine a world where humanity lives in concert with nature, protecting the delicate ecosystems that sustain life. Environmental sustainability requires us to respect the planet's limits and tread

---

This tapestry of knowledge, woven with the threads of empathy, serves as the foundation upon which the symphony of humanity will be built. The following sections will delve deeper into the core principles that will guide you in composing its intricate melody:

- **The Call for Sustainability:** A covenant with our planet. Weaving sustainability into the fabric of society ensures a harmonious future where all instruments can play in perfect resonance.
- **The Spark of Innovation:** Fueling progress with curiosity. Ignite the spark of innovation within you, for it is the creative energy that composes new movements in the symphony.
- **The Strength of Unity:** A chorus, not a cacophony. Let us stand shoulder-to-shoulder, united in purpose, and transform this symphony from a cacophony of discord into a harmonious masterpiece. Imagine humanity as a grand orchestra, each section contributing its unique voice to the powerful crescendo of human achievement.

By embracing empathy alongside these core principles, you can transform the threads of knowledge and understanding into a bridge that connects us all. Together, we can build a future where compassion reigns and harmony thrives.

lightly, ensuring that our actions today preserve its vitality for future generations.

- **Clean Air and Water as the Foundational Notes:** Envision a melody where rivers flow unpolluted and the skies remain clear, a natural symphony that sustains all other instruments.

- **Protecting Biodiversity as the Harmony of Life:** Safeguard the interconnected web of life, from the smallest insects to the grandest forests, each contributing its voice to the planet's song.

- **Renewable Energy as a Crescendo of Progress:** Shift from fossil fuels to sustainable energy sources, allowing humanity to grow without silencing the planet's natural rhythms.

Social Sustainability: A Chorus of Equity

True harmony cannot exist without equity. Social sustainability demands that we build a world where every individual has the opportunity to thrive. This is the melody of inclusion, where diversity is celebrated, and every voice finds its place in the grand composition.

- **Justice as the Steady Beat:** Advocate for systems that promote fairness, dismantle systemic inequities, and ensure access to education, healthcare, and opportunity for all.

- **Inclusion as the Universal Harmony:** Imagine a world where marginalized communities are no longer silenced but uplifted, their unique perspectives enriching the symphony.

- **Community as the Resonant Chord:** Strengthen local connections and global cooperation, creating a shared purpose that transcends boundaries.

Economic Sustainability: A Rhythm of Prosperity

Economic sustainability ensures that the pursuit of progress does not come at the expense of future generations. It calls for responsible practices that balance growth with stewardship, ensuring long-term prosperity for all.

- **Shared Success as the Steady Rhythm:** Envision a global economy where wealth is generated without depleting natural resources or exploiting labor.

- **Circular Systems as the Crescendo of Innovation:** Embrace circular economies that minimize waste and maximize reuse, keeping the planet's resources in harmony with human needs.

- **Ethical Innovation as the Melody of Progress:** Foster industries and technologies that prioritize the well-being of people and the planet, creating a sustainable cadence for growth.

The Instruments of Progress: Building a Sustainable Future

This covenant with the planet is enriched by empathy, innovation, and unity, forming the foundation upon which the symphony of humanity can be composed. The following principles act as guiding stars:

- **The Spark of Innovation:** Let innovation illuminate new pathways to sustainability, composing solutions that align with the planet's rhythms.

- **The Strength of Unity:** Imagine humanity as a grand orchestra, with environmentalists, engineers, and social advocates contributing their unique voices to a powerful crescendo of progress.

Together, these instruments create a world where humanity thrives in harmony with the Earth, a melody that grows richer with each passing generation.

A Call to Action: Will You Join the Symphony?

Sustainability is not a solo performance; it is a collective effort, a grand composition that requires every voice. By embracing the principles of sustainability, we honor our covenant with the planet and ensure a future where humanity flourishes alongside nature.

The time to act is now. Will you pick up your instrument, lend your voice, and join the symphony? Together, we can compose a masterpiece of harmony that echoes through the ages, leaving a legacy of balance, equity, and prosperity.

The melody awaits. Let us begin.

E. The Heritage of Flexibility: A Symphony of Adaptation

Cultivating Resilience and Adaptability as the Foundation for Navigating Uncertainty

As humanity weaves the tapestry of a harmonious future, it must embrace the winds of change, for they are as constant as the air we breathe. Flexibility is not a compromise; it is the cornerstone of resilience and a catalyst for enduring progress. This is the legacy we must leave for future generations—a heritage of adaptability that transforms challenges into opportunities and uncertainty into innovation.

Washington Irving's words remind us of this truth: *"Great minds have purposes, others have wishes. Little minds are tamed and subdued by misfortune, but great minds rise above them."* The civilizations that endure are those that evolve. Those who cling to rigidity crumble, but those who adapt write their legacy in the annals of progress.

The Power of Adaptation: A Song That Evolves.[5]

Flexibility is the melody that allows humanity to navigate uncharted waters. It empowers us to adjust our strategies, embrace new ideas, and confront unforeseen challenges. Imagine a world where adaptability permeates every facet of society:

- **Scientific Discoveries Driving Social Progress:** Envision breakthroughs in renewable energy seamlessly integrated into global economies, creating sustainable systems that benefit all.

- **Art and Technology Working in Harmony:** Picture artists and technologists collaborating to design solutions that are not only functional but also deeply meaningful and inspiring.

- **Resilience in Action:** Governments and communities adapting to environmental changes with proactive policies and collaborative efforts.

Adaptation is not a sign of weakness but of strength. It is the ability to evolve without abandoning core principles, ensuring that humanity rises above obstacles and continually moves forward.

A Commitment to Growth: A Melody That Rises Above

Flexibility does not mean forsaking foundational values; rather, it is about refining their application to meet the demands of an ever-

---

[5] **To overcome these challenges, it is important to cultivate a culture of innovation and experimentation. This can be achieved by:**

- **Encouraging risk-taking:** Create an environment where people feel safe to try new things and make mistakes.

- **Fostering a learning mindset:** Promote lifelong learning and encourage employees to seek out new knowledge and skills.

- **Embracing diversity:** Recognize the value of diverse perspectives and encourage collaboration across different teams and departments.

- **Building resilience:** Develop the capacity to adapt to change and bounce back from setbacks.

By addressing these challenges and embracing flexibility, we can build a more resilient, adaptable, and prosperous society.

changing world. This requires mental toughness, creativity, and foresight—the qualities that Irving attributes to great minds.

- **Learning from Mistakes:** Imagine a society that views failure not as an endpoint but as a stepping stone toward improvement. Each misstep becomes an opportunity for refinement and progress.

- **Overcoming Obstacles:** Flexibility demands dedication and courage to face immediate challenges while keeping sight of long-term goals. It requires the resolve to innovate, iterate, and persevere.

- **Embracing Continuous Growth:** A flexible society commits to lifelong learning, ensuring that individuals and institutions evolve alongside the complexities of the modern world.

This is the melody of adaptation—a song that rises above adversity, carries humanity forward, and ensures that progress endures.

Building a Brighter Tomorrow: A Symphony for the Ages

By embracing flexibility, humanity paves the way for a future rich in possibility. A society that values resilience and adaptability is better equipped to innovate, overcome crises, and navigate an ever-changing world. This is the true heritage of flexibility—the foundation upon which a symphony of human achievement can be built for generations to come.

However, embracing flexibility requires balance. Without structure, flexibility risks becoming aimless, leading to instability. Similarly, implementing a culture of adaptability may face resistance from those who prefer predictability and control. Overcoming these challenges demands:

- **A Balance Between Flexibility and Structure:** Establishing adaptable frameworks that retain a clear sense of direction.

- **Cultural Shifts:** Fostering a mindset of continuous learning and encouraging experimentation and risk-taking.

- **Organizational Resilience:** Creating environments where change is seen as an opportunity rather than a threat.

The benefits of flexibility far outweigh its challenges. A flexible society thrives by embracing innovation, solving complex problems, and building a more sustainable and resilient future.

A Call to Action: Will You Become a Maestro of Change?

The call to action has been sounded! Will you rise to the challenge and become a maestro of change? Flexibility is the guiding principle of humanity's grand symphony—a melody that adapts and evolves, shaping the future with every note.

Raise your instrument. Embrace the winds of change. Join the melody of progress. Together, we can compose a future where resilience and adaptability become the hallmarks of a thriving civilization, a legacy that echoes through the ages.

The symphony awaits. Let us begin.

II. IGNITING INDIVIDUAL POTENTIAL: SPARKS OF INNOVATION AND INGENUITY

Every great symphony begins with a single note, every masterpiece with a single stroke of the brush, and every world-changing idea with a single spark of inspiration. Progress is born in the imaginations of bold thinkers, dreamers, and doers—those who see possibilities where others see limitations.

Within each individual lies the power to ignite transformative change. Creativity, ingenuity, and courage are the embers of progress, and when fanned by curiosity and determination, they grow into a flame that lights the way forward. Eleanor Roosevelt's words resonate profoundly: *"The future belongs to those who believe in the beauty of their dreams."* This is a call to harness that belief, to transform vision into action, and to spark a brighter future.

In this section, we celebrate the courage to innovate, the curiosity to learn, and the ingenuity to create. Together, we will explore the power of individual potential to shape the world. Knowledge will be your compass, and courage will be your guide as you embark on this transformative journey.

The future demands your unique voice, your creative spark, and your unwavering determination to make a difference. Will you rise to the challenge? The symphony of progress begins with you.

A. The Spark of Innovation: A Flame that Fuels the Symphony

Encouraging Curiosity and Creativity to Ignite Transformative Advancements

As humanity strives to transform its vision into reality, the spark of innovation must be nurtured as the flame that fuels progress. Innovation, born of curiosity and creativity, is the heart of human advancement. It is the engine that propels us forward, illuminating new possibilities and empowering humanity to address its most profound challenges.

Albert Einstein once said, *"Imagination is more important than knowledge. For knowledge is limited, whereas imagination embraces the entire world."* This sentiment serves as a call to keep the embers of exploration glowing, to foster a culture where the unexpected is celebrated, and where bold ideas inspire transformative change.

Nurture a Culture of Exploration: Embracing the Unexpected

Innovation flourishes in environments where curiosity is encouraged and unconventional thinking is embraced. Imagine a symphony that transcends traditional instruments, welcoming unexpected harmonies that add richness and depth to the composition.

- **Daring Ideas as Catalysts:** Foster a world where bold and imaginative concepts are not only tolerated but celebrated. Encourage individuals to challenge the status quo and push the boundaries of what is possible.

- **Unexpected Collaborations:** Imagine a future where solutions arise from unlikely partnerships—a historian and a programmer creating a revolutionary education platform or a musician and an engineer designing sustainable energy solutions powered by sound waves.

- **Creativity as the Guiding Light:** Let creativity illuminate the path ahead, weaving threads of imagination into the fabric of progress.

Embrace the Spectrum of Innovation: Every Note Contributes to the Melody

Innovation is not solely the domain of groundbreaking inventions or technological breakthroughs. Often, it is the subtle shifts in perspective; the novel approaches persistent challenges, that drive meaningful progress.

- **Creativity Across Disciplines:** Imagine artists inspiring engineers with their boundless creativity or social workers devising innovative strategies to address systemic inequalities. Every discipline contributes a unique note to the symphony of innovation.

- **Innovation in Everyday Acts:** Recognize that transformative change begins with small, creative ideas. A single new method or process can have a ripple effect, inspiring further advancements.

The Strength of Unity: A Chorus, Not a Cacophony

Innovation is amplified through collaboration. Like a symphony that harmonizes strings, brass, and percussion, progress requires diverse perspectives working in unison.

- **Collective Action as the Foundation of Progress:** Imagine humanity as a grand orchestra, with scientists, artists, and engineers contributing their unique voices to the powerful crescendo of a brighter future.

- **Interdisciplinary Collaboration:** Envision sustainable cities designed by engineers and artists working together or equitable societies created through the combined efforts of social scientists and entrepreneurs.

United by Innovation: Composing a Brighter Future

The spark of innovation cannot be sustained by solitary effort; it thrives in collective action. Progress is a symphony that requires every instrument, every voice, and every perspective to compose its masterpiece. Innovation lies at the intersection of imagination, collaboration, and determination.

A Call to Action: Ignite Your Creative Spark

The call to action has been issued! Will you rise to the occasion, fueled by curiosity, a spirit of exploration, and the courage to challenge convention? The choice is yours: to embrace innovation, to push the boundaries of what is possible, and to compose a movement within the grand symphony of humanity.

- **Be the Catalyst:** Let your creativity take flight. Raise your instrument and contribute to a future rich in possibility and purpose.

- **Join the Symphony of Innovation:** Together, we can transform the spark of curiosity into a brilliant flame, a beacon that illuminates the path to a brighter tomorrow.

The melody awaits. Let your imagination and creativity become the fuel for humanity's enduring progress.

B. The Summoning of Ingenuity: A Call to Weave the Tapestry of Progress

Empowering Bold Thinkers to Craft Solutions That Reshape the Future

The symphony of innovation is not a solo performance—it is a collective masterpiece woven together by the ingenuity of bold thinkers from every walk of life. The winds of time carry an urgent message: *The Summoning of Ingenuity.* This is a clarion call to all who dream, create, and aspire—a call to contribute your unique threads to the grand tapestry of progress.

As Arnold Bennett reminds us, *"A single spark of inspiration has the power to energize the entire mental life."* This spark must be nurtured and transformed into ideas that push the boundaries of what is possible. The future demands boldness, a willingness to embrace challenges, and a commitment to innovation as both a necessity and a moral imperative.

The Fire Within: Fueling the Symphony's Crescendo

Ingenuity is the fire that propels humanity forward. It is the defining characteristic of thriving civilizations, distinguishing them from those that stagnate. The challenges of today are the kindling that ignites tomorrow's innovations. Embrace them as opportunities to rise, to venture into the unknown, and to chart paths that benefit generations to come.

- **Harness the Power of Imagination:** Let your mind explore uncharted territories. Picture yourself as a pioneer, discovering solutions that others dare not envision.

- **Transform Obstacles into Opportunities:** Every challenge presents a chance to innovate. From adversity springs the creativity needed to shape a brighter tomorrow.

- **Fuel the Crescendo:** Imagine the combined energy of countless innovators, each contributing their unique spark to a collective symphony of progress.

Together We Rise: A Symphony of Progress

Progress is not built in isolation; it is the result of collective effort. Ingenuity flourishes when individuals collaborate, bringing diverse perspectives to the table. This is the essence of weaving the tapestry of progress—a symphony where every voice matters.

- **Collaboration Across Disciplines:** Envision breakthroughs in medicine born from the combined efforts of biologists, engineers, and artists, who inspire empathy and understanding through their creations.

- **Uniting for a Common Purpose:** Picture humanity as an orchestra, each section contributing its distinct sound to create a masterpiece that transcends borders, cultures, and ideologies.

- **Elevating the Collective:** By summoning your ingenuity, you elevate not only yourself but the collective destiny of humanity. Every contribution enriches the tapestry of progress.

A Call to Action: Answering the Call of Ingenuity

The future is calling for your boldness, imagination, and unwavering will. This is your moment to step forward, embrace the power of innovation, and ignite the spark that will illuminate the path to a brighter tomorrow.

- **Be the Architect of Change:** Dedicate your creativity to addressing humanity's challenges and envisioning transformative solutions.

- **Join the Symphony of Progress:** Let your voice resonate within the grand composition of human achievement. Collaborate, innovate, and inspire.

- **Ignite the Spark of Ingenuity:** The fire of innovation burns within you. Feed it with determination, creativity, and the courage to dream beyond limitations.

Will You Become a Maestro of Ingenuity?

The choice is yours: to be a passive observer or to rise as a bold pioneer in the symphony of progress. Embrace your ingenuity, take up your instrument, and contribute to the masterpiece of humanity.

The call has been sounded. Let your spark of innovation ignite the flames of a brighter future. The melody awaits— join the symphony and help weave a tapestry of possibility, purpose, and progress.

C. The Courageous Chorus: A Symphony of Collaboration for a Brighter Future

Channeling Collective Courage to Confront and Overcome Global Challenges

Humanity's grand tapestry, woven from the threads of knowledge, collaboration, empathy, sustainability, and innovation, requires yet another vital strand to withstand the trials of tomorrow: courage. Courage is the compass that guides us through the unknown, the spark that ignites collective action, and the strength that propels humanity forward. Without it, progress falters, and potential remains unrealized.

Courage: The Compass in the Unknown

As we navigate uncharted territories, courage becomes the guiding light in the face of uncertainty. Joseph Campbell's words echo with timeless wisdom: *"The cave you fear to enter holds the treasure you seek."* Within every challenge lies a wellspring of opportunity, waiting to be unlocked by those who dare to act.

- **Reframing Fear as Opportunity:** Embrace uncertainties not as obstacles but as invitations to explore, learn, and innovate. Courage transforms hesitation into determination.

- **The Spirit of Exploration:** Imagine a world driven by the fearless curiosity of pioneering explorers—those who ventured beyond known horizons, sparking revolutions in thought, technology, and human connection.

- **Courage as the First Step:** Recognize that courage is not the absence of fear but the willingness to move forward despite it. It is the unwavering spirit that propels humanity toward its brightest potential.

Collaboration: The Engine Fueled by Courage

Just as a grand starship navigating the cosmos relies on the unified efforts of its crew, humanity's journey into the future demands collaboration powered by collective courage. It is through the synergy of diverse minds that humanity can confront its greatest challenges.

- **The Power of Unified Action:** Collaboration turns individual courage into collective strength. Imagine engineers, artists, and scientists uniting to solve complex global problems, their combined ingenuity creating breakthroughs that no single discipline could achieve alone.

- **Courage as a Catalyst for Ingenuity:** The courage to step beyond comfort zones fosters the spark of creativity that fuels innovation and discovery.

- **Breaking Barriers Together:** Collaboration rooted in courage dissolves divisions, allowing humanity to tackle challenges with a shared purpose and a unified vision.

Sustainability: The Foundation for a Courageous Future

Courage without sustainability is fleeting. A future built on unstable foundations cannot endure. Sustainability must be the cornerstone upon which courage and collaboration thrive.

- **A Commitment to Balance:** Imagine a world where courage extends beyond bold ideas to encompass a commitment to environmental, social, and economic sustainability. Such a foundation ensures a resilient future for generations to come.

- **Equity as a Reflection of Courage:** True courage demands a commitment to justice and opportunity for all. Clean air, water, and access to resources must be universal rights, not privileges.

- **A Legacy of Responsibility:** Sustainability ensures that the bold actions of today do not compromise the well-being of tomorrow.

A Call to Courage: Pick Up Your Thread and Join the Symphony

The symphony of humanity's future calls for courage as its driving force. By intertwining courage with knowledge, collaboration, empathy, and sustainability, humanity can chart a course toward a world brimming with possibility and shared prosperity.

- **Choose Wisely:** Recognize that the choices you make today ripple through time, shaping the destiny of future generations.

- **Embrace Boldness:** Let courage guide you to explore uncharted territories, confront challenges, and create innovative solutions.

- **Unite Through Action:** Together, we can transform visions into realities, building a future that reflects humanity's highest ideals.

The Melody of Courage: A Symphony of Human Potential

The call to action has been issued. Will you answer? The future awaits your courage, your collaboration, and your unwavering spirit. Let your courage be your compass, guiding you to illuminate the path toward a brighter tomorrow.

As the threads of courage, collaboration, and the other core principles intertwine, we will compose a symphony of human potential—a melody that echoes through the ages, inspiring progress and harmony for generations to come. The stage is set. The baton awaits. Let us begin.

D. Knowledge: The Fuel that Propels the Symphony

Promoting Universal Access to Knowledge and Lifelong Learning

At the heart of humanity's symphony lies a vital force: knowledge. It is the thread that strengthens the tapestry of progress and the fuel that propels the symphony forward. Eleanor Roosevelt's words remind us of its boundless potential: *"The future belongs to those who believe in the beauty of their dreams."* Knowledge, like a shared melody, multiplies and grows richer the more it is given.

Albert Einstein echoes this truth: *"The only true wealth is that which you give away, and it multiplies by being given."* When access to knowledge is unrestricted, its power transforms not just individuals but entire societies, enabling progress, fostering understanding, and creating a foundation for lasting harmony.

Imagine Knowledge as a Birthright

Picture a future where knowledge knows no barriers—where education transcends borders, socioeconomic limitations, and any other obstacle that hinders its flow. Imagine a world where the collective brilliance of humanity is unleashed through shared learning:

- **A Global Classroom:** Envision students from every corner of the globe learning together, exchanging ideas, and fostering a deeper understanding of our shared humanity.

- **Universal Empowerment:** Knowledge becomes a birthright, accessible to all, empowering individuals to innovate, collaborate, and create solutions that propel humanity forward.

- **Boundless Potential:** In this world, progress accelerates, fueled by curiosity and the collective ingenuity of empowered minds.

Knowledge: A Symphony of Shared Ideas

The power of knowledge extends beyond formal education; it thrives in the free exchange of ideas across disciplines and cultures. Let curiosity be the conductor, guiding humanity toward unimagined possibilities.

- **Collaborative Creativity:** Imagine scientists partnering with artists to design sustainable cities or philosophers collaborating with engineers to create ethical frameworks for artificial intelligence.

- **A Grand Composition:** Every discipline contributes its unique melody to the symphony of progress, enriching the composition with diverse perspectives.

- **Freely Flowing Currency:** Knowledge, like music, is most powerful when shared. Its free exchange fuels innovation, understanding, and a collective sense of purpose.

The Guiding Principles: Building the Foundation

To harness the transformative power of knowledge, we must uphold the core principles that guide humanity's progress:

- **Empathy is the Bridge to Understanding:** Empathy enables humanity to harmonize as a grand orchestra, where every section anticipates and responds to the others, creating a powerful and unified sound.

- **Sustainability is the Foundation of Prosperity:** A covenant with our planet ensures that environmental responsibility becomes the foundation for long-term prosperity.

- **The Spark of Innovation:** Curiosity ignites innovation, propelling humanity toward groundbreaking ideas and transformative advancements.

- **The Strength of Unity:** Unity harmonizes diverse voices, transforming potential discord into a powerful chorus of positive change.

These principles form the bedrock upon which a future fueled by knowledge and guided by purpose can thrive.

A Call to Action: Will You Pick Up the Instrument of Knowledge?

The path forward is illuminated by the light of knowledge and the collective wisdom of humanity. This is not merely an ideal—it is a call to action.

- **Be the Architect of Enlightenment:** Dedicate yourself to the pursuit and sharing of knowledge. Empower others, and in doing so, empower yourself.

- **Join the Symphony of Progress:** Take your place in the orchestra of humanity, where every voice contributes to a melody of possibility, innovation, and harmony.

- **Inspire Generations:** Use knowledge to craft solutions, build bridges, and create opportunities that echo through time.

The Melody Awaits: Begin the Composition

The future is not a distant horizon but a symphony waiting to be composed. Will you pick up the instrument of knowledge, contribute your unique voice, and help weave a tapestry of shared learning, progress, and empowerment?

The melody awaits—let us compose it together, a symphony of brilliance and possibility that will echo through generations to come.

III. STRENGTHENING COLLECTIVE FOUNDATIONS: A SYMPHONY OF UNITY AND SUSTAINABILITY

Progress is not the result of isolated efforts but the culmination of shared dreams and collective action. Just as a symphony requires every instrument to work in harmony, so too does humanity's future depend on the collaboration of diverse minds, disciplines, and cultures. Together, we are greater than the sum of our parts.

The challenges we face are vast and interconnected, demanding unity, empathy, and a commitment to sustainability. Henry Ford's words remind us: *"Coming together is a beginning; keeping together is progress; working together is success."* Through collaboration, we transcend barriers, integrate perspectives, and transform isolated efforts into a powerful force for change.

In this section, we delve into the essential pillars of collective progress: the strength of unity, the power of empathy, the necessity of sustainability, and the profound potential of interconnected knowledge. These principles are the foundation upon which humanity can build a resilient, inclusive, and thriving future.

This is not a dream—it is an invitation. Together, we can weave a tapestry of harmony, where every voice contributes to the melody of progress and every action paves the way for future generations. Will you join this symphony and help compose a legacy of shared purpose and enduring prosperity?

A. The Strength of Unity: A Symphony Forged in Collaboration

Harnessing the Collective Power of Humanity to Overcome Challenges

In the symphony of progress, unity is the unshakable rhythm that underpins every melody, every harmony, and every crescendo of human achievement. As Ken Blanchard wisely observed, *"None of us is as smart as all of us."* This truth serves as a beacon, reminding us that humanity's greatest strength lies not in individual brilliance but in the collective power of collaboration.

To weave the tapestry of a harmonious future, we must transcend divisions of race, religion, and nationality, embracing the shared humanity that binds us all. The challenges we face—environmental crises, social inequities, and economic uncertainties—are too vast for any one individual or group to overcome alone. Unity transforms these challenges into opportunities, amplifying our potential to create solutions that benefit all.

A Grand Orchestra: The Power of Unity in Action

Imagine humanity as a grand orchestra, each person contributing their unique sound to a symphony of progress. In this ensemble, there are no soloists vying for dominance, but instead, a collective harmony that celebrates the richness of diverse perspectives.

- **Collaboration Across Boundaries:** Picture a world where engineers and artists join forces to design sustainable cities that are both functional and beautiful. Imagine social scientists and entrepreneurs working together to create equitable societies, addressing systemic injustices with innovative solutions.

- **Building Bridges, Not Walls:** In the symphony of unity, walls of division crumble, replaced by bridges of understanding and cooperation. Collaboration becomes the key to unlocking the full potential of humanity's collective wisdom.

- **A Shared Purpose:** Let every voice, talent, and perspective harmonize in pursuit of a common goal—a brighter, more inclusive, and sustainable future for all.

The Future Awaits: A Masterpiece Composed by All

The future is not a predestined path but a vast, open canvas waiting to be painted. It is a masterpiece that can only be composed when every brushstroke, every note, and every contribution comes together in unity. As architects of this future, your choices, actions, and collaborations will determine the legacy humanity leaves behind.

- **Courageous Choices:** Be bold in weaving this tapestry. Let compassion and purpose guide your actions, ensuring that every decision contributes to the greater good.

- **A Shared Vision:** Imagine a future where humanity thrives, united by shared values and a commitment to progress. This is the masterpiece we are called to create together.

The Call to Action: Will You Conduct the Symphony of Humanity?

This is not a mere whisper from the future—it is a clarion call to action. Will you rise to the occasion? Will you become the artist who transforms this vision into reality? The choice is yours, and the stakes could not be higher.

- **Be the Conductor:** Imagine yourself not as a single musician but as the conductor of this grand symphony, uniting diverse talents and perspectives into a harmonious whole.

- **Answer the Call:** Embrace the synergy of knowledge, the power of empathy, the call for sustainability, the spark of innovation, and the strength of unity. Together, these principles form the foundation of a future where humanity thrives.

A Future Illuminated by Collective Brilliance

The symphony of unity is waiting to be composed, its melody brimming with possibility and illuminated by the collective brilliance of humanity. This is your moment to contribute—to transform the abstract into the tangible, the vision into reality.

Raise your baton, unite the orchestra, and let the symphony of progress resound through the ages. Together, we can compose a future where harmony, progress, and purpose prevail. The melody awaits. Let us begin.

B. The Harmony Engine: A Symphony of Collaboration for a Brighter Future

Uniting Disciplines, Sectors, and Cultures to Achieve Shared Goals

As humanity weaves the tapestry of a harmonious future, one force stands out as the engine of progress: collaboration. Henry Ford's timeless words remind us, *"Coming together is a beginning; keeping together is progress; working together is success."* True progress is not the product of isolated effort but of collective brilliance, where diverse minds and disciplines converge to achieve extraordinary feats.

Weaving the Tapestry of Progress

Collaboration is not merely a strategy—it is the foundation of human achievement. Imagine a world where boundaries between disciplines, sectors, and cultures dissolve, and a shared purpose unites humanity's most creative and innovative minds.

- **A Fellowship of Change:** Picture a fellowship of scientists, engineers, artists, and social workers—a team united by the common goal of creating sustainable cities that inspire awe, foster equity, and propel humanity forward. This is collaboration at its finest: a symphony where every instrument contributes to a grand and transformative composition.

- **The Invisible Force of Collaboration:** Through collaboration, every thread in the tapestry becomes stronger, every voice more resonant, and every solution more profound. It is the harmony engine that powers progress and ensures that humanity thrives.

The Conductor of Harmony

True collaboration requires more than cooperation; it demands a culture of respect, openness, and mutual celebration of individual strengths. To foster this culture is to become a Conductor of Harmony—one who inspires, unites, and elevates the voices around them.

- **Celebrating Unique Strengths:** Each individual brings a unique perspective, talent, and voice. Collaboration is about weaving these differences into a cohesive melody that enriches the whole.

- **Fostering Mutual Respect:** By creating an environment where diverse voices are valued and empathy bridges divides, you ensure that collaboration becomes a source of strength, not conflict.

- **Empowering Through Unity:** A Conductor of Harmony does not lead by command but by empowering others to play their part in the symphony, encouraging the best from every contributor.

The Strength of Unity: A Chorus in Perfect Pitch

Building upon the foundation of unity, collaboration transforms individual efforts into a chorus in perfect pitch. Like a grand orchestra, collaboration allows each section to anticipate and respond to the others, creating a harmonious and powerful sound.

- **Diverse Perspectives as a Source of Strength:** Through collaboration, diversity becomes an asset. The combination of varied experiences and viewpoints leads to innovative solutions and creative breakthroughs.

- **Empathy as the Bridge:** Empathy allows individuals to understand and appreciate the contributions of others, fostering a unified spirit that ensures harmony.

- **A Unified Spirit:** A shared vision ensures that everyone works in harmony, striving toward a future where humanity thrives together.

The Call to Action: Becoming the Conductor of Progress

The Harmony Engine is powered by collaboration, empathy, and a shared commitment to progress. To ensure humanity thrives, we must embrace these principles and act as stewards of collaboration.

- **Fuel Progress with Knowledge:** Let knowledge drive innovation, ensuring that collaboration leads to solutions that address humanity's most pressing challenges.

- **Foster Collaboration as the Engine of Change:** Unite disciplines, sectors, and cultures in a shared mission to build a better future.

- **Uphold Core Principles:** Empathy, sustainability, and a unified spirit must remain at the heart of every effort, ensuring that collaboration creates lasting and meaningful progress.

A Future Composed Together

By embracing collaboration, you have the power to shape a brighter future where humanity thrives in harmonious cooperation. Will you pick up your instrument, join the orchestra, and become a Conductor of Progress? Together, we can compose a symphony of unity, innovation, and achievement that will echo through generations to come.

The melody awaits—let us create it together.

C. Weaving the Tapestry of Progress: A Symphony of Empathy and Unity

Celebrating Diversity as the Driving Force Behind Progress

Humanity is not a collection of isolated threads; it is a grand tapestry woven from the essence of progress. Each principle—knowledge, collaboration, sustainability, and innovation—contributes to this intricate design. Yet, the shimmering thread that binds them all, the one that gives the tapestry its true strength and beauty, is empathy.

Empathy: The Bridge to a Harmonious Future

Empathy is the bridge that unites us, transcending differences in culture, belief, and background. Nelson Mandela's timeless words remind us: *"No one is born hating another person because of the color of his skin, or his background, or his religion. People must learn to hate, and if they can learn to hate, they can be taught to love, for love comes more naturally to the human heart than its opposite."*

Imagine a future where empathy enables us to see the world through the eyes of others, to walk a mile in their shoes. This is a world where walls of misunderstanding crumble, replaced by bridges of compassion and mutual respect. Empathy transforms coexistence into collaboration and connection into unity.

- **Celebrating Shared Humanity:** Recognize that the richness of diversity is humanity's greatest strength. From unique perspectives arise innovative solutions and transformative progress.

- **Replacing Walls with Bridges:** Envision a future where compassion dissolves barriers and understanding becomes the mortar that binds us together.

A Symphony Strengthened by Empathy

Empathy is the melody that harmonizes humanity's diverse voices, transforming differences into a chorus of shared purpose. Like a grand orchestra, where each instrument contributes its unique voice, empathy ensures that every perspective adds depth and richness to the symphony of progress.

- **Diverse Perspectives in Harmony:** Imagine an artist's empathy inspiring a biologist's work on conservation or a social worker's understanding shaping a programmer's educational innovations. These collaborations, driven by compassion, spark solutions that elevate all of humanity.

- **Respect as the Bedrock of Collaboration:** Empathy fosters respect for our differences, creating a common ground where bridges are built, and divides are bridged.

- **Unity Through Understanding:** The true strength of humanity lies in its ability to harmonize diverse perspectives, each contributing to a shared melody that soars on the wings of mutual understanding.

Weaving the Tapestry Together

To create a future where progress and unity thrive, empathy must be the thread that binds the tapestry of humanity. Knowledge fuels innovation, collaboration drives action, sustainability ensures balance, and empathy bridges the gaps. Together, these principles illuminate the path forward.

- **A Future of Shared Purpose:** This vision is not a distant dream but a symphony waiting to be composed, a tapestry waiting to be woven.

- **Your Contribution Matters:** Every thread, every voice, every perspective adds to the richness of this grand design.

The Call to Action: Will You Weave Your Thread?

The future calls upon each of us to pick up our threads, imbued with the power of empathy, and join the movement to weave a harmonious tomorrow.

- **Be the Architect of Understanding:** Let empathy guide your actions, ensuring that compassion and unity become the foundation of progress.

- **Join the Symphony of Humanity:** Take up your instrument, contribute your unique voice, and help compose the melody of a brighter future.

The Loom Awaits: Begin the Tapestry

The conductor's baton is raised. The stage is set. The greatest human symphony—a future brimming with possibility, understanding, and shared purpose—is ready to begin.

Will you pick up your thread and join the movement? Together, we can weave a tapestry that resonates with the harmony of humanity and endures for generations to come.

D. Building a Future in Harmony: The Pillars of Sustainability

Embedding Environmental and Social Responsibility into the Foundations of Growth

Imagine humanity not as a fragmented collection of threads but as a grand tapestry woven with the vibrant colors of progress. Each principle—knowledge, collaboration, empathy, and innovation—contributes to its intricate patterns. Yet, the foundation that ensures its strength, longevity, and beauty is sustainability. Without it, the tapestry would fray, its brilliance dimmed by imbalance and neglect.

Sustainability: The Bedrock of a Thriving Future

Sustainability is not an ideal to strive for—it is the foundation upon which humanity's future must be built. Mahatma Gandhi's profound words serve as a timeless reminder: *"The Earth has enough for everyone's needs, but not for everyone's greed."* Living in harmony with the planet is not a luxury but a necessity. It is the cornerstone of a truly unified and prosperous humanity.

Sustainability is more than a principle—it is a symphony in its own right, with three vital movements:

- **Environmental Sustainability: A Song of Balance**

  o Imagine a future where clean air and water are universal birthrights, not privileges. Picture thriving ecosystems that hum with life, their health ensuring the vitality of all living things.

  o This movement calls for respect, restoration, and protection of the planet's delicate balance, ensuring that humanity exists in harmony with nature.

- **Social Sustainability: A Chorus of Equity**

- ○ The second movement envisions a just and equitable society where inclusion and opportunity are woven into the fabric of everyday life.

- ○ Imagine communities built on understanding, where walls of division crumble, and education empowers every individual to add their voice to the melody of progress.

- ○ Social sustainability is the harmony of human connection, ensuring that every thread in the tapestry contributes to its brilliance.

- **Economic Sustainability: A Rhythm of Responsibility**

  - ○ The final movement demands responsible economic practices that prioritize long-term prosperity over short-term gain.

  - ○ Picture a world where economic growth aligns with environmental stewardship, and innovation fuels solutions that meet present needs without compromising the well-being of future generations.

Together, these movements form a symphony that resonates with the well-being of humanity and the planet—a foundation for true prosperity and progress.

A Symphony of Sustainability: Building a Brighter Future

To achieve this vision, sustainability must permeate every decision, every innovation, and every action. It is the thread that weaves resilience into the tapestry of progress, ensuring that humanity thrives in harmony with the Earth.

- **Knowledge as the Fuel:** Empower individuals with the knowledge to make informed and responsible choices.

- **Collaboration as the Engine:** Unite disciplines, sectors, and cultures to create sustainable solutions that benefit all.

- **Empathy as the Bridge:** Foster a culture of care, ensuring that sustainability addresses not only the planet's needs but also the well-being of every individual.

- **A Unified Spirit:** Let humanity's shared purpose guide the melody of sustainability, harmonizing environmental, social, and economic goals.

The Call to Action: Will You Weave Your Thread?

This vision is not a utopian dream; it is a clarion call to action. The loom is ready, and the threads of sustainability await your contribution. Together, we can compose the greatest symphony of human achievement—a future where progress soars, harmony thrives, and prosperity is shared.

- **Embrace the Challenge:** Take up your thread and join the movement to build a sustainable future.

- **Be the Architect of Balance:** Design solutions that respect the planet, uplift humanity, and ensure economic equity.

- **Contribute to the Melody:** Every action, no matter how small, adds a vital note to the symphony of sustainability.

The Loom Awaits: Begin the Tapestry

The stage is set. The instruments are tuned. The greatest human symphony—a future brimming with possibility, balance, and shared prosperity—is ready to begin.

Will you pick up your thread and join the movement? The melody awaits. Together, we can weave a tapestry that shines with the brilliance of humanity and endures for generations to come.

E. Weaving the Tapestry of Progress: A Symphony of Interconnected Knowledge

Integrating Diverse Fields and Perspectives to Create Holistic Solutions

Humanity is not a collection of isolated threads but a grand tapestry woven from the essence of progress. Each principle—knowledge, collaboration, empathy, sustainability, and innovation—plays a vital role, yet the foundation upon which this tapestry rests is the transformative power of interconnected knowledge. It is knowledge, interwoven and harmonized, that provides the strength and depth required to address humanity's greatest challenges.

Knowledge as a Tapestry: A Symphony of Interconnected Wisdom

Leonardo da Vinci, a master of uniting art and science, offers a timeless truth: *"Study the science of art. Study the art of science. Learn how to see. Realize that everything connects to everything else."* In this spirit, knowledge is not merely a collection of facts; it is the thread from which the tapestry of our future is woven.

- **Beyond Accumulation:** A mere collection of knowledge, like unspun wool, holds potential but lacks purpose. True power lies in weaving these threads into a cohesive design through interdisciplinary learning.

- **Intersections of Insight:** Imagine historians and scientists collaborating to predict the societal impacts of technological advancements. Picture artists and engineers design structures that are not only functional but also awe-inspiring and sustainable.

In these intersections lie the seeds of solutions that transcend traditional boundaries. Knowledge, when interwoven across disciplines, creates a tapestry far greater than the sum of its parts.

The Power of Interdisciplinary Brilliance

The future demands holistic solutions—answers that arise from the confluence of diverse perspectives and expertise. This is the essence of a symphony of interconnected knowledge.

- **Artists and Biologists for Conservation:** Imagine biologists collaborating with artists to create conservation campaigns that touch the human spirit, inspiring action to protect the natural world.

- **Engineers and Philosophers for Ethical Progress:** Picture engineers and philosophers uniting to design technologies that prioritize human well-being while advancing innovation.

- **Scientists and Social Advocates for Global Impact:** Envision scientists working alongside social advocates to address climate change, combining technical expertise with community-driven solutions.

By integrating diverse fields, humanity harnesses the full spectrum of creativity and intelligence, crafting solutions that resonate with both logic and emotion.

The Loom Awaits: Contributing to the Tapestry

The tapestry of interconnected knowledge is not complete without your contribution. Your perspective, your curiosity, and your dedication to learning are essential threads in the grand design.

- **Pick Up Your Thread:** Let your unique perspective enrich the broader composition. Whether through art, science, philosophy, or advocacy, your contribution strengthens the whole.

- **Commit to Lifelong Learning:** Embrace curiosity as your compass, guiding you to explore, question, and connect ideas across disciplines.

- **Foster Collaboration:** Build bridges between fields, uniting efforts to address humanity's most pressing challenges.

A Symphony for the Ages

This is the call to action: to weave a future where knowledge transcends silos, where disciplines unite, and where humanity thrives on the brilliance of its collective wisdom. Imagine the melody of interdisciplinary brilliance echoing through the ages, a testament to the power of knowledge that connects us all.

Will you pick up your thread and join the symphony? The loom is ready, the tapestry awaits, and the future beckons. Together, let us create a masterpiece of progress, harmony, and boundless possibility.

IV. THE CALL TO ACTION: IGNITING THE TORCH OF CHANGE

The future is not a distant shore but a vast and uncharted ocean, waiting for the courage, will, and collective resolve of humanity to navigate its depths. The time for passive observation has passed; the time for action is now. *The Call to Action* is a resounding symphony that invites each of us to step forward, pick up the torch of change, and illuminate the path toward a brighter tomorrow.

Throughout history, progress has been forged not by chance but by the bold actions of individuals and communities who dared to believe in a better world. This belief, paired with courage, empathy, and determination, is the spark that ignites revolutions of thought, innovation, and unity. As Annie Besant reminds us, *"Knowledge is essential to conquest; only according to our ignorance are we helpless."* The power to shape the future lies in the hands of those who refuse to let ignorance, apathy, or fear dictate the narrative of humanity.

The Symphony of Progress: A Collective Awakening

This moment demands more than vision; it demands a symphony of action. Every voice, every choice, and every contribution becomes a vital note in the melody of change. From the voice of tomorrow calling us to rise to the clarion call of unconquerable will urging us to persevere, each principle strengthens the harmony of humanity's journey forward.

- **The Voice of Tomorrow:** Recognize your role as a catalyst for progress and embrace the knowledge that fuels transformation.

- **A Clarion Call to Will:** Let determination and resilience guide you through adversity, transforming challenges into opportunities.

- **Guardianship Through Vigilance:** Stand as a vigilant protector of progress, dismantling biases and building bridges across divides.

- **Empathy in Action:** Let compassion be the unifying melody that binds diverse perspectives, fostering collaboration and understanding.

- **Sustainability as the Foundation:** Commit to the stewardship of our planet, ensuring that the legacy we leave is one of care and balance.

The Call to Rise: Be the Change You Seek

This call is not a whisper but a clarion cry to awaken the hearts and minds of humanity. It challenges each of us to move beyond the safety of complacency, to recognize our collective power, and to act with purpose. The world we seek to create—a world of unity, justice, and harmony—depends on the courage and commitment of those who dare to pick up the torch and illuminate the way.

- **A Future Forged Together:** This is not a solitary journey but a shared endeavor. Together, we will compose a symphony of progress that celebrates diversity, empowers the marginalized, and uplifts the human spirit.

- **Your Role in the Symphony:** The melody of change cannot reach its crescendo without your voice. You are not a passive observer but an active participant, a guardian, and a builder of the future.

The Torch Awaits: Will You Ignite It?

The path forward is illuminated by the light of knowledge, courage, and collaboration. The torch of change is in your hands, ready to set ablaze the possibility of a brighter tomorrow. Will you answer the call?

Let your actions resonate with purpose. Let your voice harmonize with others in a chorus of progress. Together, we can compose a legacy that echoes through the ages—a testament to the unyielding spirit of humanity and the torchbearers who dared to ignite the future. The symphony awaits. The stage is yours. Let the torch of change shine brightly.

A. The Voice of Tomorrow: A Call to Action

Inspiring Individuals to Recognize Their Role as Catalysts for Progress

Knowledge is the key to unlocking human potential. As Annie Besant once proclaimed: *"Knowledge is essential to conquest; only according to our ignorance are we helpless. Thought creates character. A character can dominate conditions. Will creates circumstances and environment."* These words echo across time, a clarion call urging each of us to rise as catalysts for progress.

The future is not an abstract dream; it is a symphony waiting to be composed, a tapestry waiting to be woven. It is built upon principles that empower the collective good, ignite individual potential, and demand vigilance and foresight. As we stand on the threshold of possibility, the voice of tomorrow calls out, asking us to recognize our power to shape what lies ahead.

Embrace Knowledge: The Fuel for Progress

Knowledge is more than power—it is the compass that guides us through uncharted territory, the fuel that drives innovation, and the light that illuminates the path forward. To embrace knowledge is to embrace progress itself.

- **Breaking Boundaries:** Imagine a world where education transcends borders and limitations, fostering curiosity and critical thinking. Picture global classrooms where minds meet, ideas flow freely, and solutions arise from diverse perspectives.

- **Informed Choices:** Knowledge empowers us to make choices that shape a brighter future. By seeking understanding, we create a foundation for progress that is thoughtful, inclusive, and enduring.

Thought Shapes Character: A Bridge Across Divides

The character of a society is forged by the collective thoughts and actions of its people. By embracing critical thinking, challenging assumptions, and fostering open-mindedness, we build a bridge to a more empathetic and inclusive world.

- **Cultivating Understanding:** Thought shapes the way we see others and the world around us. Let informed thought be the bridge that replaces walls with compassion, creating connections that transcend divides.

- **A Unified Spirit:** Imagine a society where empathy and understanding are guiding principles, where diverse perspectives are celebrated, and where progress is driven by mutual respect.

Will Creates Circumstances: The Power of Collective Action

The future is not a preordained script but a canvas waiting for your brushstrokes. Willpower—the ability to act with courage and determination—creates the circumstances and environment in which progress thrives.

- **Transforming Challenges into Opportunities:** Together, we can turn the challenges of today into the building blocks of tomorrow. Imagine a world where collaboration is the engine of progress, where voices harmonize into a symphony of innovation.

- **The Strength of Unity:** By uniting our efforts, we amplify our impact, proving that the collective will is greater than the sum of its parts.

The Tapestry of Progress Awaits Your Threads

This call to action is more than an invitation—it is a demand for engagement, creativity, and courage. The principles within this vision—knowledge, empathy, collaboration, and more—are the threads that will guide you on this journey.

- **Weaving a Shared Future:** Imagine a tapestry where knowledge empowers, empathy unites, and collective will shapes a future brimming with possibility. Every thread you contribute strengthens the fabric of humanity's progress.

- **Answering the Call:** Will you rise to the challenge? The conductor's baton awaits your touch, and the symphony of human potential is ready to begin.

A Call to Action: Let Your Voice Shape Tomorrow

The future is not an echo of the past but a melody waiting to be composed. Let your voice rise above the noise, your thoughts inspire progress, and your actions forge paths toward a brighter tomorrow.

Pick up your thread and join the symphony. Let your melody of progress resonate across generations, creating a legacy of innovation, compassion, and unity. Together, we can compose a symphony of human potential that echoes through the ages.

B. Beyond the Dream: A Clarion Call to Unconquerable Will

Encouraging Resilience, Determination, and Purpose in Facing Adversity

The power of will is humanity's most enduring force—a driving energy that transforms dreams into reality and adversity into opportunity. Thomas Fowell Buxton once proclaimed: *"The longer I live, the more deeply I am convinced that that which makes the difference between one man and another… is energy, invincible determination, a purpose once formed and then death or victory."* These words resonate as a rallying cry, urging humanity to embrace resilience, determination, and purpose as the bedrock of progress.

This vision is more than an abstract ideal; it is a call to action—a challenge to rise above uncertainty, to summon unwavering will, and to channel collective purpose into the tapestry of a brighter future. Together, we can compose a symphony of determination, a melody that echoes with the power of human potential.

Embrace the Call to Action: Together We Rise

Unwavering will and clear purpose have propelled individuals to achieve greatness throughout history. Imagine if these qualities, shared collectively, could propel all of humanity toward an enlightened future.

- **Collaboration as a Force of Progress:** Picture a world where collaboration is not just an ideal but the engine of transformation—where diverse voices unite to solve complex challenges and create groundbreaking solutions.

- **Unity in Action:** Let the principles of knowledge, empathy, and innovation converge with determination to build a future that is sustainable, inclusive, and prosperous for all.

- **The Strength Within You:** Recognize the power you hold. You are not a passive observer in humanity's narrative but an active participant—a builder of tomorrow.

The Power of Resilience: A Purpose Formed

Determination is not merely about enduring challenges; it is about transforming them into stepping stones for progress. Resilience is the courage to adapt, to persevere, and to grow stronger in the face of adversity.

- **Overcoming Challenges Together:** Imagine a future where resilience is woven into the fabric of society, enabling humanity to overcome crises with unity and resolve.

- **A Future of Purpose:** Let purpose be your guiding light—a shared commitment to creating a world that thrives on balance, understanding, and innovation.

The Architects of Tomorrow: A Collective Symphony

You are not merely a thread in the tapestry of humanity; you are its weaver, its designer, and its architect. The future depends on your determination to pick up the thread and contribute to the grand composition of progress.

- **Designing a Legacy of Will:** Let your actions today shape a future that reflects humanity's highest ideals—resilience, innovation, and unity.

- **A Symphony of Unyielding Spirit:** Together, our collective will can transform whispers from the future into a resounding symphony of human achievement.

A Call to Unconquerable Will: Will You Rise?

This is the moment to answer the call of the future. Will you channel your energy, determination, and purpose into building a brighter tomorrow? The conductor's baton awaits, and the stage is set for a performance that will resonate through time.

Pick up your thread, imbued with the spirit of collaboration, resilience, and unwavering will. Let us compose a symphony of human potential—a melody of progress, innovation, and unity that echoes through the ages. The stage is yours. The time is now. Let the symphony begin.

C. The Guardians of Progress: A Symphony of Vigilance and Action

Fostering Active Participation and Ensuring Progress Through Collective Effort

Humanity's role in shaping the future is not one of passive observation but of active guardianship. Each individual, like an instrument in a grand orchestra, plays a vital role in creating the symphony of progress. Knowledge, empathy, sustainability, innovation, and collaboration each contribute their unique melody, but without vigilance and action, the harmony falters.

Plato, a philosopher of self-mastery, offers a timeless reminder: *"The first and best victory is to conquer self; to be conquered by self is, of all things, the most shameful and vile."* Vigilance requires introspection, foresight, and the courage to overcome internal and external challenges. Progress is not guaranteed—it must be actively pursued and protected.

The Guardians of Progress: Vigilance and Foresight

The path to a brighter tomorrow is fraught with challenges, and the greatest threats often emerge from within. Biases, misconceptions, and complacency can erode the foundations of progress if left unchecked. History offers countless lessons of societies that fell not from external pressures but from their inability to confront internal flaws.

- **Self-Mastery as a Collective Virtue:** Vigilance begins with self-awareness—acknowledging biases, questioning assumptions, and fostering critical thinking.

- **A Cautionary Tale:** Let the lessons of history guide us, reminding us that short-sightedness and inaction are the enemies of progress.

The Magic Talisman: Courage and Perseverance

Progress requires more than awareness; it demands bold action. Courage and perseverance are the "magic talismans" that empower humanity to dismantle flawed systems and champion ideals that advance the greater good.

- **Challenge the Status Quo:** When systems or traditions no longer serve humanity's collective interests, let courage guide you to question and transform them.

- **Commit to the Long Game:** True progress rarely unfolds overnight. Persevere through setbacks, understanding that the greatest advancements are born from unwavering dedication.

- **Courage in Action:** Imagine dismantling barriers of prejudice, inequality, and ignorance while building bridges of understanding and cooperation.

The Power of Action: Dismantling Walls and Building Bridges

Active participation is the cornerstone of progress. Knowledge, empathy, and collaboration are tools in your arsenal, empowering you to think critically, challenge biases, and foster understanding.

- **Knowledge as a Weapon:** Use knowledge to dispel misconceptions, illuminate truths, and guide informed decision-making.

- **Empathy as a Bridge:** Build connections across divides, fostering collaboration and mutual respect.

- **Interdisciplinary Learning:** Embrace diverse perspectives to dismantle rigid mindsets and craft holistic solutions.

A Call to Action: Will You Play Your Part?

The symphony of progress calls for vigilant and active participants. As guardians of the future, you hold the responsibility to protect and advance the ideals that ensure humanity's prosperity.

- **Be the Architect of Change:** Use courage and perseverance to challenge injustice, uphold truth, and champion progress.

- **Join the Orchestra of Humanity:** Let your actions harmonize with others, creating a melody of resilience, innovation, and shared purpose.

The Symphony Awaits: Compose the Future

This is your moment to step forward. Will you pick up the instrument of courage and perseverance, joining the orchestra that safeguards progress? The conductor's baton is raised, and the stage is set for a symphony of human potential.

Let your courage be the crescendo, your perseverance the driving rhythm. Together, we will compose a future illuminated by knowledge, action, and hope—a symphony of progress that echoes through the ages. The time is now. The symphony awaits.

D. The Guardians of Progress: A Symphony of Empathy and Action

Embedding Empathy into Governance and Societal Frameworks to Inspire Collaboration

Imagine humanity not as a collection of isolated instruments but as a grand orchestra playing a vital symphony for the future. Each section—knowledge, collaboration, sustainability, innovation, and courage—contributes its unique melody. Yet, the harmony of this composition relies on a unifying force that transcends boundaries and divisions: empathy. Without it, the symphony falters; with it, the melody of progress soars.

Cultivate Empathy to Bridge Divides: The Unifying Power of Compassion

Empathy is the thread that binds humanity together, transforming disconnected voices into a unified chorus. Abraham Lincoln's words remind us of its profound significance: *"The mystic chords of memory, stretching from every battlefield and patriot grave to every living heart and hearth-stone, all over this broad land, will yet swell the chorus of the Union, when again touched, as surely they will be, by the angel hands of peace."* In a world growing ever more interconnected, empathy is not merely an ideal but a cornerstone of thriving societies.

- **Understanding Beyond the Surface:** Empathy calls us to look deeper, to walk a mile in another's shoes, and to feel their joys and sorrows. This capacity to connect with others fosters understanding and cooperation across divides.

- **Celebrating Diversity:** Imagine a world where cultural differences are not merely tolerated but celebrated. Empathy transforms differences into opportunities for growth and innovation, strengthening the bonds of humanity.

- **Resolving Conflict Through Compassion:** Envision conflicts resolved through dialogue and mutual understanding rather than violence. Empathy is the bridge that unites hearts and minds, creating a foundation for lasting peace.

The Power of Empathy in Action: Building Bridges Across Divides

Empathy is not a passive sentiment; it is a call to action that demands courage and persistence. By embedding empathy into governance, societal frameworks, and individual actions, we can transform how humanity addresses its most pressing challenges.

- **Wielding Knowledge Against Prejudice:** Use knowledge to challenge biases, dispel misconceptions, and foster understanding across cultural and ideological boundaries.

- **Creating Systems Rooted in Empathy:** Imagine governments, corporations, and communities that prioritize compassion in their policies and practices, ensuring that every voice is heard and valued.

- **Building Bridges Through Interdisciplinary Collaboration:** Combine empathy with interdisciplinary learning to dismantle rigid mindsets and craft holistic solutions.

A Call to Action: Becoming Guardians of Empathy

The symphony of progress calls for guardians who champion empathy as the unifying melody of humanity. As a guardian, your role is to bridge divides, foster understanding, and ensure that progress is guided by compassion.

- **Be the Architect of Understanding:** Let empathy shape your actions, decisions, and interactions, ensuring that humanity moves forward together.

- **Join the Orchestra of Progress:** Pick up your instrument of empathy and understanding and harmonize with others to create a future of unity and purpose.

The Symphony Awaits: Compose a Future of Compassion

The greatest human achievement—a future illuminated by knowledge, action, and compassion—depends on your contribution. Let empathy be the melody that unites humanity, transforming diverse perspectives into a powerful harmony.

Will you pick up the baton of empathy and lead the symphony of progress? Together, let us compose a melody that resonates with understanding, a harmony that bridges divides, and a future that thrives on compassion. The stage is set. The orchestra awaits. Let the symphony begin.

E. The Guardians of Progress: A Symphony for a Sustainable Future

Committing to Long-Term Strategies for Planetary Stewardship

Humanity stands not as a collection of solo performers but as the guardians of progress, united in a grand orchestra playing a symphony for the future. Each principle—knowledge, collaboration, courage, empathy, and innovation—contributes to its melody, but the harmony of this symphony rests on a secure foundation: sustainability. Without sustainability, the melody falters, and the future is left vulnerable.

Chief Seattle's profound words remind us of our collective responsibility: *"We do not inherit the Earth from our ancestors; we borrow it from our children."* Sustainability is not merely a principle; it is a legacy of care, a commitment to ensure that the choices we make today create a thriving world for generations to come.

Prioritize Sustainability for a Legacy of Care

Sustainability is the foundation upon which a harmonious future is built, encompassing environmental, social, and economic dimensions.

- **Environmental Sustainability: A Song of Balance**
  Respect the delicate balance of our planet. Imagine a future where clean air and water are universal birthrights, ecosystems thrive with vibrant life, and humanity exists in harmony with nature.

- **Social Sustainability: A Chorus of Equity**
  Build a just and equitable society where every individual can thrive. Picture a world where inclusion, opportunity, and understanding form the pillars of social progress.

- **Economic Sustainability: A Rhythm of Responsibility** Foster responsible economic practices that align growth with environmental stewardship. Envision a future where innovation drives prosperity without compromising the well-being of future generations.

This is the promise of a sustainable future—a legacy that reflects humanity's care for the planet and all who call it home.

The Power of Action: Building Bridges to a Sustainable Future

Sustainability requires more than awareness; it demands action. Knowledge, empathy, and collaboration are the tools that will help dismantle the barriers to progress and build a thriving, balanced future.

- **Knowledge as a Catalyst:** Use knowledge to inspire critical thinking and informed decision-making, empowering societies to adopt sustainable practices.

- **Empathy as a Bridge:** Foster a global culture of care where understanding and compassion guide policies, innovations, and collaborations.

- **Collaboration as the Engine:** Unite disciplines, sectors, and cultures to design solutions that integrate environmental, social, and economic priorities.

These tools empower humanity to dismantle prejudice, rethink rigid mindsets, and embrace sustainability as the foundation for progress.

The Call to Action: A Symphony Woven with Purpose

By embracing these principles, you do more than listen to whispers from the future—you become the architects who shape its reality. The future is not a predetermined path; it is a canvas awaiting your bold brushstrokes.

- **Fuel Progress with Knowledge:** Use education and understanding to drive sustainable innovation and decision-making.

- **Let Empathy Guide You:** Ensure compassion and equity are at the heart of every action and initiative.

- **Anchor Progress in Sustainability:** Build a future that balances growth with care for the planet and its people.

The Future Awaits: Will You Answer the Call?

The tools are in your hands, the orchestra is poised, and the conductor's baton awaits. Together, we stand on the precipice of tomorrow with the power to create a world brimming with possibility and rooted in sustainability.

Let your choices be bold, your actions guided by compassion, and your creativity flourish. Together, we can weave a tapestry of knowledge, empathy, and purpose—a symphony of progress that echoes through the ages, leaving a thriving, harmonious world as our legacy. The stage is set. The time is now. Let the symphony begin.

V. THE ETHOS OF LEADERSHIP: GUIDING THE SYMPHONY

Leadership is the unseen hand that shapes the course of humanity's symphony. It is the guiding force that harmonizes diverse voices, orchestrates collective action, and ensures that progress resonates with purpose and integrity. True leadership does not command—it inspires. It does not divide—it unites. As John Quincy Adams once said, *"If your actions inspire others to dream more, learn more, do more, and become more, you are a leader."*

The ethos of leadership is more than a collection of traits; it is a moral and visionary compass that points the way forward. In a world facing complex challenges, leadership must embody courage, wisdom, and collaboration to guide humanity toward a brighter future. Leadership is not reserved for a select few—it is a call that each of us can answer, shaping the symphony of progress through our actions and example.

The Three Pillars of Leadership: Conducting Humanity's Symphony

In this section, we explore three pillars of leadership that illuminate the path to a harmonious and thriving future. Each pillar reflects a unique aspect of leadership, yet all are interconnected, working together to guide humanity's collective potential.

- **Visionary Leadership:** The conductor of humanity's symphony, visionary leaders inspire collective action and cultivate shared purpose. They illuminate the possibilities of tomorrow, guiding others toward a common goal.

- **Ethical Leadership:** The moral compass that ensures power is wielded with integrity and trust. Ethical leaders set the standard for fairness, accountability, and compassion, building a foundation of trust that strengthens communities and societies.

- **Global Leadership:** The symphony of nations united in purpose. Global leaders transcend borders, fostering international collaboration to address humanity's most pressing challenges and building a harmonious future for all.

Leadership as a Catalyst for Transformation

Leadership is not simply about authority; it is about responsibility. It is the ability to inspire, uplift, and unite others in pursuit of a vision greater than any individual. Leadership is the spark that transforms ideas into action, the force that turns potential into progress.

- **Inspire Action:** Leadership ignites the courage and determination needed to face adversity and overcome barriers.

- **Unite Perspectives:** A true leader brings people together, harmonizing diverse voices into a cohesive and powerful melody.

- **Build a Legacy:** Leadership creates a ripple effect, empowering others to become leaders themselves and ensuring that progress endures across generations.

The Call to Leadership: Will You Answer?

The world is in need of leaders—visionary thinkers, ethical guides, and global collaborators—who will rise to the challenge of shaping a brighter tomorrow. This is not a call for titles or positions; it is a call for action, courage, and purpose.

- **Lead with Vision:** Illuminate the possibilities of a future shaped by shared goals and collective efforts.

- **Lead with Integrity:** Be the moral compass that upholds trust, accountability, and fairness.

- **Lead with Unity:** Foster collaboration across borders, disciplines, and cultures, building a symphony of nations that harmonizes progress with purpose.

The Symphony Awaits: Guiding Humanity Toward Harmony

Leadership is the baton that conducts the symphony of humanity. With vision, ethics, and unity, we can guide the world toward a future that resonates with harmony, progress, and hope.

Will you take up the baton of leadership? Let your actions inspire, your principles guide, and your vision unite. Together, we can compose a legacy of progress that echoes through the ages. The orchestra awaits. The stage is set. Let us lead the symphony forward.

A. Visionary Leadership: The Conductor's Role

Inspiring Collective Action and Cultivating a Shared Vision for the Future

Leadership is the baton that guides humanity's symphony, aligning diverse voices into a harmonious composition. Visionary leaders do more than manage; they inspire, unify, and amplify the potential of those they guide. As Henry Ford reminds us, *"The whole secret of a successful life is to find out what one's destiny is to do and then do it."* In the context of leadership, this destiny is to be the conductor—a guiding force that elevates individual efforts into collective greatness.

The Conductor's Role: Inspiring Collective Action

Visionary leaders understand that progress is not achieved alone but through the collective power of unified action. Their role is to inspire others, providing the clarity and direction needed to turn a shared vision into reality.

- **Unifying Diverse Perspectives:** Leadership is about weaving together the unique strengths of every individual into a cohesive whole. Imagine a conductor harmonizing instruments of different tones, tempos, and volumes to create a powerful symphony.

- **Illuminating the Path Forward:** Visionary leaders articulate a clear and compelling vision, inspiring others to see the possibilities and potential that lie ahead.

- **Empowering Others to Rise:** Effective leaders empower those they guide, fostering a culture of trust, accountability, and shared purpose.

The Power of Shared Vision: Cultivating a Future of Possibility

Visionary leaders do more than lead—they cultivate a vision that others can believe in, contribute to, and take ownership of. This shared vision becomes the foundation for collective action and progress.

- **Envisioning a Brighter Future:** Imagine leaders who see not just the challenges of the present but the opportunities of the future. These leaders inspire innovation and bold thinking.

- **Encouraging Collaboration:** Visionary leadership fosters an environment where individuals feel valued and motivated to contribute their unique perspectives and skills.

- **Aligning Purpose and Action:** By connecting individual aspirations to a collective mission, leaders ensure that every effort contributes to the greater good.

A Call to Leadership: Will You Take the Baton?

The symphony of progress requires conductors—leaders who inspire, unite, and elevate. This is not a role confined to those in positions of authority; it is a call for anyone willing to guide others toward a shared vision.

- **Lead with Purpose:** Let your vision inspire action, aligning the efforts of those around you with a common goal.

- **Empower and Uplift:** Recognize and celebrate the strengths of others, ensuring that every voice is heard and valued.

- **Foster Collaboration:** Encourage open dialogue and mutual respect, creating an environment where collective potential thrives.

The Symphony Awaits: Compose a Legacy of Leadership

This is your moment to take the baton and guide humanity's symphony toward harmony and progress. Visionary leadership is not about command—it is about connection, inspiration, and shared purpose.

Will you step into the role of conductor? Let your leadership inspire others, your vision illuminate the path, and your actions compose a legacy of unity, innovation, and progress. The stage is set. The symphony awaits. Let us lead together.

B. Ethical Leadership: The Moral Compass

Balancing Power with Responsibility to Uphold Trust and Integrity

Leadership is not merely the exercise of power but the embodiment of responsibility, trust, and integrity. Ethical leaders act as the moral compass of humanity's symphony, ensuring that progress is guided by principles rather than personal ambition. As Mahatma Gandhi reminded us, *"The best way to find yourself is to lose yourself in the service of others."* Ethical leadership is a call to serve—not command—and to balance power with accountability to foster a future built on trust and fairness.

The Moral Compass: Guiding Progress with Integrity

Ethical leaders prioritize the well-being of those they serve over personal gain, setting the tone for progress that is both sustainable and just.

- **Power as a Stewardship:** Leadership is not ownership—it is stewardship. Ethical leaders understand that power is a tool for service, not self-interest.

- **Cultivating Trust:** Trust is the foundation of effective leadership. Imagine a society where leaders' actions consistently reflect their words, building bridges of credibility and respect.

- **Upholding Integrity:** Ethical leaders lead by example, setting standards of fairness, honesty, and accountability that inspire those they guide.

Balancing Power with Responsibility

The greater the power, the greater the responsibility to use it wisely. Ethical leaders navigate this balance by aligning their decisions with principles that prioritize the collective good.

- **Accountability as a Pillar of Leadership:** Ethical leaders are transparent, embracing accountability for their actions and decisions.

- **Empowering Others Through Fairness:** By fostering equity and inclusion, ethical leaders empower individuals to thrive within a framework of justice and respect.

- **Making Decisions with Empathy:** Ethical leadership considers the human impact of every decision, ensuring that progress does not come at the expense of dignity or well-being.

A Call to Ethical Leadership: Will You Be the Compass?

Ethical leadership is not a title but a mindset—a commitment to guiding humanity with principles that honor trust, integrity, and shared purpose.

- **Lead by Example:** Let your actions reflect your values, inspiring those you guide to follow principles over personal gain.

- **Build with Integrity:** Create systems, policies, and practices that uphold fairness, transparency, and respect for all.

- **Be the Guardian of Trust:** Recognize that trust is not given but earned through consistent, principled action.

The Symphony Awaits: A Legacy of Ethical Leadership

The future calls for leaders who balance power with responsibility and progress with integrity. Ethical leadership is the guiding light that ensures humanity's symphony resonates with harmony, equity, and trust.

Will you take the baton of ethical leadership? Let your principles guide you, your integrity inspire others, and your actions compose a legacy of fairness and progress. Together, we can lead a symphony of trust and hope that echoes through the ages. The stage is set. The orchestra awaits. Let us lead with integrity.

C. Global Leadership: A Symphony of Nations

Fostering International Collaboration to Address Global Challenges

Humanity's challenges are not confined by borders, nor are the solutions. Global leadership calls for nations to come together as a grand orchestra, each contributing its unique strengths to compose a harmonious response to shared challenges. As John F. Kennedy once said, *"Our problems are man-made—therefore, they can be solved by man. And man can be as big as he wants."* The symphony of nations requires leaders who embrace collaboration, prioritize unity, and guide the world toward a shared vision of progress.

A Symphony of Nations: Uniting for Common Purpose

Global leadership is about fostering cooperation among nations, transcending differences to create a collective response to challenges that affect us all.

- **Collaboration Across Borders:** Imagine a world where nations come together to address climate change, global health crises, and economic inequality—not as competitors but as allies in the pursuit of shared goals.

- **A Shared Vision:** Global leaders articulate a vision that transcends individual national interests, inspiring collective action for the greater good.

- **Harmony in Diversity:** Like an orchestra blending distinct instruments, global leadership thrives when diverse perspectives, cultures, and resources unite in pursuit of a common purpose.

The Role of Global Leaders: Catalysts for Cooperation

Global leaders act as catalysts for international collaboration, building bridges of trust and mutual respect to address pressing global issues.

- **Diplomacy as a Bridge:** Effective global leadership leverages diplomacy to resolve conflicts, foster understanding, and build enduring partnerships.

- **Equity in Leadership:** True global collaboration ensures that every nation, regardless of size or power, has a voice in shaping the world's future.

- **Championing Collective Action:** Leaders prioritize solutions that benefit all, ensuring that progress is inclusive and equitable.

Addressing Global Challenges Together

The complexity of global challenges requires solutions that are as interconnected as the problems themselves. Global leadership must inspire nations to rise above divisions and act with unity.

- **Environmental Stewardship:** Imagine nations working together to combat climate change, preserving the planet for future generations.

- **Global Health Initiatives:** Picture a world where countries collaborate to share resources, research, and innovations to tackle pandemics and improve healthcare access.

- **Economic Balance:** Envision global trade systems and policies designed to reduce inequality and foster sustainable growth.

A Call to Global Leadership: Will You Join the Symphony?

Global leadership is not confined to presidents and diplomats—it is a call for all individuals to recognize their role as citizens of a shared planet. By fostering unity, empathy, and collaboration, we can address the challenges that transcend borders.

- **Be a Citizen of the World:** Advocate for policies and practices that prioritize global cooperation and equity.

- **Lead with Compassion:** Promote understanding and respect for diverse cultures and perspectives.

- **Inspire Collective Action:** Encourage your community, organization, or nation to contribute to global efforts for progress.

The Symphony Awaits: Composing a Harmonious World

The future depends on the ability of nations to act as one, addressing global challenges with unity, determination, and vision. Global leadership is the baton that guides this symphony, transforming division into harmony and potential into progress.

Will you answer the call of global leadership? Let your actions inspire unity, your voice advocate for collaboration, and your vision compose a symphony of nations working together to create a brighter future. The stage is set. The orchestra is ready. Let us lead as one.

VI. CULTIVATING HUMAN POTENTIAL: THE WELLSPRING OF ENLIGHTENMENT

Human potential is the most precious resource humanity possesses, a boundless wellspring from which innovation, compassion, and progress flow. Each individual carries within them the seeds of greatness—the capacity to dream, create, and contribute to the collective tapestry of progress. As Johann Wolfgang von Goethe once said, *"Treat people as if they were what they ought to be, and you help them become what they are capable of being."*

Cultivating human potential is both a moral imperative and a transformative act. It is the foundation of enlightenment, the key to unlocking the brilliance within each person, and the driving force behind a thriving and harmonious world. To achieve this, we must empower minds through education, spark creativity through imagination, and nurture the well-being of both individuals and communities.

A Wellspring of Empowerment: Unlocking the Human Spirit

The journey toward enlightenment begins with education. Education is not merely a tool for knowledge but a beacon that illuminates the path to empowerment and opportunity. By breaking down barriers to learning and fostering emotional intelligence, we create a world where curiosity flourishes, and every individual can contribute to the collective good.

A Symphony of Creativity: Transforming Imagination into Progress

Creativity is the spark that ignites progress, a force that propels humanity beyond the boundaries of what is and into the realm of what could be. By fostering artistic expression and interdisciplinary thinking, we inspire individuals to dream boldly and transform challenges into opportunities.

A Foundation of Flourishing: Nurturing Holistic Well-being

Human potential cannot thrive without a strong foundation of mental and physical well-being. Resilience, vitality, and emotional balance are the cornerstones of a flourishing society. By prioritizing holistic health for individuals and communities, we create the conditions for enduring progress and harmony.

The Call to Cultivate: Will You Nurture the Future?

The potential of humanity is limitless, but it must be nurtured to thrive. This is a call to action—not just for leaders and educators, but for every individual who seeks a brighter future. Together, we can ignite the spark of enlightenment, ensuring that human potential becomes the wellspring from which progress flows.

- **Empower Minds:** Advocate for equitable access to education and foster a culture of lifelong learning.

- **Inspire Creativity:** Encourage bold thinking and support the arts as a vital part of progress.

- **Champion Well-being:** Prioritize mental and physical health, ensuring that humanity flourishes in every sense.

The Wellspring Awaits: A Symphony of Human Potential

Humanity's future depends on its ability to cultivate the potential within each individual. Education, creativity, and well-being are not luxuries—they are the foundation of enlightenment, the keys to unlocking a brighter tomorrow.

Will you join the effort to nurture this wellspring of potential? Let your actions inspire minds, your vision ignite creativity, and your compassion build a foundation of well-being. Together, we can compose a symphony of human progress, a legacy of enlightenment that resonates through the ages.

A. Education as Empowerment

Promoting Equitable Access to Knowledge and Fostering Emotional Intelligence

Education is the spark that ignites human potential, the wellspring from which enlightenment flows. It empowers individuals to dream, innovate, and build a better world. As Nelson Mandela wisely said, *"Education is the most powerful weapon which you can use to change the world."* It is through education that societies break barriers, overcome inequities, and unlock the boundless creativity of their people.

True empowerment through education extends beyond knowledge acquisition. It nurtures emotional intelligence, cultivates empathy, and fosters resilience, ensuring that individuals are not only equipped to succeed but to contribute meaningfully to the collective progress of humanity.

Education as the Key to Opportunity

Equitable access to education is not a privilege but a right—a foundation upon which a fair and thriving society is built.

- **Breaking Barriers:** Imagine a world where socioeconomic limitations, geographical constraints, and cultural biases no longer restrict access to education. Envision global classrooms where students from diverse backgrounds learn and grow together.

- **Fostering Curiosity:** Education awakens curiosity and encourages critical thinking, providing individuals with the tools to explore new ideas and challenge assumptions.

- **Empowering the Underserved:** By ensuring education reaches every corner of the globe, we can uplift marginalized communities and create opportunities for all.

Nurturing Emotional Intelligence: The Heart of Empowerment

Education must nurture not only the intellect but also the heart. Emotional intelligence—the ability to understand and manage one's emotions and empathize with others—is essential for building meaningful relationships and driving collaborative progress.

- **Building Empathy:** Imagine an education system that prioritizes compassion, teaching students to understand diverse perspectives and foster unity.

- **Encouraging Resilience:** Education equips individuals to navigate adversity with confidence, transforming challenges into opportunities for growth.

- **Fostering Purpose:** By connecting knowledge with real-world impact, education instills a sense of purpose, inspiring individuals to contribute to the greater good.

A Call to Action: Championing Education for All

The transformative power of education lies in its ability to shape individuals and societies alike. To cultivate human potential, we must ensure that education is accessible, inclusive, and empowering.

- **Promote Access to Knowledge:** Advocate for policies and initiatives that eliminate barriers to education, ensuring that every individual has the opportunity to learn and grow.

- **Redefine Success:** Champion an education system that values emotional intelligence, creativity, and social responsibility alongside academic achievement.

- **Inspire Lifelong Learning:** Encourage a culture of curiosity and continuous growth, where education is a journey that lasts a lifetime.

The Wellspring Awaits: Will You Empower the Future?

Education is the foundation of enlightenment, the wellspring from which progress flows. By empowering individuals with knowledge, empathy, and resilience, we can unlock humanity's full potential.

Will you champion education as the key to a brighter future? Let your advocacy inspire, your actions empower, and your vision guide the way. Together, we can cultivate a world where learning knows no boundaries and human potential

knows no limits. The symphony of enlightenment awaits—let us play our part.

B. Fostering Creativity and Imagination

Encouraging Artistic Expression and Interdisciplinary Thinking as Catalysts for Progress

Creativity is the lifeblood of progress, the force that breathes life into innovation and transforms challenges into opportunities. It is the power to envision what does not yet exist, to explore beyond boundaries, and to weave imagination into reality. As Albert Einstein observed, *"Imagination is more important than knowledge. For knowledge is limited, whereas imagination embraces the entire world."*

By fostering creativity and interdisciplinary thinking, humanity can unlock new dimensions of progress. Artistic expression fuels innovation, and when combined with scientific and technical disciplines, it becomes a catalyst for groundbreaking solutions and transformative change.

Creativity as a Catalyst for Progress

Creativity is not confined to the arts—it is a universal skill that drives innovation in every field. By nurturing creative thinking, societies empower individuals to see the world through new lenses and reimagine what is possible.

- **Unleashing Artistic Expression:** Imagine a world where artistic expression flourishes, inspiring empathy, curiosity, and new ways of thinking. Art serves as a mirror for society, reflecting its hopes, struggles, and aspirations.

- **Encouraging Bold Ideas:** Creativity thrives in environments that embrace experimentation and risk-taking. Picture spaces where individuals feel empowered to challenge norms and push boundaries.

- **Fueling Innovation:** From engineering to education, creativity sparks solutions that bridge gaps, solve problems, and advance humanity.

Interdisciplinary Thinking: The Fusion of Ideas

Progress flourishes at the intersection of disciplines, where diverse perspectives combine to create holistic solutions. Interdisciplinary thinking is the art of connecting disparate ideas to address complex challenges.

- **Art Meets Science:** Imagine scientists and artists collaborating to create sustainable urban designs that are both functional and inspiring. Picture engineers working with musicians to harness sound as an energy source.

- **Breaking Down Silos:** Foster collaboration across fields, encouraging individuals to bring their unique expertise to shared goals. This integration generates ideas that are richer and more impactful than those born in isolation.

- **Seeing the Bigger Picture:** Interdisciplinary thinking teaches individuals to view problems from multiple angles, leading to solutions that are innovative and inclusive.

A Call to Action: Ignite the Spark of Creativity

To foster creativity and imagination, we must create environments where individuals feel free to dream, explore, and innovate. These environments must embrace diversity, celebrate curiosity, and encourage collaboration.

- **Champion Artistic Expression:** Support arts education, public art initiatives, and cultural exchanges that inspire creative thinking and community connection.

- **Promote Interdisciplinary Collaboration:** Break down barriers between disciplines, creating opportunities for people from different fields to work together on shared challenges.

- **Nurture a Culture of Innovation:** Encourage curiosity, experimentation, and resilience, fostering a mindset where mistakes are stepping stones to success.

The Wellspring of Creativity Awaits

Creativity and imagination are humanity's most powerful tools for shaping the future. They allow us to dream beyond what is and strive toward what could be. By fostering these qualities, we create a world where progress is not just possible but inevitable.

Will you embrace the power of creativity and imagination? Let your artistic vision inspire, your interdisciplinary ideas transform, and your boldness ignites a spark that fuels progress for generations to come. Together, we can compose a masterpiece of human ingenuity. The symphony of creativity awaits—let us begin.

C. Mental and Physical Well-being: The Foundation of Flourishing

Prioritizing Holistic Health and Resilience for Individuals and Communities

True progress cannot be achieved without a foundation of well-being. Mental and physical health are the cornerstones of a flourishing society, empowering individuals to live meaningful lives and contribute to the collective progress of humanity. As the ancient Roman poet Virgil wrote, *"The greatest wealth is health."* By prioritizing holistic health and resilience, we not only enhance individual potential but also strengthen the fabric of our communities.

In a world facing unprecedented challenges, from environmental changes to social inequalities, the well-being of individuals and communities is both a moral imperative and a practical necessity. A flourishing future begins with healthy minds and bodies.

Holistic Health: The Cornerstone of Prosperity

Holistic health encompasses mental, physical, and emotional well-being. It is the foundation upon which individuals and communities can thrive.

- **Mental Resilience:** Imagine a world where mental health is destigmatized and supported through accessible resources, fostering resilience and emotional intelligence. Envision communities that prioritize mindfulness and self-awareness as integral parts of education and daily life.

- **Physical Vitality:** Physical health enables individuals to pursue their goals and contribute to society. Picture cities designed to promote active lifestyles, with green spaces, walkable neighborhoods, and accessible healthcare.

- **Emotional Balance:** Emotional well-being is the thread that weaves together our interactions, decisions, and personal growth. Support systems that nurture emotional health create communities that are compassionate and cohesive.

Resilience as a Pillar of Progress

Resilience is the ability to adapt, recover, and thrive in the face of adversity. It is an essential skill for navigating the complexities of the modern world.

- **Building Personal Resilience:** Encourage practices such as mindfulness, physical activity, and meaningful social connections to help individuals build inner strength.

- **Fostering Community Resilience:** Resilient communities are those that support their members in times of need, respond to challenges collectively, and grow stronger through shared experiences.

- **Preparing for the Unknown:** Resilience enables societies to face future challenges with confidence and creativity, transforming obstacles into opportunities for growth.

A Call to Action: Cultivating Well-being for All

Promoting mental and physical well-being requires a commitment to creating environments and systems that prioritize health, resilience, and inclusivity.

- **Design for Health:** Advocate for policies and initiatives that make mental and physical health resources accessible to all. This includes healthcare, education, and infrastructure that supports active, balanced lifestyles.

- **Support Community Well-being:** Foster a culture of care where communities prioritize support, understanding, and collaboration.

- **Promote Balance and Purpose:** Encourage individuals to find balance in their lives, connecting personal goals with contributions to the greater good.

The Foundation Awaits: Will You Build a Thriving Future?

The well-being of individuals and communities is not a luxury—it is the foundation of a thriving, resilient, and harmonious world. By prioritizing health and resilience, we create the conditions for humanity to flourish.

Will you champion the cause of well-being? Let your actions inspire health, your commitment foster resilience and your vision guide humanity toward a flourishing future. Together, we can build a foundation of thriving minds, bodies, and communities. The symphony of well-being awaits—let us compose it together.

VII. TECHNOLOGY AS A STEWARD OF PROGRESS

Technology is the vessel that carries humanity toward the horizon of possibility. It is the steward of progress, holding the potential to address humanity's greatest challenges and amplify its brightest dreams. Yet, the power of technology is not in its mere existence but in how we guide it—shaped by ethical principles, driven by shared purpose, and anchored in a commitment to the greater good.

As Alan Kay famously said, *"The best way to predict the future is to invent it."* Technology grants humanity the tools to invent the future, but its impact depends on the choices we make today. Will it divide or unite? Will it exploit or empower? Will it serve a privileged few or uplift all of humanity? The answers to these questions lie in our hands.

The Three Pillars of Technological Stewardship

This section explores how technology can become a steward of progress, not by chance but through intentionality and purpose. Each pillar offers a vision of how technology, guided by humanity's highest ideals, can become a force for positive change:

- **The Promise of Ethical Innovation:** Technology must be grounded in equity, transparency, and accountability. Ethical innovation ensures that progress uplifts humanity protects its dignity, and honors its diversity.

- **Technology for Planetary Stewardship:** The planet is humanity's shared home, and technology is a powerful tool for its preservation. From combating climate change to fostering sustainable development, technology can help restore the Earth and protect it for generations to come.

- **Humanity and AI: A Harmonious Coexistence:** Artificial intelligence holds immense potential, but its true power lies in enhancing human creativity and problem-solving. A harmonious coexistence with AI ensures that it serves humanity as a partner, not a replacement.

Technology as a Force for Good

When guided by ethics and purpose, technology becomes more than a tool—it becomes a force for good, addressing humanity's most urgent needs and inspiring transformative progress. It can be a bridge between cultures, a catalyst for innovation, and a beacon of hope for a better tomorrow.

The Call to Stewardship: Will You Guide the Future?

The future of technology is not predetermined; it is a blank canvas awaiting the brushstrokes of humanity's collective will. This is a call to action for visionaries, innovators, and leaders to rise as stewards of progress, ensuring that technology reflects humanity's highest ideals.

- **Champion Ethical Principles:** Advocate for technology that serves humanity with fairness, inclusivity, and integrity.

- **Use Technology to Heal the Planet:** Leverage innovation to address environmental challenges and foster a sustainable relationship with the Earth.

- **Shape AI with Wisdom and Purpose:** Ensure that artificial intelligence amplifies human potential and aligns with ethical values.

The Symphony Awaits: A Legacy of Technological Harmony

Technology is not a force beyond our control—it is an extension of humanity's ingenuity and values. Its potential to transform the world is limitless, but its direction depends on the choices we make today.

Will you become a steward of progress? Let your vision guide innovation, your ethics anchor its development, and your actions shape a future where technology serves humanity and the planet. Together, we can compose a symphony of technological harmony—a legacy that uplifts, empowers, and unites. The stage is set. The future awaits. Let us create it together.

A. The Promise of Ethical Innovation

Ensuring Technology Serves Humanity Through Equity, Transparency, and Accountability

Technology is a powerful force capable of shaping the future in profound and unprecedented ways. It holds the potential to solve humanity's greatest challenges, from eradicating disease to mitigating climate change, yet it also carries the risk of deepening inequalities and amplifying harm if left unchecked. Ethical innovation is the promise that technology will serve humanity, guided by principles of equity, transparency, and accountability.

As Tim Berners-Lee, the inventor of the World Wide Web, once said, *"We need diversity of thought in the world to face the new challenges."* This sentiment underscores the need for intentional and ethical innovation—an approach that prioritizes human dignity, fairness, and the greater good.

Ethical Innovation: The Compass for Progress

Innovation without ethics is a ship that is adrift, directionless, and dangerous. Ethical principles provide the compass that ensures technology enhances lives rather than exploits them.

- **Equity as the Foundation:** Ethical innovation ensures that technology benefits all, not just the privileged few. Imagine a world where technological advancements address disparities, providing access to education, healthcare, and opportunities for everyone.

- **Transparency as the Guiding Light:** Transparency builds trust. Envision systems where algorithms, data, and decisions are open to scrutiny, ensuring fairness and preventing misuse.

- **Accountability as the Safeguard:** Accountability holds creators and users of technology responsible for its impact. Picture a future where companies, governments, and individuals work together to ensure that technology aligns with humanity's highest ideals.

The Role of Technology: A Steward, Not a Master

Technology should act as a steward of progress, amplifying humanity's potential while safeguarding its values.

- **Empowering Humanity:** Imagine AI systems designed to enhance creativity, augment education, and solve complex global challenges while respecting human agency.

- **Ethical Design:** Envision engineers and ethicists collaborating to develop technologies that prioritize safety, privacy, and inclusivity.

- **Sustainability Through Innovation:** Picture breakthroughs in renewable energy, sustainable agriculture, and environmental conservation, all driven by ethically guided technology.

A Call to Action: Building a Future of Responsible Innovation

Ethical innovation is not an ideal to strive for—it is a necessity. To ensure technology serves humanity, we must advocate for principles that prioritize fairness, inclusion, and accountability.

- **Champion Ethical Standards:** Advocate for policies and practices that require ethical considerations at every stage of technological development.

- **Foster Inclusive Innovation:** Ensure that diverse voices are involved in shaping technology, creating solutions that reflect humanity's full spectrum of needs and perspectives.

- **Engage in Critical Reflection:** As users, creators, and regulators of technology, we must continuously evaluate its impact, asking not only what is possible but what is right.

The Promise Awaits: Will You Be Its Keeper?

Technology is a tool, a means to an end, but it is humanity's responsibility to determine the direction it takes. The promise of ethical innovation lies in ensuring that every advancement contributes to a brighter, more equitable future.

Will you commit to the promise of ethical innovation? Let your principles guide your creations, your voice advocate for fairness, and your vision ensure that technology serves as a steward of progress. Together, we can compose a legacy where technology amplifies humanity's potential while

safeguarding its values. The future awaits—let us shape it with care and integrity.

B. Technology for Planetary Stewardship

Leveraging Innovation to Address Environmental Challenges and Create Sustainable Solutions

The planet is humanity's shared home, and its preservation is both a moral obligation and a necessity for survival. Technology holds the power to transform humanity's relationship with the Earth, offering solutions to some of the most pressing environmental challenges of our time. By leveraging innovation for planetary stewardship, we can create a future where humanity thrives in harmony with nature.

Rachel Carson, the pioneering environmentalist, warned us decades ago: *"Man is a part of nature, and his war against nature is inevitably a war against himself."* These words resonate even more profoundly today, urging us to embrace technology as a tool not for dominance but for partnership with the planet.

Technology as a Steward of the Planet

Technology, when guided by purpose and ethics, can play a pivotal role in safeguarding the Earth's ecosystems and resources.

- **Sustainable Energy Solutions:** Imagine a future powered entirely by renewable energy sources such as solar, wind, and geothermal, reducing humanity's reliance on fossil fuels and curbing greenhouse gas emissions.

- **Climate Mitigation Innovations:** Envision technologies that capture carbon from the atmosphere, restore degraded ecosystems, and protect vulnerable habitats from the effects of climate change.

- **Resource Efficiency:** Picture a world where AI and IoT optimize resource usage, reducing waste in agriculture, water management, and urban planning.

Innovation for Conservation and Renewal

Beyond mitigating harm, technology can help restore and regenerate the planet's natural systems, ensuring their vitality for generations to come.

- **Reforestation through Technology:** Drones and satellite imagery can support large-scale reforestation efforts, tracking growth and identifying areas in need of restoration.

- **Ocean Health Initiatives:** Advanced technologies like underwater robots and data analytics can monitor and restore marine ecosystems, addressing issues like overfishing and coral bleaching.

- **Circular Economy Systems:** Imagine a future where technology supports circular economies, minimizing waste and ensuring that materials are reused and repurposed instead of discarded.

A Call to Action: Innovating for Sustainability

Planetary stewardship through technology is not an abstract vision—it is a necessity. By aligning innovation with sustainability, humanity can reverse the damage caused by industrialization and build a future that honors the planet's delicate balance.

- **Invest in Green Technology:** Advocate for funding and policies that prioritize research and development in sustainable technologies.

- **Adopt and Scale Innovations:** Encourage widespread adoption of technologies that reduce environmental impact and improve efficiency.

- **Collaborate Across Sectors:** Foster partnerships between governments, businesses, and communities to ensure technological solutions are implemented equitably and effectively.

The Planet Awaits: Will You Be Its Steward?

The Earth has sustained humanity for millennia, but its future depends on the actions we take today. Technology offers the tools to protect, preserve, and renew our shared home, but its power must be guided by purpose and responsibility.

Will you harness innovation to safeguard the planet? Let your ingenuity drive sustainable solutions, your vision inspire global stewardship, and your actions restore the balance between humanity and nature. Together, we can compose a symphony of renewal, a legacy of care that echoes across generations. The Earth is calling—let us answer with innovation and commitment.

C. Humanity and AI: A Harmonious Coexistence

Enhancing Human Creativity and Problem-Solving Through Ethical AI Integration

Artificial intelligence (AI) is one of humanity's most powerful tools—an innovation with the potential to revolutionize creativity, problem-solving, and decision-making. Yet, its true promise lies in harmonious coexistence: leveraging AI to enhance human capabilities while safeguarding ethical principles and human dignity. As Stephen Hawking wisely said, *"Success in creating AI could be the biggest event in the history of our civilization. But it could also be the last unless we learn how to avoid the risks."*

To realize the full potential of AI, humanity must guide its development and integration with foresight, care, and an unwavering commitment to ethical principles. AI should not replace humanity but amplify its potential, ensuring progress that benefits all.

Enhancing Creativity and Problem-Solving Through AI

AI's power lies not in replacing human ingenuity but in augmenting it, providing tools that unlock new realms of possibility.

- **AI as a Creative Partner:** Imagine AI collaborating with artists, musicians, and writers to push the boundaries of creativity, generating novel ideas and reimagining traditional forms of expression.

- **Solving Complex Challenges:** Envision AI analyzing vast amounts of data to identify solutions to global issues, from climate change to healthcare disparities, at speeds impossible for humans alone.

- **Personalized Learning and Innovation:** Picture education systems where AI tailors learning experiences to individual needs, fostering creativity and critical thinking in students worldwide.

Ethical AI Integration: Safeguarding Humanity's Values

The integration of AI into society must prioritize ethics, ensuring that technological advancements respect humanity's core values of fairness, inclusivity, and accountability.

- **Transparency and Trust:** Imagine AI systems designed with open, interpretable algorithms, enabling users to understand how decisions are made and fostering trust.

- **Bias-Free Innovation:** Ethical AI development requires rigorous efforts to eliminate biases in data and algorithms, ensuring equitable outcomes for all individuals and communities.

- **Human-Centered Design:** Envision AI systems that prioritize the well-being of their users, designed not to exploit but to empower.

AI as a Force for Good

AI's potential extends beyond efficiency and innovation; it has the capacity to be a transformative force for good, addressing humanity's most pressing needs.

- **Advancing Healthcare:** Imagine AI diagnosing diseases earlier, personalizing treatments, and supporting medical research to improve outcomes globally.

- **Sustainability Solutions:** Picture AI optimizing energy usage, predicting environmental risks, and supporting efforts to combat climate change.

- **Building Inclusive Communities:** Envision AI fostering inclusivity by enabling greater accessibility for individuals with disabilities and enhancing global connectivity.

A Call to Action: Shaping a Harmonious Future with AI

Harmonious coexistence with AI requires proactive stewardship. It is not enough to create intelligent systems; humanity must guide their development to align with ethical principles and the greater good.

- **Advocate for Ethical AI Development:** Support policies and initiatives that prioritize transparency, accountability, and inclusivity in AI systems.

- **Promote Collaboration Across Fields:** Foster partnerships between technologists, ethicists, artists, and policymakers to ensure AI serves humanity holistically.

- **Empower the Next Generation:** Equip future leaders with the skills and values needed to shape AI's development responsibly and effectively.

The Symphony Awaits: Will You Conduct the Harmony?

AI is not a solitary instrument but a powerful section in humanity's symphony. When integrated thoughtfully and ethically, it harmonizes with human ingenuity to create a brighter, more inclusive future.

Will you join the effort to shape a harmonious coexistence with AI? Let your creativity drive its potential, your principles guide its integration, and your actions ensure its legacy serves all of humanity. Together, we can compose a symphony where humanity and AI thrive side by side. The baton is yours—the harmony awaits.

VIII. A LEGACY FOR THE AGES: THE TIMELESS IMPACT OF TOMORROW

A legacy is more than what we leave behind—it is the promise we make to the future. It is the bridge between generations, the enduring impact of our choices, and the echo of our actions that resonates across time. To build a legacy for the ages is to recognize that the decisions we make today will shape not only our world but the lives of those yet to come. As Maya Angelou wisely said, *"Your legacy is every life you've touched."*

This is a call to think beyond the immediacy of the present and embrace a long-term vision rooted in responsibility, creativity, and foresight. It is an invitation to create enduring systems, timeless ideas, and a shared future that reflects humanity's highest aspirations.

The Three Pillars of a Lasting Legacy

The creation of a timeless impact requires a commitment to three interconnected pillars, each essential to ensuring that humanity thrives not only today but for generations to come:

- **Intergenerational Responsibility:** Recognize the profound impact of your actions on future generations. By investing in long-term prosperity and safeguarding cultural heritage, we lay the foundation for a thriving future.

- **The Path to Immortality:** Ideas and innovations that endure are humanity's greatest monuments. Through the creation of transformative systems and the sharing of timeless wisdom, we can inspire progress that transcends the boundaries of time.

- **Preparing for the Unknown:** The future is uncertain, but preparation ensures that humanity can adapt, explore, and expand its potential. By developing resilience and embracing exploration, we secure a legacy of courage and adaptability.

A Legacy Beyond Time: The Promise of Possibility

To create a legacy for the ages is to act with the understanding that our time is but one chapter in humanity's story. It is the willingness to imagine a brighter future and take bold steps to bring it to life.

- **Investing in Tomorrow:** Let every action you take reflect a commitment to progress that endures, ensuring that the world we leave behind is richer and more resilient.

- **Inspiring Through Wisdom:** Share knowledge, values, and stories that guide and empower future generations, ensuring that they carry forward the lessons of today.

- **Exploring the Boundless Unknown:** Dare to look beyond the horizon, preparing humanity to thrive in the face of uncertainty and discover its place among the stars.

The Call to Legacy: Will You Shape the Future?

The creation of a timeless legacy is not the work of one individual—it is a collective effort that requires courage, vision, and unity. Each choice, no matter how small, contributes to the tapestry of progress.

- **Be the Guardian of Tomorrow:** Protect and nurture the resources, values, and wisdom that future generations will inherit.

- **Build Bridges Across Time:** Create systems, innovations, and ideas that connect today's progress to tomorrow's possibilities.

- **Dream Boldly and Act Wisely:** Embrace the unknown with curiosity, determination, and an unwavering commitment to humanity's potential.

The Symphony Awaits: Compose a Legacy That Echoes

The legacy of humanity is written in the lives we touch, the ideas we create, and the future we prepare. It is a melody that spans generations, a testament to the power of collective action and enduring vision.

Will you answer the call to shape a legacy for the ages? Let your actions resonate with purpose, your ideas inspire timeless progress, and your courage prepare humanity for the

unknown. Together, we can compose a symphony of impact—a legacy that echoes through time, illuminating the path for generations to come. The baton is yours. Let the symphony begin.

A. Intergenerational Responsibility

Investing in Long-Term Prosperity and Safeguarding Cultural Heritage

The legacy we leave behind is not just the culmination of our actions but the foundation upon which future generations will build. Intergenerational responsibility is the commitment to invest in long-term prosperity and protect the cultural heritage that defines who we are. It is the recognition that the decisions we make today echo through time, shaping the lives of those who come after us.

As the Haudenosaunee (Iroquois) philosophy reminds us, *"In every deliberation, we must consider the impact of our decisions on the next seven generations."* This principle calls us to act not for immediate gain but with foresight, ensuring that the torch of progress is passed forward, burning brighter with each new hand that carries it.

The Stewardship of Prosperity

Intergenerational responsibility is rooted in the idea that prosperity is not a fleeting achievement but a sustained effort that benefits all.

- **Building Long-Term Systems:** Imagine governments, businesses, and communities investing in infrastructure, education, and healthcare systems designed to endure and evolve, ensuring opportunities for generations to come.

- **Balancing Present and Future Needs:** Envision a world where policies prioritize sustainability, ensuring that today's actions do not deplete the resources needed by tomorrow's inhabitants.

- **Fostering Innovation for Continuity:** Picture innovations designed with long-term adaptability, creating solutions that evolve alongside humanity's needs.

Preserving Cultural Heritage: The Story of Humanity

Our cultural heritage is the story of who we are—a tapestry of traditions, values, and knowledge that connects us to our past and guides our future.

- **Protecting History:** Imagine historical landmarks, art, and literature preserved not only as relics but as living lessons for future generations to learn from and build upon.

- **Celebrating Diversity:** Envision a world where the unique traditions and identities of every culture are celebrated and safeguarded, enriching humanity's collective identity.

- **Teaching Wisdom Across Generations:** Picture elders sharing their experiences and values with younger generations, creating a continuum of knowledge that informs progress.

A Call to Action: Leaving a Lasting Legacy

Intergenerational responsibility demands action. It is not enough to hope for a better future; we must actively shape it, ensuring that the legacy we leave is one of prosperity, understanding, and unity.

- **Invest in the Future:** Advocate for policies and initiatives that prioritize education, sustainability, and equitable opportunities for all.

- **Preserve Cultural Richness:** Support efforts to protect cultural heritage, ensuring that humanity's story remains vibrant and accessible.

- **Act with Foresight:** Consider the long-term impact of your choices, acting not only for immediate benefit but for the well-being of future generations.

The Tapestry Awaits: Will You Weave the Future?

The legacy we create is the greatest gift we can offer to those who come after us. By acting with responsibility and foresight, we ensure that the foundation we lay today becomes a stepping stone for tomorrow's progress.

Will you embrace the responsibility to shape a lasting legacy? Let your actions invest in prosperity, your vision preserve heritage, and your choices inspire generations to come. Together, we can compose a legacy that resonates through the ages—a timeless impact that defines humanity's potential. The loom is ready. Let us weave the future.

B. The Path to Immortality: Ideas that Endure

Building Enduring Monuments of Progress and Passing Down Timeless Wisdom

Humanity's greatest achievements are not bound by time but live on as enduring legacies—monuments to progress, ideas that shape the world, and wisdom that guides generations. Immortality is not found in the fleeting moments of life but in the lasting impact of ideas and actions that ripple across time. As Marcus Aurelius wisely said, *"What we do now echoes in eternity."*

The path to immortality lies in the creation of enduring ideas, innovations, and values that inspire future generations to dream bigger, think deeper, and strive for greater heights. It is the art of building a legacy that transcends the present, weaving the brilliance of today into the fabric of tomorrow.

Enduring Monuments of Progress

The most profound monuments are not made of stone or steel but of ideas that endure—concepts, systems, and creations that continue to shape the world long after their inception.

- **Innovations That Transform:** Imagine technologies, scientific discoveries, and artistic creations that redefine possibilities and inspire humanity for generations. These are the monuments of progress that leave an indelible mark on history.

- **Institutions That Last:** Picture systems of governance, education, and healthcare built on principles of equity and adaptability, ensuring they evolve with humanity's changing needs.

- **Cultural Treasures:** Envision art, music, and literature that encapsulate the essence of an era, preserving its values, struggles, and triumphs for those who follow.

Timeless Wisdom: The Gift of Knowledge

Wisdom is humanity's most enduring inheritance. By passing down knowledge, values, and lessons learned, we create a bridge between generations, ensuring that progress is informed by the experiences of the past.

- **Lessons from History:** Imagine a world where historical insights guide decisions, helping societies avoid the pitfalls of the past while building on its successes.

- **Teaching Values That Transcend Time:** Picture a culture where empathy, integrity, and resilience are passed down as guiding principles, shaping the character of future generations.

- **Mentorship as a Legacy:** Envision individuals sharing their expertise and life experiences to empower others, creating a ripple effect of growth and enlightenment.

A Call to Action: Composing a Legacy That Lasts

Creating enduring monuments of progress and passing down timeless wisdom is not the task of a chosen few—it is a call to action for everyone. Each contribution, no matter how small, adds to humanity's collective legacy.

- **Create with Purpose:** Let your work reflect values and ideas that stand the test of time, inspiring others to continue what you begin.

- **Share Your Knowledge:** Act as a mentor, teacher, or guide, ensuring that the wisdom you've gained becomes a resource for others.

- **Build for Tomorrow:** Design solutions, systems, and structures that prioritize sustainability, adaptability, and long-term impact.

The Legacy Awaits: Will You Shape Immortality?

Immortality is not a promise but a choice—the decision to create something greater than oneself, to invest in ideas and actions that endure. The monuments of progress and the wisdom we pass down become the echoes of our lives, resonating through the ages.

Will you contribute to humanity's enduring legacy? Let your ideas inspire, your wisdom guide, and your creations stand as monuments to progress. Together, we can compose a symphony of timeless impact—a legacy that ensures humanity thrives long after we are gone. The path to immortality awaits—let us begin.

C. Preparing for the Unknown

Developing Strategies for Uncertainty and Expanding Humanity's Reach Beyond Earth

The unknown is humanity's greatest frontier—a vast, uncharted expanse that holds both challenges and opportunities. To prepare for the unknown is to embrace uncertainty with courage, foresight, and adaptability. It is the call to imagine beyond the present, to innovate solutions for challenges we cannot yet foresee, and to expand humanity's reach beyond the confines of Earth. As Carl Sagan profoundly said, *"Exploration is in our nature. We began as wanderers, and we are wanderers still."*

The journey into the unknown requires resilience, creativity, and a collective will to confront the unforeseen with boldness. By embracing uncertainty as a catalyst for progress, humanity can transform the unpredictable into the extraordinary.

Strategies for Navigating Uncertainty

The future is inherently uncertain, but preparation ensures that humanity can adapt and thrive in the face of the unexpected.

- **Building Resilient Systems:** Imagine societies designed with flexibility and foresight, capable of adapting to environmental, social, and technological changes without losing their foundation of stability.

- **Harnessing the Power of Innovation:** Picture innovations that address unforeseen challenges—AI systems that predict and mitigate natural disasters, or healthcare advancements that prepare for future pandemics.

- **Fostering a Mindset of Adaptability:** Envision education systems that emphasize critical thinking, creativity, and problem-solving, equipping individuals with the skills to navigate an ever-changing world.

Expanding Humanity's Reach Beyond Earth

To prepare for the unknown is also to look beyond our planetary boundaries, exploring the vast universe that lies ahead. The stars call to us, offering both inspiration and the promise of survival.

- **Space Exploration as a Catalyst:** Imagine missions to Mars, the Moon, and beyond, advancing humanity's understanding of the universe while unlocking technologies that benefit life on Earth.

- **Ensuring Humanity's Survival:** Picture colonies on other planets, safeguarding humanity against existential threats while fostering a spirit of exploration and discovery.

- **The Search for Knowledge:** Envision space exploration not as an escape but as an expansion, a journey to uncover the mysteries of existence and connect with the cosmos.

The Power of Collective Preparation

Preparing for the unknown requires a united effort—governments, scientists, educators, and communities working together to anticipate challenges and seize opportunities.

- **Collaborative Innovation:** Encourage partnerships across disciplines, nations, and cultures to tackle humanity's greatest uncertainties with collective wisdom.

- **Global Resilience Initiatives:** Advocate for global policies and practices that prioritize preparedness, sustainability, and equity.

- **Inspiring a Visionary Spirit:** Foster a culture that celebrates curiosity and exploration, inspiring future generations to dream boldly and think expansively.

A Call to Action: Embracing the Unknown

The unknown is not a barrier but a gateway—a call to prepare, to explore, and to create. It challenges humanity to think beyond immediate needs, to envision what could be, and to act with purpose and resilience.

- **Plan for Possibilities:** Develop strategies that embrace flexibility and adaptability, ensuring readiness for the challenges of tomorrow.

- **Dream Beyond Boundaries:** Support exploration, innovation, and discovery that push humanity to new heights and broaden our understanding of the universe.

- **Inspire the Next Generation:** Encourage young minds to embrace uncertainty as an opportunity for growth, creativity, and adventure.

The Future Awaits: Will You Prepare?

The unknown holds infinite potential, but its promise can only be realized through intentional action. Preparing for the future means building a legacy of resilience, exploration, and adaptability—a foundation for progress that transcends the limits of today.

Will you rise to meet the unknown? Let your imagination guide you, your preparation empower you, and your courage inspire others to join the journey. Together, we can compose a future that thrives in the face of uncertainty and reaches for the stars. The symphony of the unknown awaits—let us play it boldly.

IX. THE FINAL MOVEMENT: A WORLD UNITED IN PURPOSE

The greatest symphony humanity will ever compose is one of unity—a harmonious melody where every voice matters, every perspective is valued, and every action contributes to a shared vision of progress. In this final movement, we are called not only to recognize our interconnectedness but to act on it, transcending borders, cultures, and generations to create a world united in purpose. As Martin Luther King Jr. eloquently said, *"We are caught in an inescapable network of mutuality, tied in a single garment of destiny. Whatever affects one directly affects all indirectly."*

This is the culmination of humanity's collective journey—a moment to weave together the threads of knowledge, empathy, courage, and vision into a tapestry that reflects the very best of who we are. It is a call to embrace the symphony of one humanity, to ensure that the progress of today becomes the foundation for the dreams of tomorrow, and to leave behind a legacy that inspires future generations to reach even greater heights.

The Symphony of One Humanity: Transcending Borders

Humanity's challenges know no boundaries, and neither should our solutions. By transcending divisions and celebrating diversity, we can create a global identity rooted in shared values and collective action.

- **Unity as Strength:** Imagine a world where nations, cultures, and individuals come together to address shared challenges, transforming differences into opportunities for collaboration.

- **Diversity as Harmony:** Picture a global chorus where each culture, tradition, and voice adds depth and beauty to the melody of progress.

- **Shared Goals:** Envision united humanity striving toward equity, sustainability, and justice for all.

The Legacy We Leave Behind: Building for Tomorrow

The final movement is not just about what we achieve today but about the foundation we lay for the future. It is the promise we make to generations yet to come—a commitment to leave the world better than we found it.

- **Progress as a Gift:** The advancements we make today must inspire hope and opportunity for those who follow.

- **Wisdom as a Guide:** By passing down knowledge, traditions, and values, we empower future generations to continue humanity's story with resilience and purpose.

- **Dreams as the Compass:** The legacy we leave is not just a reflection of our past but a beacon that guides the imaginations of tomorrow's leaders and dreamers.

A Call to Unity: The Final Movement

This is the moment for humanity to come together as one, to act not as isolated individuals or nations but as a unified force for good. Each of us has a role to play in composing the final movement of this symphony—a legacy of unity, progress, and shared purpose.

- **Be the Architect of Harmony:** Foster connections across divides, building bridges of understanding and cooperation.

- **Inspire the Next Generation:** Act with foresight and generosity, ensuring that the dreams of tomorrow are built on the progress of today.

- **Embrace the Universal Melody:** Recognize that humanity's collective strength lies in its diversity and interconnectedness.

The Symphony Awaits: Will You Join the Chorus?

The final movement is more than an idea; it is a call to action, a challenge to each of us to contribute to the melody of a world united in purpose. It asks us to imagine a future where unity is not an aspiration but a reality, where progress is not fleeting but enduring, and where humanity stands together, bound by shared values and dreams.

Will you add your voice to the symphony of one humanity? Let your actions harmonize with others, your vision inspire unity, and your legacy guide the world toward a brighter future. Together, we can compose a final movement that echoes through the ages—a testament to what humanity can achieve when united in purpose. The baton is raised. Let us play as one.

A. The Symphony of One Humanity

Transcending Borders to Create a Global Identity Rooted in Shared Values

Humanity's greatest achievements are born not in isolation but in unity. The challenges we face—climate change, inequality, and conflict—are universal, and so too must be the solutions. To compose the symphony of one humanity is to transcend borders, celebrate diversity, and create a global identity rooted in shared values and collective purpose. As Ban Ki-moon reminds us, *"Saving our planet, lifting people out of poverty, advancing economic growth... these are one and the same fight. We must connect the dots between climate change, water scarcity, energy shortages, global health, and food security. Solutions to one problem must be solutions for all."*

This symphony is a call for humanity to act as one, to embrace its shared destiny, and to harmonize its efforts in pursuit of a brighter future.

Transcending Borders: A Shared Global Identity

Borders are lines drawn on maps, but the connections between people transcend those divisions. The symphony of one humanity envisions a world where collaboration replaces conflict, and unity becomes the foundation for progress.

- **A Universal Perspective:** Imagine a future where people see themselves not just as citizens of nations but as members of a global community, working together to address shared challenges.

- **Celebrating Diversity:** Diversity is not a barrier but a strength. Picture a world where cultural differences enrich the global identity, fostering creativity, understanding, and innovation.

- **Global Goals, Local Action:** Envision nations aligning their policies and actions to contribute to collective global goals, from sustainability to human rights.

Shared Values: The Harmony of Humanity

A united world is rooted in shared values—principles that reflect the common aspirations of all people and guide humanity toward collective flourishing.

- **Equity and Justice:** Imagine a world where access to resources, opportunities, and rights is not determined by geography or circumstance but by the inherent dignity of every human being.

- **Empathy and Understanding:** Picture societies that prioritize compassion and understanding, fostering connections across cultural, ideological, and geographical divides.

- **Sustainability and Stewardship:** Envision global efforts to protect the planet, ensuring that humanity thrives in harmony with the Earth and its ecosystems.

A Call to Action: Composing the Symphony of One Humanity

To transcend borders and create a united world, we must act with intention, courage, and collaboration. Each individual has a role to play in building bridges, fostering understanding, and contributing to a global identity.

- **Advocate for Unity:** Champion policies, initiatives, and actions that prioritize collaboration over division and shared progress over individual gain.

- **Celebrate Diversity:** Embrace cultural differences as a source of strength, promoting exchanges that enrich humanity's collective identity.

- **Lead with Empathy:** Let compassion guide your actions, ensuring that progress benefits all members of the global community.

The Final Movement: Will You Join the Symphony?

The symphony of one humanity is not a dream—it is a vision within our grasp, a melody waiting to be composed through shared purpose and collective action. To unite the world is to recognize that what binds us is greater than what divides us and that our shared future depends on our ability to act as one.

Will you join the symphony of one humanity? Let your actions transcend borders, your vision inspire unity, and your values guide the way. Together, we can compose a legacy of harmony, justice, and hope—a final movement that echoes through the ages. The orchestra awaits. Let us play as one.

B. The Legacy We Leave Behind

Ensuring the Progress of Today Becomes the Foundation for the Dreams of Tomorrow

A legacy is not merely the sum of what we achieve; it is the promise we make to the future. It is the bridge between generations, carrying the wisdom of the past and the progress of the present into the dreams of tomorrow. The legacy we leave behind is our greatest gift—a foundation upon which future generations can build, dream, and thrive. As John F. Kennedy profoundly stated, *"We celebrate the past to awaken the future."*

This is a call to ensure that the progress we make today is not fleeting but enduring. It is a call to act with purpose, to create with intention, and to leave behind a world that inspires hope, fosters growth, and reflects the best of humanity.

Building a Foundation for the Future

The progress of today must serve as a sturdy foundation for tomorrow, providing the tools and opportunities for future generations to thrive.

- **Sustainability as the Cornerstone:** Imagine a world where environmental stewardship ensures that the planet's resources are preserved and nurtured for generations to come.

- **Education as a Catalyst:** Picture systems of education that not only impart knowledge but inspire curiosity, creativity, and critical thinking in every individual.

- **Innovation as a Legacy:** Envision technologies and systems designed to evolve, adapting to humanity's changing needs while addressing the challenges of the future.

Inspiring the Dreams of Tomorrow

The legacy we leave is not just what we build but how we inspire. By fostering a culture of hope, resilience, and possibility, we can ignite the imaginations of those who will shape the world to come.

- **Empowering Future Generations:** Imagine young minds equipped with the tools, resources, and confidence to dream boldly and innovate fearlessly.

- **Preserving Cultural Identity:** Picture a world where traditions, art, and stories are preserved as living legacies, guiding humanity's path forward while celebrating its roots.

- **Creating Opportunities:** Ensure that the doors of opportunity are open to all, breaking down barriers and empowering every individual to contribute to humanity's collective progress.

A Call to Action: Crafting a Timeless Legacy

The legacy we leave behind is shaped by the choices we make today. To ensure the progress of today becomes the foundation for tomorrow's dreams, we must act with foresight, responsibility, and unity.

- **Act with Intention:** Make decisions that prioritize long-term impact over short-term gains, building systems that endure and inspire.

- **Empower and Uplift:** Advocate for equity and opportunity, ensuring that the progress we make benefits all members of society.

- **Celebrate the Present, Invest in the Future:** Recognize the value of today's achievements while laying the groundwork for tomorrow's possibilities.

The Legacy Awaits: Will You Build It?

The legacy we leave is not a reflection of our past but a beacon for the future. It is an invitation to contribute, to inspire, and to ensure that humanity's progress continues to resonate across generations.

Will you shape the legacy of tomorrow? Let your actions reflect purpose, your vision ignite inspiration, and your choices create a foundation for dreams yet to be imagined. Together, we can compose a legacy of progress and possibility—a testament to humanity's enduring potential. The baton is yours. Let us begin.

X. REWEAVING THE FABRIC OF HUMANITY

Humanity's story is an ever-evolving composition, a symphony woven from the threads of countless lives, aspirations, and shared dreams. Yet, in moments of dissonance—amidst challenges that divide and crises that test our resilience—it becomes clear that the fabric of our narrative must be reimagined. This is not a call to abandon the progress of the past but to reweave it into a tapestry that reflects the values of harmony, inclusivity, and collective purpose. As Desmond Tutu once said, *"My humanity is bound up in yours, for we can only be human together."*

To reweave the fabric of humanity is to redefine progress, not as the triumph of a few but as the harmonious endeavor of all. It is to rewrite the score of humanity, crafting a melody that celebrates unity, respects diversity, and aspires to a future where every voice contributes to the grand composition of progress.

The Fabric of Humanity: Threads of Connection

The threads that bind us—empathy, equity, and shared purpose—are the foundation of a thriving and resilient world. By strengthening these connections, we create a society where collaboration replaces conflict and compassion overcomes division.

- **Building Trust:** Imagine a world where understanding and respect guide interactions, fostering bonds that unite communities and transcend borders.

- **Celebrating Diversity:** Picture a tapestry enriched by the unique contributions of every culture, perspective, and individual, creating a collective identity that is both vibrant and enduring.

- **Shared Aspirations:** Envision a future where progress is defined by the well-being of all, not the success of a few.

A New Symphony: Rewriting the Narrative

To rewrite the score of humanity is to challenge old paradigms and reimagine what progress can mean. It is an opportunity to harmonize our ambitions with our values, ensuring that the melody of the future reflects our highest ideals.

- **Progress as a Collective Endeavor:** Redefine success as the achievement of shared goals, where no one is left behind, and every effort contributes to the greater good.

- **Unity in Action:** Foster global collaboration to address humanity's most pressing challenges, transforming differences into strengths.

- **A Vision of Hope:** Craft a narrative that inspires generations to dream boldly, act with compassion, and believe in the power of unity.

The Call to Reweave: Will You Join the Movement?

This is humanity's moment to act—to reweave the threads of connection, rewrite the narrative of progress, and create a future where harmony prevails. The baton is in our hands, and the symphony awaits our contributions.

- **Reweave the Tapestry:** Strengthen the bonds that connect humanity, ensuring that the fabric of our society reflects compassion, equity, and resilience.

- **Redefine Progress:** Advocate for a vision of success that prioritizes inclusivity, sustainability, and shared prosperity.

- **Inspire Through Leadership:** Be a voice that calls others to action, demonstrating the values of empathy, collaboration, and hope.

The Symphony Awaits: Let Us Reimagine Together

The fabric of humanity is not frayed beyond repair—it is ready to be rewoven, stronger, and more harmonious than ever before. By embracing this moment, we can create a legacy of unity and progress that echoes through the ages.

Will you help rewrite the score of humanity? Let your actions compose a melody of hope, your vision inspire a narrative of purpose, and your courage reweave the fabric of our shared story. Together, we can create a future where humanity's greatest symphony is yet to be played. Let us begin.

A. Rewriting the Score of Humanity

Redefining the Narrative of Progress as a Harmonious and Collective Endeavor

Humanity's narrative is one of resilience, creativity, and boundless potential. Yet, as we confront the challenges of the modern age—climate change, inequality, and fractured societies—it is clear that the score we have followed needs to be rewritten. Progress must no longer be defined by competition or individual gain but by harmony, collaboration, and shared purpose. As Barack Obama once said, *"The arc of the moral universe may bend toward justice, but it doesn't bend on its own."*

Rewriting the score of humanity means reimagining our collective story. It is a call to reweave the fabric of our societies with threads of empathy, equity, and innovation, crafting a melody that celebrates connection and shared achievement.

Redefining Progress: A Collective Melody

The narrative of progress must shift from one of isolated accomplishments to one of collective success, where every voice contributes to a harmonious whole.

- **From Competition to Collaboration:** Imagine a world where nations, communities, and individuals unite to solve shared challenges, prioritizing mutual benefit over rivalry.

- **Progress for All:** Picture a future where no one is left behind, where opportunities are created for everyone to thrive, and where success is measured by the well-being of all.

- **Harmony in Diversity:** Envision societies that celebrate differences, understanding that diversity is the key to resilience and creativity.

The Fabric of Humanity: Weaving Connection

Reweaving the fabric of humanity requires us to strengthen the bonds that connect us, fostering trust, understanding, and cooperation across every divide.

- **Building Bridges, Not Walls:** Let empathy guide us in dismantling barriers of prejudice, ignorance, and fear, replacing them with connections that unite.

- **Amplifying Shared Stories:** Celebrate the stories and contributions of all people, creating a narrative that reflects the richness and complexity of humanity.

- **Cultivating Global Citizenship:** Encourage individuals to see themselves as part of a global community responsible for the well-being of both their neighbors and the planet.

A Call to Reimagine Humanity's Score

The score of humanity is not set in stone—it is a living composition, one that can be rewritten to reflect our highest ideals and aspirations. This is a call to action for all of us to become the composers of a new symphony, one that harmonizes progress with purpose and innovation with compassion.

- **Embrace the Power of Unity:** Actively seek opportunities to collaborate across cultures, disciplines, and perspectives, creating solutions that serve the greater good.

- **Redefine Success:** Advocate for a definition of progress that prioritizes equity, sustainability, and shared prosperity.

- **Inspire Through Action:** Lead by example, demonstrating the values of empathy, inclusion, and collective responsibility.

The Final Composition: Will You Rewrite the Score?

This is humanity's moment to redefine its narrative and reimagine progress as a shared endeavor that uplifts and unites. The future depends on our willingness to rewrite the score, ensuring that the melody of humanity reflects its greatest strengths—resilience, creativity, and compassion.

Will you help reweave the fabric of humanity? Let your vision inspire a new narrative, your actions compose a harmonious melody, and your courage guide us toward a collective future.

Together, we can rewrite the score of humanity—a symphony of unity and progress that echoes through the ages. The baton is in your hand. Let us begin anew.

Closing Reflection: A Light to Guide the Generations

This chapter, *Whispers from the Future: A Guide to an Enlightened Tomorrow*, serves as both a roadmap and a call to action—a guide for those who seek to shape a brighter, more harmonious future. Within its pages, the principles of progress, empathy, resilience, and sustainability intertwine to create a symphony of human potential. It is a legacy of wisdom and a testament to what humanity can achieve when united in purpose and driven by shared values.

The Guardians of Progress: Humanity's Greatest Symphony

As we conclude this symphony of ideas, we envision humanity as a grand orchestra, each individual contributing a unique melody to the performance. The instruments—knowledge, collaboration, courage, empathy, innovation, and sustainability—combine to create a masterpiece greater than the sum of its parts. Together, they compose the music of progress, a sound that transcends time, borders, and divisions.

This is the promise of an enlightened tomorrow: a world where unity strengthens diversity, where progress uplifts all, and where the whispers of the future inspire boundless possibilities.

A Torch for the Generations to Come

To those who inherit this vision: you are the stewards of humanity's symphony, the guardians of a legacy built upon the principles presented here. Your choices will shape the destiny of the world, just as the actions of those before you have laid the foundation for your journey.

Let courage guide you, for the path forward may be fraught with challenges. Let empathy unite you, for progress is born from understanding. Let knowledge empower you, for wisdom is the light that illuminates the unknown. Let sustainability ground you, for the Earth is your shared home, and its stewardship is your greatest responsibility.

Together We Ascend: A Symphony of Human Potential

Picture a future where these principles are not merely ideals but lived truths—a world where individual potential harmonizes with collective action, creating a melody that resonates with hope and triumph. The echoes of tomorrow call upon you to embrace persistence, nurture these principles, and become the virtuosos of humanity's greatest composition.

The baton is raised, the orchestra assembled, and the opening notes of a brighter future hang in the air. The stage is set for the generations to come to carry forth the symphony of progress.

The Choice Is Yours: Will You Join the Symphony?

The whispers of the future are not faint—they are a clarion call urging humanity to rise to its highest potential. This is your moment to answer, pick up your instrument, and join the chorus of progress. Will you be a passive observer, or will you take your place as a conductor, leading humanity toward a harmonious and enlightened tomorrow?

The baton is in your hands. The music awaits. Let your actions compose a legacy of hope, let your vision inspire a symphony of progress, and let your courage echo through the ages. Together, we can create a future that stands as

humanity's greatest triumph—a symphony for the ages. The choice is yours. Let us begin.

REWEAVING THE FABRIC OF HUMANITY

ઠ૭ઠ૭ઠ૭

I n the grand symphony of existence, humanity stands poised at the precipice of a new era. The dissonant chords of division and discord threaten to overwhelm the melody of our shared destiny, yet within the discord lies an unyielding truth: the power to compose a brighter tomorrow rests within us all.

This is not the first time we have faced such a cacophony. History whispers of civilizations that transcended the chaos of their times, uniting under banners of empathy, wisdom, and innovation. They built not just monuments of stone but of spirit—gleaming testaments to human potential and resolve. Let us draw strength from their legacy as we craft our own.

Imagine a world reborn, where knowledge flows freely like the rivers that nourish the earth, where verdant cities hum with the harmony of nature and innovation. Picture the brilliance of diverse minds converging, creating a tapestry that celebrates every culture, every story, every voice. These are not distant dreams but blueprints waiting to be realized, echoes of a future that calls to us.

The Weavers of Tomorrow

We are the architects of this vision, the weavers tasked with mending the fabric of humanity. Let empathy be the golden thread that binds us, and let collaboration form the loom upon which our shared destiny is crafted. Together, we must compose a melody that bridges divides, celebrates diversity, and rises above the dissonance.

Like the travelers in ancient tales embarking on perilous quests to restore balance, we, too, must embrace our role as stewards of progress. Knowledge is our compass, empathy our anchor, and innovation our guiding star. Each of us holds an instrument, and every note we play contributes to the harmony of our collective endeavor.

A Symphony of Progress

The challenges before us are profound—climate change, social inequity, and existential uncertainty. Yet within each challenge lies the seed of transformation. As we face these trials, let us remember that no single voice can carry the melody alone. It is through unity that we find strength, through diversity that we find innovation, and through collaboration that we achieve greatness.

Imagine disagreements transformed into opportunities for counterpoint, where differing perspectives weave a richer tapestry of solutions. Envision innovation ignited by the sparks of shared ideas, transcending borders and barriers. Picture a humanity that does not merely survive but flourishes, reaching heights once deemed impossible.

The Call to Action

Rise, Guardians of the Future! Let this moment be the overture to a grand symphony of progress. Pick up your instruments—your knowledge, your creativity, your compassion—and play your part. The world needs your melody, your harmony, and your unwavering commitment to the collective good.

The conductor awaits, baton raised. The first note hangs in the air, trembling with anticipation. This is your moment to join the orchestra and contribute your voice to the masterpiece that will echo through the ages.

Together, we can rewrite the score of humanity, crafting a legacy of hope, resilience, and boundless potential. Let us rise, not as isolated notes, but as a unified chorus. Let us reforge the destiny of humanity with purpose and passion.

The symphony of a united world awaits. Play your part. The future depends on it.

CONCLUSION TO THE ARCANUM OF AWARENESS SERIES

EVOLVING INTO ENLIGHTENMENT: A NEW ERA OF HUMANITY

ᲖᲔᲖᲔᲖᲔ

In the name of Allah, the Entirely Merciful, the Especially Merciful.

[By the ʿpassage ofʾ time! (1) Surely humanity is in ʿgraveʾ loss, (2) Except those who have faith, do good, and urge each other to the truth, and urge each other to perseverance. (3)]

– Holy Quran: Surah Al-Aser 1-3

ᲖᲔᲖᲔᲖᲔ

The final stroke of the pen does not mark an ending but the stirring of a grand new beginning. What has been written here is not a conclusion but the foundation of a greater journey—a threshold into an era where the seeds of awareness take root and blossom into enlightenment.

The **Arcanum of Awareness** series has served as a celestial compass, pointing humanity toward its vast and untapped potential. Through its pages, we have journeyed into the depths of the mind, traversing the uncharted territories of thought, imagination, and selective awareness. These books have been more than companions; they have been architects of higher consciousness, alchemists transforming latent potential into boundless possibility.

Now, as the ink dries on the final page, we stand united at the precipice of transformation. This is not a call to stand and admire the horizon—it is a summons to cross it. The wisdom revealed within these volumes is the spark to ignite a new civilization—one that transcends limitation and builds bridges between the realms of knowledge, empathy, and innovation.

The Birth of the New Humanity

Humanity stands as a sculptor before an infinite block of marble, poised to carve a masterpiece of harmonious existence. The insights gleaned from these teachings have awakened a collective imagination, one that dreams of a future unshackled by fear, division, or stagnation. We have learned that greatness arises not from isolated triumphs but from the symphony of interconnected minds, each note resonating with a unique voice yet harmonizing with a shared purpose.

In this era of renewal, we see cities as vibrant ecosystems of collaboration and creativity where the digital and natural coexist in seamless harmony. Governance evolves into stewardship, with leaders as visionaries guided by ethical compasses, ensuring that justice, equity, and sustainability are the foundations of progress.

The Legacy of Awareness

The journey through the **Arcanum of Awareness** was not just a discovery of what we are but an unveiling of what we can become. The creative spark has been lit in every individual; the labyrinth of thought has been traversed with clarity, and selective awareness has honed our ability to focus on what truly matters. We now carry the tools to reimagine our existence to elevate not only ourselves but the entire human family.

This is the era of *conscious innovation*, where technological marvels serve not as masters but as allies in the quest for balance and well-being. This is the epoch of *enlightened empathy*, where the barriers of race, creed, and culture dissolve, leaving a unified humanity striving toward common goals. This is the age of *purposeful progress*, where every step forward is a testament to our commitment to the flourishing of life in all its forms.

The Eternal Symphony

The **Arcanum of Awareness** closes, but the melody it began continues to swell. Each reader, thinker, and creator who embarks on this journey becomes a part of the grand orchestra that composes humanity's future. Let this symphony resound with the brilliance of curiosity, the strength of unity, and the courage to pursue the unknown.

As Ralph Waldo Emerson observed, "What lies behind us and what lies before us are tiny matters compared to what lies within us." And within us lies the power to ascend, to illuminate the world with the light of our collective awareness, and to write a legacy that will echo through eternity.

A Call to the Architects of Tomorrow

The responsibility is now ours to carry forward. Let every action be guided by the truths uncovered in these pages. Let us build bridges where there are divides, foster creativity where there is stagnation, and shine light into the shadows of ignorance.

Rise, architects of the future! Take the alchemy of thought, the forge of imagination, and the precision of awareness, and shape a world that reflects the best of who we are. Dream with courage. Innovate with conviction. Above all, we should live with purpose, for the symphony of humanity has only just begun.

As we embark upon this odyssey, let the stars above and the truths within guide us, united in our journey toward a horizon ablaze with the dawn of enlightenment.

THE LAST HORIZON: A NEW BEGINNING

❧❧❧

As they embark upon a voyage reflecting the trials of existence,
youthful spirits set forth, with hope illuminating their path.
Through trials and tribulations, they understood that every
stumble heralded the dawn of a fresh tale.

At the intersection of destiny, a whisper would echo, "Begin
afresh, for within your soul, mysteries flow." With hands
brimming with promise, they set out on their way, For the secrets
of the cosmos dwelled deep within their essence.

"You perceive yourself as a fleeting mote," they pondered, "Yet
within you, the universe does float." Unbeknownst to the tapestry
of existence, Within their essence, the deepest mysteries did dwell.[6]

"In humility, strength finds its place," they discovered with a
gentle embrace, "In this truth, the joy of life you trace." With each
dawn, a vow unfolds as the sun ascends with unwavering grace. In
this cadence, they discovered the essence of existence.

---

[6] Adopted from One of the most beautiful sayings attributed to the Commander of the
Faithful, Ali ibn Abi Talib: "Your cure is within you, and you do not perceive it; your ailment
is from you, and you do not feel it... Do you claim that you are a small entity while the greater
world is contained within you? And you are the clear book, in which the hidden is revealed
by its letters."

Life, akin to blossoms, shall flourish and fade, A ballet of luminescence and darkness, the eternal embrace of twilight and dawn. Upon a journey of quietude, selflessness, and profundity, they would discover a haven where their spirit could rest unbound.

Mariners lost upon the ocean of moments, Harmonizing tales of yesteryears in melodic verses. With a gentle goodbye to urban landscapes and expansive heavens, they journeyed forth to meet new horizons, casting aside what once was.

In every harbor, they wove a story of determination, Confronting life's tempests with unwavering resolve. They clung to the whisper of dawn, a heavenly omen, And in this faith, their happiness unfurled like petals in the sun.

For within them, the cosmos's secrets lay, Leading them through shadowed nights and radiant days. 'Do not surrender,' the stars appeared to murmur, 'For within your soul, resides the power to navigate your own destiny.'

ॐॐॐ

END OF ARCANUM OF AWARENESS SERIES...